Masculinity & Femininit
Their Psychological Dimensions, Correlates, & Antecedents

By Janet T. Spence & Robert L. Helmreich

University of Texas Press, Austin & London

Library of Congress Cataloging in Publication Data
Spence, Janet Taylor.
    Masculinity and femininity.
    Bibliography: p.
    Includes index.
    1. Femininity (Psychology).   2. Masculinity (Psychology).
I. Helmreich, Robert, joint author.   II. Title.
BF692.2.S68   155.33   77-10693
ISBN 0-292-76443-X (cloth); 0-292-75052-8 (paper)

Printed in the United States of America

Second Cloth Printing, 1979
First Paperback Printing, 1979

*To our respondents, who gave
so generously of themselves
and made this book possible.*

Contents

Preface

Psychologists, like other scientists, tend to pride themselves on the objectivity of their investigations and on attempts to build value-free theoretical models, driven by empirical data rather than personal beliefs and prejudices. However, by eschewing analyses of their own ideological commitments, many of which they share with society at large, they often fall unwitting prey to them. Psychological research on masculinity and femininity conducted over the past three or four decades serves as a prime example. Much of this research appears to have been guided by the conventional wisdom of its time: the traditional division of labor between the sexes reflects, if not the biological destiny of men and women, then an arrangement whose functional value is unquestionable; men and women differ sharply in their psychological make-up, differences that both explain and justify the roles which each sex is assigned; those who try to break out of the mold are unhappy, maladjusted individuals, if not worse. Men are men and women are women and *vive la différence*.

Ironically, it was a self-conscious political movement that has caused psychologists to begin to be aware of the unexamined suppositions which shaped their empirical research. Thus the rise in the 1960s of the feminist movement, with its frontal attack on the political, economic, and social institutions that differentiated between men and women, has led a growing number of psychologists to reappraise critically premises about masculinity and femininity and to suggest alternative theoretical models.

A central target of these criticisms has been the so-called bipolar conception of masculinity and femininity: the notion that the psychological properties stereotypically associated with men and with women essentially preclude each other, thus yielding a single dimension with masculinity (and most men) at one extreme and femininity (and most women) at the other. Writers such as Bakan (1966), Carlson (1971), Block (1973), and Constantinople (1973) began to question this formulation, particularly as it touches on personality characteristics, suggesting instead a dualistic model in which masculinity and femininity are conceived as separate dimensions which vary more or less independently.

Given impetus by this ongoing reexamination of the nature of the psychological differences between the sexes and spurred by the empirical work on stereotypes of Paul Rosenkrantz, the Brovermans, and their colleagues (e.g., Rosenkrantz, Vogel, Bee, Broverman, & Broverman 1968), we began in 1972 to study stereotypic beliefs about the personality differences between the sexes and the relationship between the socially desirable "masculine" and "feminine" attributes which people report in themselves. This work led us to the development of an objective self-report instrument, the Personal Attributes Questionnaire, containing separate masculinity and femininity scales (Spence, Helmreich, & Stapp 1974, 1975). Given the zeitgeist, it was not surprising that a similar measure was concurrently being developed by Sandra Bem (1974) and that her work and ours have turned out to supplement and complement each other.

Using our instrument, we found in our initial investigation that, in college students, masculinity and femininity were indeed essentially independent. An additional finding was that, contrary to accepted beliefs, greater self-esteem and social competence were associated with higher levels of masculinity and femininity in *both* sexes.

These data suggested that traditional ways of thinking about masculinity and femininity required radical restructuring. However, a critical issue was whether these results were unique to middle-class, American college students, the major inheritors of the feminist movement, or would, in fact, hold true across a broader spectrum of ages and backgrounds. Accordingly, we began to amass data from a number of diverse groups both in the U.S. and in other cultures. The largest and most extensive data set came from a sample of more than 1,500 high school students, who provided a more representative profile of social and economic strata. Having faith that our original findings would be replicated, we simultaneously extended our research to explore some of the correlates of masculinity and femininity, most notably achievement motivation and some of the parental variables associated with these clusters of characteristics.

As the sheer mass of data accumulated, we were faced with a decision about the form of its publication. It appeared to us that releasing the findings in bits and pieces in a series of journal articles rather than together would not reveal effectively the rich and complex network of interrelationships found in the data as a whole. The thought of presenting them in an extended monograph, however, made us aware of how sprawling this corpus of data was. While some of our findings were solidly tied down, others were tentative and demanded still further exploration. Although some of our instruments were refined to a level that satisfied us, others clearly demanded further psychometric development. While the social, ideological, and theoretical context for this area of investigation could be explicated, and some convergence could be reached about some sources and kinds of data, a "last chapter," integrating the causes and consequences of the phenomena at hand, could not be written.

As we reached the decision to present in a single monograph the collection of data that we and our colleagues had gathered, we found ourselves yielding to the temptation of testing just one more sample or of exploring just one more implication of an intriguing finding. But a halt had to be called. Too many relationships were being uncovered too fast in too many directions and we despaired of reaching the point in any reasonable period of time where we could present a neat and tidy empirical and theoretical package.

The reader will thus find the following chapters to be part finished product and part progress report, an account of where we have been and where the data seem to be directing us. Despite the profusion of empirical analyses and tabular summaries we present, the range of the data has been only partially explored. We have not discussed, for example, the effects of birth order and family size on masculinity and femininity and the other attitudes and attributes we have measured. We have given these factors a cursory examination and have found no evidence of direct effects or influence, but more complex analyses may reveal that important effects are present. Such analyses, however, could well require a monograph of their own.

So many colleagues and students have given us invaluable assistance in the accumulation of these data and preparation of the manuscript that it is hard to single out individuals for recognition. We owe a particular debt to Dr. Joy Stapp, now at the University of California at Los Angeles, who was our early collaborator and who has continued to contribute to the project in innumerable ways.

We wish to thank the teachers and administration of Hamden High School, Hamden, Connecticut, and the following Massachusetts schools: Belmont High School, Bunker Hill Community College, Marblehead Regional High School, Wachusett Regional High School, and Waltham High School for their cooperation in allowing us access to their students and their assistance in administering the test battery, and we wish to thank Janet Jameson and Sally Styvco, who so ably stagemanaged several of these efforts.

A number of other individuals generously gave of their data and their time, especially Avi and Debbie Blattstein, Edward Connolley, Cecil Harris, Joel Saegert, and Waneen Spirduso. We are grateful to our students, who have helped us clarify our ideas and who have labored on the mass of data. Special acknowledgment is due John Wilhelm, who meticulously assembled the computer data archive and aided in the data analysis throughout, and Darryl Gowan, who ably assisted in the later stages of the project. We appreciate the patience and skill of Kathy Underwood and Carol Austin, who deciphered our often unintelligible scrawls and produced superbly typed manuscripts.

Our work was greatly facilitated by the support of a number of granting agencies and institutions. Parts of the research were funded by the National Science Foundation, Grant SOC 73-09197 (J.T.S.) and Grant BNS 76-17316 (J.T.S. and R.L.H.), and the National Aeronautics and Space Administration, Grant NSG 2065 (R.L.H.). Our work was also made possible by the award of a Faculty Research Leave, University of Texas Research Institute (R.L.H.), and a Ford Foundation Fellowship in Women's Studies (J.T.S.). Thanks are also due to Harvard University, where Janet Spence was in residence as Visiting Research Associate while many of the high school data were collected.

Austin, Texas   J.T.S.

June 20, 1977   R.L.H.

Masculinity & Femininity
Their Psychological Dimensions,
Correlates, & Antecedents

1. Gender, Sex Roles, and the Psychological Dimensions of Masculinity and Femininity

The research to be reported in this volume centrally concerns the psychological dimensions of masculinity and femininity: clusters of socially desirable attributes stereotypically considered to differentiate males and females and thus to define the psychological core of masculine and feminine personalities. We will present extensive normative data from adolescents and adults on the occurrence of these constellations of attributes in females and males as well as some of the other characteristics, attitudes, and behaviors we have found to be related to them. We will also inquire into some of the familial antecedents of these dimensions, most particularly some of the perceived parental behaviors that may be correlated with individual differences in masculinity and femininity and patterns of parent-child resemblance on these same characteristics.

In this chapter, some of the assumptions underlying our inquiries will be outlined and contrasted with the conceptualizations that have guided most prior research.

In brief, the view that masculine and feminine attributes are essentially bipolar opposites has dominated the writings of social and behavioral scientists until recently. The presence of feminine attributes tends to preclude the appearance of masculine ones, if indeed the absence of a feminine attribute is not by definition equivalent to masculinity. Conversely, masculine attributes are assumed to preclude feminine ones and their absence to define femininity. Further, the prevalent view has been that the appropriate goal of socialization is to inculcate sex-appropriate characteristics in members of each sex so that they may be capable of executing successfully the sex roles society has assigned them. Indeed, the tie between masculine and feminine characteristics and sex roles has implicitly been assumed to be so strong that these psychological dimensions are often discussed under the general sex-role rubric.

In opposition to this theoretical model, it will be our contention that the psychological dimensions of masculinity and femininity should not only be conceptually distinguished from masculine and feminine sex roles but that masculine and feminine attributes, while they differentiate the sexes to some degree, are not bipolar opposites but in each sex are separate and essentially orthogonal dimensions. Finally, we will argue that, at least in contemporary society, these psychological dimensions are only weakly related within each sex to the broad spectrum of sex-role behaviors.

Before presenting these arguments in detail, we will discuss briefly some of the social forces that appear to influence the nature and intensity of sex-role differentiation, the changes in our society that are bringing about role restructuring, and the implications of these changes for the psychological dimensions of masculinity and femininity.

The Social Context of Sex-Role Differentiation

Sex-role differentiation is universal among human societies: women and men are assigned different tasks, rights, and privileges and are likely to be subject to different rules of conduct, particularly in interaction with each other. Reflecting this division of roles along sexual lines, men and women are typically assumed to possess different temperamental characteristics and abilities—distinctive sets of attributes whose existence is used to justify the perpetuation of the society's role structure or whose inculcation is believed to be necessary if members of each sex are to fulfill their assigned functions.

The data of anthropologists and sociologists make it abundantly clear that across societies the differentiations between the sexes vary widely in their particulars and yet exhibit certain similarities. In the modal society, whether preliterate or postindustrial, women are given primary responsibility for caring for children and the family dwelling, while men are given the primary responsibilty for providing for the family's economic well-being. Parsons and Bales (1955) have characterized this division of labor as representing a distinction between instrumental and expressive roles, men charged with being the family's representatives in the outside world and acting in its behalf, women accorded responsibility not only for ministering directly to the physical needs of the family members but also for attending to their emotional needs and maintaining harmonious interactions among them. Paralleling these divisions, men are expected to develop independence, self-reliance, and other instrumental skills that will permit them to discharge their responsibilities to their families and to society as a whole; women are expected to develop the nurturant, expressive characteristics needed to carry out their interpersonal tasks.

Differences also exist in most societies in the power relations between the sexes—men typically being expected to be dominant over their wives and to have greater control of economic resources. Even in societies in which the interactions within the family are relatively egalitarian, men in their extrafamilial relationships are likely to be accorded positions of greater power and prestige than women (Stephens 1963).

The diversities among societies are as remarkable as their similarities. While men are usually assigned the most physically arduous tasks, in some agricultural groups, such as the Bamenda (Kaberry 1952) or the Arapesh (Mead 1935), women do all the heavy work. Inversions between what are typically considered "masculine" and "feminine" personality characteristics have also been reported. For example, in her classic study of sex and temperament in three New Guinea tribes, Mead (1935) reported that among the Arapesh men as well as women were trained to be nonaggressive and responsive to the needs of others while, among the Mundugumor, both sexes were ruthless and aggressive. Unlike the members of these two tribes, women and men of the Tchambuli tribe did exhibit personality differences, but the pattern was a reversal of what is typical in the western world: women being dominant, impersonal, and managing and men being more emotional and less independent and responsible.

Explanation of the origins of sex-role differentiations and the factors that maintain them, as well as of observed patterns of personality distinguishing the typical male and female within a given society, continue to be the subject of scientific controversy. At one extreme are those who argue that the near-universal regularities in societal arrangements can be attributed to profound, genetically determined differences in the psychological makeup of males and females (e.g., Tiger & Fox 1971). The other extreme is represented by those who, more impressed by the variability of human societies, claim that the origins of sex-role differentiations lie in a more limited set of innate differences between the sexes (e.g., Murdock 1949; D'Andrade 1966). These genetic differences include the superior physical capacities of men, such as their greater physical strength and higher metabolic rate, and factors associated with child bearing in women, such as their reduced mobility because of the necessity of nursing and caring for young children. Among such theorists, interest thus becomes focused not merely on describing the similarities in sexual differentiations across societies or historical periods but also on determining the kinds of historical and contemporary factors responsible for variations among them.

Definitive data are lacking regarding the existence of genetically determined differences in the temperamental makeup of men and women. There is evidence in abundance, however, to indicate that human personality is highly malleable. Observed differences in the personalities of the two sexes in a given society can be shown to be heavily influenced by the sex-specific child-rearing practices and by the nature and severity of sex-role differentiation imposed by that society. These differentiations, in turn, can be shown to be related to political, sociological, and economic forces. For example, in an ethnographic survey, primarily of nonliterate societies, Barry, Bacon, and Child (1957) found that, while boys tended to be trained in self-reliance and achievement and girls in nurturance and obedience, the magnitude of the sex differences in socialization practices was associated with the degree to which the society's economy demanded superior physical strength and the development of motor skills requiring strength. Similarly, Haavio-Mannila (1975) has compiled evidence from several European countries suggesting that sex-role differentiation, as related to participation in the labor force, is related to rate of industrialization.

Once established, sex-role differentiations tend to persist long after evolutions in societal conditions have diluted or changed their original functional significance. If the social arrangements between the sexes become maladaptive or come to conflict with the contemporaneous value system of the society, realignment may be expected to occur, sometimes slowly and sometimes rapidly, in response to an accumulation of social pressures or to shifts in political ideology. In this country both evolutionary and revolutionary changes in sexual differentiations have taken place over the past 150 years, ferment being particularly marked during the present decade. Changes in societal attitudes and practices have most visibly taken the form of sex-role broadening and permissiveness for women and have centered about our conceptions of the "traditional" family and the nature of women's participation in the labor force.

According to the (idealized) vision of the family to which our society has traditionally subscribed, women are not only responsible for the maintenance of the home but are also confined to it. The duty of their husbands, if they are to be considered a success, is to provide both the economic support of their families and the economic means to relieve their wives of arduous domestic chores. This narrow view of women's place is of relatively recent origin, arising during the Industrial Revolution as an urban and largely middle-class phenomenon (Janeway 1971; Scott & Tilly 1975). In agricultural communities, women's labor continued to be required in a broader sphere, while in poor urban families women could not afford the luxury of staying at home and were forced to seek employment in an outside world not prepared to offer them anything but the most menial, low paying kinds of work. With the spread of industrialization and the rise of the middle class, however, the economic contribution of increasing proportions of women was to be found solely within the home. The division along sexual lines between instrumental and expressive functions was thrown into high relief and, along with it, expectations that women and men should possess contrasting personal qualities.

The immediate impact of industrialization and increasing middle-class affluence was thus to decrease the burden placed upon many women by confining their labors to domestic chores. However, the same technological developments that made industrialization possible simultaneously made less compelling the justifications for excluding women from the work force or from masculine occupations that were based on their inferior physical capacities.

Increasingly, occupational competency has depended less on superior physical strength and stamina and more on formal education and vocational training. Although women were allowed to seek advanced education and to study the same curriculum as men only after overcoming men's misgivings about their lack of appropriate intellect and the frailty of their constitutions, their educational level has risen over the past century, along with that of men. The changing nature of work has also eliminated much of the adaptive significance of the cleavage between the sexes in the socialization of personality traits.

Attention has been called, for example, to the implications of the shift in postindustrial societies from entrepreneurial to bureaucratic organizations (Miller & Swanson 1958; Hacker 1956). In bureaucracies, successful job performance places less premium on such conventionally masculine traits as aggressiveness and dominance and more on interpersonal skills that promote harmonious relationships and group cooperation—skills traditionally regarded as feminine. Men (and women) thus may require expressive, "feminine" characteristics as well as instrumental "masculine" ones to be maximally effective in the vocational sphere.

The instrumental skills women must possess if they are to rear their children effectively and manage their households efficiently have undoubtedly been systematically underestimated. Certainly the variety of tasks inside and outside the home that contemporary housewives have been permitted or have been expected to assume, including their volunteer work for schools, civic organizations, and philanthropic groups, cannot be successfully accomplished with expressive characteristics alone. Several investigators (Barry, Bacon, & Child 1957; Bott 1957) have further suggested that, in nuclear families (the mode in industrialized societies), sex-role differentiations cannot be permitted to be too great, since each partner must be prepared to assume the duties of the other in the other's absence or incapacity. Women in particular must be able to take on all the day-to-day responsibilities for their children and the running of their household, both during the lengthy daily periods while their husbands are at work and during such prolonged disruptions of the marital partnership as may occur during husbands' military tour of duty or when marriages are terminated. Although seldom fully acknowledged, for some time there has also been a societal expectation that women stand ready to seek paid employment outside the home when needed. Women have always been used as a reserve labor force, urged to enter the job market during manpower shortages, particularly during wartime. (When needed, they have even entered into combat, as, for example, in the Spanish Civil War.)

Even when such external pressures are minimal, women's participation in the labor force has been systematically rising. Currently nearly two-fifths of married women with children under six years and more than half of those with school age children are gainfully employed, and women as a group make up approximately two-fifths of the labor force.[1] In accepting outside employment, however, women have been expected to retain most of their traditional domestic responsibilities. Although working wives tend to receive more household help from their husbands than wives with no outside employment (Hall & Schroeder 1970), they continue to assume the major burden. Even in industrialized societies such as Sweden and the USSR, where there is governmental commitment to sex-role equality, women who

1. U.S. Department of Labor, Wage and Labor Standards Administration, Women's Bureau. Woman Workers Today. 1976.

hold full-time jobs also perform the bulk of the work within the home, a state of affairs many women regard as not being entirely equitable (Haavio-Mannila 1975).

The factors that have increasingly led women in the United States to seek employment can be briefly outlined. With the development and acceptance of effective methods of contraception, family size has become progressively smaller, especially for the increasingly large middle class. In addition, rising affluence, combined with technological advances, which include improved nutritional standards and medical care, has made household work less arduous and time-consuming and has slowed the aging process and increased the life span. This constellation of factors has resulted in women ending their child bearing at a chronologically earlier age, physiologically younger and with a greater life expectancy than women in previous eras.

Women who orient their activities around the home may frequently find themselves underemployed, both in terms of time, particularly as their children grow older, and in terms of the level of activity for which their intellectual capacities and education have prepared them. Many married women find enjoyment and fulfillment in hobbies or community activities. A substantial number seek paid employment, some for self-expression but many because of the greater economic contribution they can thereby make to their family's well-being.

For many women, even their status as wives is uncertain.[2] Divorce is becoming more common and socially acceptable at all age and class levels. Being widowed at a relatively young age is also an all too realistic possibility. The average life span for women is approximately eight years longer than for men, and, by custom, women marry men their own age or older. In addition, divorced and widowed women are significantly less likely to remarry than men in a similar position. For many this single state is involuntary: women wishing to remarry must hope to find a mate in a pool of men their age or older whose numbers, relative to their own, continue to shrink. According to estimates, there are in this country over 12 million once married women, many of them quite young, who are currently without husbands.

When women were part of an extended family system, loss of a husband had less social and economic impact since they could be absorbed into the family unit. In our contemporary society, middle-aged women without spouses (or an equivalent) tend far more than men to be excluded from the social activities of the married. Further, the vast majority of widowed and divorced women have limited financial resources and are expected to work to support themselves and, often, their minor children. We also take for granted that women who have not married will be self-supporting although, in the not too distant past, it was considered respectable for single women to live with their parents before marriage and to seek employment only if their families could not afford to support them.

2. Convenient summaries of relevant statistics occur in such sources as Leslie and Leslie (1977).

Although women are represented in large numbers in the labor force, occupations continue to be strongly sex-typed and, though on the wane, discrimination against women in hiring, promotion, and salary in the more prestigious fields traditionally occupied by males has yet to disappear. Similarly, women still receive less encouragement than men to seek positions of political power and influence or to obtain the training necessary to enter traditionally masculine occupations. Explanations of this occupational sex typing cannot be based on differences between women and men in their physical capacities and cognitive abilities, particularly in highly valued fields, since strength and endurance are largely if not completely irrelevant to successful job performance and sex differences in intellectual abilities, if they exist at all, are minor (Maccoby & Jacklin 1974). Arguments have been advanced about temperamental differences between men and women (e.g., men are more rational and women too emotional) to justify the present discrepancy, differences that are often implied to have a genetic basis. The evidential support for such claims is, at best, weak. Even if genetic differences did exist, however, their effects appear to be exaggerated rather than minimized by the differential socialization practices that parents tend to employ with boys and girls (e.g., Sears, Maccoby, & Levin 1957; Block 1973) and, as noted earlier, to have lost much of the functional utility they may once have possessed.

One explanation offered by sociologists (e.g., Parsons 1942) for the continuance of a social structure in which men possess greater economic and political power than women is that it serves as a device for preserving marriage as a stable, monogamous institution. However, the institution of marriage, about which men have always had a certain ambivalence, has already been weakened by the growing ease of divorce, coupled with women's demonstration that they are able to be self-supporting and men's enthusiasm for their former wives (if not their present wives) working at well-paid jobs that relieve them of financial obligation. Accompanying changes in sexual morality that tolerate cohabitation without the benefit of legal sanction (changes brought about in part because of the availability of contraceptives) have further weakened marriage as a social institution.

Still another countervailing force exists in our democratic political institutions. Although response may be sluggish and not accomplished without strife, our society has historically yielded to the claims for social justice of groups who have systematically suffered from social, economic, or political discrimination. In this connection, Holter has suggested that when the net advantages and disadvantages of sexual differentiation "violate common standards of justice, or the burdens of some groups exceed certain absolute limits of tolerance, dissatisfaction with sex differentiation may arise and . . . weaken the system of differentiations" (1970, p. 33). Contemporary society and its governmental institutions have been relatively receptive to the feminist movement, in comparison to their hostility to its precursors in the

1800s and the early part of this century. Such events as the passage of federal legislation forbidding discrimination on the grounds of gender and compelling affirmative action programs suggest that women, like blacks, have achieved the status of individuals rather than objects or property and that they are therefore coming to be treated by common democratic standards of justice. They also suggest that changes in a general system of social values make less valid the rigid maintenance of traditional distinctions between the sexes.

While the future is difficult to foretell, the political, economic, and social changes over the past decades have led to a blurring of the formerly sharp division between the roles of women and men. Although no data bearing on the contention exist, men and women may also be in the process of coming closer together in their personality makeup. The current recodification of normative expectations for the two sexes may be less a blueprint for the future than a belated recognition of contemporary societal realities.

Assumptions Concerning Gender, Sex Roles, and Masculinity-Femininity

Anthropologists and sociologists have concentrated their efforts on describing the normative expectations underlying observed differences in the behavior of the typical female and male within and among various cultures and subcultures and, also, on isolating the kinds of factors that determine and maintain sexual differentiations. Psychologists, particularly those concerned with social behavior, have tended to accept as given the complex set of gender-related phenomena that exist in our society and to focus their attention on the processes by which its members come to correspond in their behaviors and attributes to the typical or expected man or woman in their cultural or subcultural group. Psychologists have also been concerned with variability among the individuals they study, seeking to isolate the factors that facilitate or interfere with the development of appropriate patterns of behavior in children, particularly factors that reside within the family.

In the past these psychological inquiries have largely been predicated on the supposition that biological gender, masculine and feminine sex-role behaviors, and the psychological attributes of masculinity and femininity are tightly intercorrelated. Thus the categorical variable of biological gender has been widely regarded as being so intimately associated with masculine and feminine role behaviors and with the presumed psychological differences between men and women that the distribution of the sexes on the latter variables has implicitly been assumed to be strongly bimodal—that is, sexual differentiation of modal females and males is marked and the sexes exhibit relatively little overlap. Further, those who exhibit sexually appropriate personality characteristics are typically expected to exhibit appropriate sex-role behaviors. A usual corollary of this assumption is that the display of cross-sex behaviors and attributes is in some sense pathological, having negative implications for the individual's level of adjustment or for sexual behavior and preferences.

A frequent conviction, at least among nonprofessionals, is that sex-role behaviors are not merely correlated with psychological characteristics and sexual proclivities but that they also have causal interconnections. Parents, particularly of boys, often insist that their children behave according to traditional sex-role standards (such as playing only with the "right" kind of toys) lest they grow to resemble the opposite sex psychologically or to become sexual deviants. Similarly, attempts of the schools to develop a unisexual nonacademic curriculum have occasionally led to resistance from some segments of the community because of the corrupting influence such a curriculum may have on the character structure of their participants; boys who are taught to cook, for example, will be robbed of their masculinity, while girls who participate in "male" sports or manual arts training are likely to be "masculinized." Traditionalists have recently expressed the same fears in stating their reservations about admitting women to the military service academies.

Perhaps as a consequence of such assumptions, psychologists have tended not to distinguish conceptually or empirically among sex-role behaviors, the psychological attributes of masculinity and femininity, and other similar gender-related phenomena, lumping them together under the heading of "sex roles." Reflecting this state of affairs, psychometric measures of masculinity and femininity have typically included (often within the same instrument or observational set) items that refer to such varied phenomena as attitudes, motives, vocational interests, leisure activities, duties within the home, patterns of interpersonal interaction, and personality attributes believed to distinguish between the sexes.

Although significant correlations may be found among these heterogeneous domains, the magnitude of the association may be expected to vary with the sharpness of sexual differentiations within a society and the severity of the negative sanctions imposed for violating them. The blurring of the distinctions between the sexes that has been taking place in our society suggests that, whatever may have been true in the past, gender-related phenomena are becoming increasingly dissociated. More specifically targeted investigations, based on finer grained conceptual analyses of sexual differentiations, may well reveal relationships both weaker and more complex than have previously been suspected.

Gender, Role, Sexual Orientation, and Characteristics of the Self

We have intimated that considerably more clarity can be brought to the study of sexual differentiation by distinguishing between four domains: biological gender, sexual orientation, sex role, and masculinity and femininity as self-variables or inner characteristics of the individual.

GENDER

With rare exception, human organisms are readily and unambiguously classified as female or male at birth or before and retain this biological status through the life span. Relatively early, children develop the cognitive capacity to acquire the concept that in nature biological gender is constant and learn to assign themselves and others to the correct category (e.g., Kohlberg 1966; Slaby & Frey 1975). At first this assignment is based on superficial characteristics, but later appropriate anatomical distinctions are made. In addition to developing cognitive knowledge about their biological gender, children almost always acquire what Green (1974) describes as a basic conviction of being male or female. Among the exceptions are transsexuals who commonly report the long-standing feeling that they have been trapped in a body of the wrong sex. Individuals may also vary in the degree to which they enjoy or resent their biological gender (a reaction that should be distinguished from individuals' enjoyment or resentment of the roles and opportunities that society makes available to their gender) but the vast majority, including the majority of homosexuals, appear to be content with the sexual category into which they have been born and have no wish to change. While it might be useful to develop distinctive labels for these various psychological components, we shall label the degree to which individuals are aware of and accept their biological sex *gender identification*.

SEXUAL ORIENTATION

By *sexual orientation* we mean the individual's preference for a sexual partner of the same or opposite sex. Valuable distinctions, such as between a felt preference and actual sexual behavior, or between conscious and unconscious desires, are often made, but further elaboration of the concept is unnecessary here.

SEX ROLE

Delineation of the meaning of *sex role* is more difficult. The term, although ubiquitous, has seldom been clearly defined, and those definitions that have been offered are frequently inconsistent. Part of the confusion, as Gordon (1966) and Angrist (1969) have noted, has been brought about because a number of factors have been subsumed under the heading of sex role, with the disciplines of anthropology, sociology, and psychology tending to stress different components. In an attempt to clarify the manner in which the concept has been employed, Angrist has identified three core usages that have appeared in the literature, and also the particular discipline with which each has tended to be associated. The first usage, stressed by anthropologists, refers to normative expectations that members of a given culture or subculture hold about the *position* men and women should occupy. Position emphasizes the division of labor between the sexes and the societal tasks assigned to each and is located in structured social settings. The second usage, associated with sociology, Angrist identifies as *relationship*. Relationship concerns the process of role taking, emphasizes socialization, and is located in dyads or larger groups with varying structure. The third usage, employed most frequently by psychologists, refers to the distinguishing characteristics of women and men themselves—to differences in behavior, personality, abilities, preferences, and the like.

While this classificatory scheme helps bring understanding to a muddled literature regarding the use of the term, the concept of sex role has more utility if restrictions upon its usage are imposed. A variety of stereotypes exists about behavioral differences between the sexes (which may or may not be factually valid). Literally speaking, these stereotypes constitute different "expectations" about the ways typical men and women behave. Not all these presumed differences are related to shared beliefs about how society *ought* to be structured and the positions females and males *ought* to be assigned. We suggest that references to sex-role expectations be restricted to these beliefs about *appropriate* behaviors for the two sexes, that is, behaviors that are positively sanctioned for members of one sex and ignored or negatively sanctioned for members of the other. Inclusion of all types of behavioral differences between the sexes (or beliefs about such differences) under the heading of "sex roles" compromises the usefulness of the role concept and of role theory as proposed by sociologists and anthropologists, without adding any descriptive clarity or explanatory power to the topic of sex differences.

Still another distinction that we propose is between the acting out of role expectations, on the one hand, and the internal properties of the actor on the other. This distinction has a number of implications that it will be useful to explore in detail.

As Angrist (1969) has noted, "sex role" involves not one but a multitude of roles and role combinations that vary across social settings and across the life span. Role behaviors are not only variable in these senses but are also highly diverse in their nature, referring to vocational and avocational activities, styles of dress, rules of social interaction, responsibilities within the home, and so forth. These behaviors differ in the importance attached to them, role violation being severely punished in some instances and a matter of relative indifference in others. Overall judgments about whether individuals exhibit role appropriate or inappropriate behavior can be expected to be determined primarily by the nature of the behavior patterns high in this hierarchy of significance, with the sheer number of types of role behaviors exhibited being of secondary importance. The existence of this hierarchy has several consequences. There is no reason to expect that the correlations between all categories of role behaviors will necessarily be high, i.e., that a given man or woman manifesting one kind of role behavior has a high probability of exhibiting another. Low correlations are particularly likely among behaviors low in the hierarchy, especially in an era in which there is increasing sex-role permissiveness and restructuring.

The variables leading to individual differences in the enactment of sex roles include not only situational factors—what resources exist in the person's environment—but also such internal dispositions as attitudes toward the appropriateness of maintaining traditional sex-role distinctions, personal preferences for certain kinds of activities, and perceptions (realistic or unrealistic) of the positive or negative consequences of acting in certain ways. This group of self-variables is most directly responsible for the degree to which an individual exhibits masculine or feminine sex-role behavior in a given situation. However, as we noted earlier, it is also commonly assumed that women and men differ in their personality characteristics. Typical characterizations of the sexes are that women are dominated by their emotions and a desire to nurture others, while men are independent, self-assertive, and rational.

These "masculine" and "feminine" attributes or beliefs about them have frequently been labeled by psychologists (e.g., Bem 1974; Rosenkrantz, Vogel, Bee, Broverman, & Broverman 1968, among others) as "sex roles" or "sex-role" stereotypes. If one refers only to overt behavior in situations containing role demands, we have no quarrel with this label. However, we consider it critical to distinguish conceptually between this category of "role" variables and other content domains. The failure to do so has probably encouraged the questionable assumption that there is a high degree of correlation between these behaviors and other types of role behaviors. Knowledge of the degree to which an individual possesses or manifests masculine or feminine personality characteristics does not necessarily permit inferences about how sex-typed the individual is in interest patterns, for example, or in any other category of role-related behaviors.

A theoretical note. In the formulation of many psychologists, as Angrist (1969) has noted, "sex role" has become an all-purpose label for all the ways females and males are assumed to differ, used not merely to identify observable behavior but also to identify (hypothetical) internal properties, such as personality characteristics, differentiating the sexes. We propose, however, that a clear distinction be made between sex-role *behavior* and properties of the behaving organism, a distinction often made by role theorists (e.g., Parsons & Bales 1955; Horrocks & Jackson 1972).

In making this proposal, we are advocating the general usefulness of a theoretical approach to psychological phenomena, as opposed to a purely empirical one. We should also interject at this point, in anticipation of our discussion of masculine and feminine personality attributes, our view that it is also useful to postulate relatively stable predispositions (given such labels as attitudes, motives, aptitudes, and personality characteristics) that have some degree of situational generality and whose nature or intensity differentiates among individuals. Vigorous attacks have been launched against this position (e.g., Jones & Nisbett 1972; Mischel 1970), the claim being made that individual differences in dispositional tendencies are likely to be highly situation-specific. Recent evidence (e.g., Bem & Allen 1974; Cartwright 1975), however, has suggested that there may be substantial intraindividual consistencies across broad categories of socially significant situations and even the severest critics of the trait approach appear to be moderating their position (e.g., Mischel 1977). Nevertheless, it should be acknowledged that behavior is determined by a multiplicity of factors so that the correlation between an internal disposition and a particular act in any given situation or limited type of situation is likely to be low. Substantial correlations, however, may be found if a wide range of behaviors and situations is assessed (e.g., Fishbein & Ajzen 1974). The literature thus suggests the utility of traitlike notions when one's intent is to understand the implications of individual differences for broad areas of real-life functioning.

A useful distinction permitted by differentiating between the internal characteristics of the individual and their overt expression in behavior is between what Horrocks and Jackson (1972) call *role taking* and *role playing*. In role taking, the behavior is congruent with the performer's self-concept and is thus an overt manifestation of some aspect of the self. The individual who is role playing, on the other hand, is performing the behaviors specified by a set of role expectations but is consciously or unconsciously acting in a way contrary to her or his self-concept.

Sex-role playing is a frequent phenomenon, individuals yielding to situational demands to avoid externally imposed penalties, using appropriate role behaviors in order to achieve some desired outcome, or responding in line with their value system about correct sex-role behaviors. Men, for example, have been demonstrated to inhibit certain types of emotional expression, except in limited circumstances, apparently because of a fear of negative reactions if they do not (e.g., Derlega & Chaikin 1976). On the other hand, women on occasion may consciously or unconsciously elect to conceal their competence, assertiveness, and other "masculine" characteristics or actively to feign the role of "helpless, dependent female" in order to influence others or to gain their assistance and attention. An interesting experimental example is provided by Zanna and Pack (1975). These investigators led college women to believe that they would be interacting with an attractive, unattached male peer who preferred either traditional or nontraditional women and that he would be supplied with their answers to a "personality" questionnaire that actually contained items describing stereotypically masculine and feminine traits and role behaviors. When their responses were compared with their preexperimental responses to the same questionnaire items, these women were found to distort their answers in the man's preferred direction. Women led to believe they would be interacting with a less attractive, unavailable man showed no such distortion.

The distinction between role taking and role playing is implicit in Lynn's (1969) proposal that individual differences in sex-role preference be distinguished from sex-role adoption. Sex-role preference, according to Lynn, refers to an individual's *desire* to adopt the sex-typed behavior of one sex or the other, while sex-role adoption refers to the actual acting out of behavior.

Individuals also differ in their more abstract attitudes toward appropriate sex roles: what rights, privileges, and behaviors women and men ought to have or be permitted in relationship to one another (e.g., Spence & Helmreich 1972b). There is no reason to assume that these attitudes will necessarily be related to the individual's personal choices, particularly if their attitudes are relatively egalitarian. Women who choose not to work outside the home, for example, may believe that women should be able to work if they please and not be subject to discrimination in employment on account of their sex.

Attempts to classify individuals according to the degree to which their role preferences and adoptions are gender-appropriate have frequently been based on measures tapping limited types of sex-linked behaviors, such as children's preference for "masculine" or "feminine" toys. The concepts of sex-role preferences or adoptions are global, however. Whether one is measuring preferences, adoptions, or attitudes, useful measures are more likely to be obtained when inquiries are made about a broad sample of sex-typed behaviors of a socially significant nature.

MASCULINE AND FEMININE PERSONALITY VARIABLES

A number of writers have attempted to describe the essential psychological dimensions that distinguish between males and females. For example, in a speculative, semiphilosophical treatise Bakan (1966) has proposed that two fundamental modalities characterize living organisms: the sense of agency and the sense of communion. Agency reflects a sense of self and is manifested in self-assertion, self-protection, and self-expansion. Communion, on the other hand, implies selflessness, a concern with others and a desire to be at one with other organisms. He further identifies agency with "male principles" or masculinity and communion with "female principles" or femininity. Other writers have proposed similar male and female principles, such as outer vs. inner space (Erikson 1964), instrumentality vs. expressiveness (Parsons & Bales 1955), field dependence vs. independence (Witkin 1974), and allocentric vs. autocentric (Gutman 1965), all clearly intending, as did Bakan, to provide fundamental distinctions between the sexes that have, if not universal, at least considerable transcultural validity.

Investigators in this country have conducted formal empirical research in which individuals are asked to identify the socially desirable characteristics that distinguish between women and men. This research has produced a core set of attributes confirming the implications of these speculative accounts (e.g., Jenkin & Vroegh 1969; Bem 1974; Spence, Helmreich, & Stapp 1974). The ideal woman tends to be described by such adjectives as emotional, sensitive, and concerned with others (a cluster of attributes most clearly labeled by Bakan's term: a sense of communion) and the ideal man by such adjectives as competitive, active, and independent (Bakan's sense of agency).[3] The data also indicate that, when men and women are asked to describe themselves on these ideal characteristics or are asked their beliefs about the typical man and woman, significant differences between the sexes are typically found in the same direction (e.g., Bem 1974; Rosenkrantz et al. 1968; Spence, Helmreich, & Stapp 1974, 1975).

The anthropological literature, some of which was surveyed above, suggests that, while all cultures do not produce women who tend to be more communal in their personal characteristics than men and men who tend to be more agentic than women, the vast majority do. Thus the agency-communion dichotomy and its conceptual equivalents appear to have considerable generality in describing the core attributes that societies expect to differentiate women and men.

BIPOLAR VS. DUALISTIC CONCEPTIONS OF MASCULINITY
AND FEMININITY

A pervasive view of these clusters of masculine and feminine attributes is that they are bipolar opposites. That is, masculine characteristics essentially preclude the appearance of feminine ones, so that individuals who possess one set of characteristics are likely to be relatively deficient in the other. Women, for example, are often described not only as interpersonally sensitive and concerned with others but therefore also as dependent and noncompetitive. Conversely, independence and competitiveness are thought to be associated with a relatively low degree of sensitivity and concern with others. Thus femininity is equated with lack of masculinity and masculinity with lack of femininity. What emerges is a single bipolar scale, with women being clustered toward the feminine pole and men toward the masculine pole.

This bipolar conception of masculinity and femininity has historically guided the research efforts of psychologists. Until recently, as Constantinople (1973) has pointed out, the major psychometric instruments devised to measure masculinity and femininity have been set up as a single masculinity-femininity scale. She also notes that

3. Despite frequent statements to the contrary, as Stricker (1977) has noted, these empirical studies do not, however, support the conclusion that the ideal woman is typically characterized by the absence of masculine, agentic attributes (e.g., dependent, passive) or the ideal man by the absence of feminine communal attributes (e.g., nonemotional, unconcerned with others). Rather, the ideal individual tends to be characterized as possessing both sets of attributes, the socially desirable differences between the sexes being viewed as one of degree rather than kind (Jenkin & Vroegh 1969; Spence, Helmreich, & Stapp 1974). The simultaneous belief that the possession of masculine or feminine attributes precludes one another thus presents something of a paradox, as will be discussed in Chapter 8.

masculinity-femininity is treated as a uni- rather than as a multi-dimensional phenomenon and that no attempt has been made to provide a conceptual definition to guide item selection or to distinguish between the inherently important and the trivial aspects of behavior. The governing criterion for inclusion of items has been their capacity to distinguish between men and women and also, in some instances, between homosexuals and heterosexuals. This approach is, of course, perfectly justified if one assumes that sex roles, sexual orientation, masculine and feminine aspects of the self, and other gender-related phenomena are not only bipolar but also strongly correlated or that one's intent is to obtain a global measure of an individual's masculinity or femininity in all its myriad facets.

While the bipolar approach to the psychological aspects of masculinity and femininity has been dominant, dualistic conceptions have also been proposed: masculinity and femininity are separate principles and may coexist to some degree in every individual, male or female. In the psychoanalytic tradition, for example, Jung distinguished between masculine *animus* and feminine *anima* and proposed that both were significant aspects of the psyche. More recently, Bakan (1966) has offered agency and communion as coexisting male and female principles that characterize all living organisms to some degree. These fundamental modes of existence, he further asserts, must be balanced if the society or the individual is to survive. Either, unchecked, is destructive. Since men tend to be dominated by a sense of agency and women by a sense of communion, the developmental task of each is different: men must learn to "mitigate agency with communion," women the reverse.

The research to be reported in this volume, as we noted earlier, has the psychological attributes of masculinity and femininity as its central theme. Along with such other investigators as Bem (1974), Carlson (1971), and Block (1973), we have been particularly influenced by Bakan's (1966) formulation. The core properties of femininity, we propose, can be usefully labeled or conceptualized as a sense of communion and the core properties of masculinity as a sense of agency. We have also adopted, at least partially, a dualistic approach to masculinity and femininity, conceiving of them as separate aspects of the personality that may vary more or less independently.

This position has in part guided our previous research and in part emerged from it. In the following chapter, we will review the findings of this research and describe the purposes of the investigations whose results we will subsequently report.

2. Previous Research and Overview of the Study

In this chapter we will briefly describe first the Personal Attributes Questionnaire (PAQ; Spence, Helmreich, & Stapp 1974, 1975)—the psychometric instrument we have devised to measure the psychological dimensions of masculinity and femininity—and then some of the variables that have been found to be associated with this questionnaire and other similar instruments. We will conclude the chapter by indicating the general directions in which the investigations to be reported here have taken us.

Prior Studies of the Psychological Dimensions of Masculinity and Femininity

The PAQ, whose development is described in considerable detail in Chapter 3, is a self-report instrument consisting of a number of trait descriptions, each set up on a bipolar scale. Each item describes a characteristic stereotypically believed to differentiate the sexes. The questionnaire is divided into three separate scales, labeled Masculinity (M), Femininity (F), and Masculinity-Femininity (M-F). The Masculinity scale contains items that our data suggest are considered to be socially desirable characteristics for both sexes but that males are believed to possess in greater abundance than females (e.g., independence). Conversely, the Femininity scale contains items describing characteristics considered to be socially desirable in both sexes but that females are believed to possess to a greater degree than males (e.g., gentleness). Items on the third, Masculinity-Femininity scale consist of characteristics whose social desirability appears to vary in the two sexes (e.g., aggressiveness is judged to be desirable in males and nonaggressiveness desirable in females). As suggested by these examples, the content of the M and F scales turned out to support our theoretical preconceptions, the former containing items referring to instrumental, agentic characteristics and the latter to expressive, communal characteristics. The M-F scale, however, contained both agentic and communal characteristics, many of the latter seeming to refer to emotional vulnerability (e.g., feelings easily hurt).

INTERCORRELATIONS AMONG THE SCALES

When we examined self-report scores on the PAQ for two independent samples of college students, we found significant differences between the means of the two sexes on every item, men scoring higher on the M and M-F items, scored in a masculine direction, and lower on the F items, scored in a feminine direction (Spence, Helmreich, & Stapp 1975). The veridicality of stereotypes about personality differences between the sexes was thus essentially validated for the particular characteristics appearing on the questionnaire, an outcome that justified its use as a measure of masculinity and femininity. Next, data relevant to the bipolar conception of masculinity and femininity were examined. According to this view, scores on the M and M-F scales should have been strongly related in a negative direction to scores on the F scale. The correlations between the M and F scales, however, were not only relatively low but *positive* in both sexes, thus providing striking disconfirmation of a bipolar conception of masculinity and femininity and supporting instead a dualistic interpretation. Low correlations between masculinity and femininity scales have also been reported by Bem (1974), who has used a self-report instrument (Bem Sex Role Inventory, BSRI) whose rationale resembles that on which the PAQ is based. Our M-F scale, however, provided some support for the bipolar model, having a moderately high positive correlation with M and, more critically, a lower but still substantial negative correlation with F. Since additional analyses convinced us that the M-F scale was not a psychometric accident and since we suspected that it might yield significant information not available from the other scales, we have retained it, despite the conceptual embarrassment of having to embrace simultaneously a dualistic and a bipolar model of masculinity and femininity.

RELATIONSHIPS WITH STEREOTYPES, ATTITUDES TOWARD
WOMEN'S ROLES, AND CONVENTIONAL M-F MEASURES

Several additional measures were obtained from members of these student samples. After rating themselves on each of the items on the three PAQ scales, the students were asked to rate the degree to which the typical adult female and male differed on each attribute of the PAQ on a scale whose bipolar extremes ranged from much more characteristic of males to much more characteristic of females. Stereotype scores were derived for each student from these ratings, and these scores were then correlated with self-ratings on the M, F, and M-F scales. The correlations were low and most were nonsignificant, suggesting that individuals' perceptions of themselves are not distorted by their perceptions of modal differences between the sexes on these attributes.

Data were also obtained from the Attitudes toward Women Scale (AWS; Spence & Helmreich 1972b), an instrument designed to tap beliefs about the rights and roles of women, vis-à-vis men, in a number of areas. Moderately high correlations were found between scores on this scale and the students' PAQ stereotype scores, those perceiving large differences in the characteristics of the sexes having more traditional sex-role attitudes. The same kind of relationship had previously been obtained by Ellis and Bentler (1973), employing similar attitudinal and stereotyping measures. The causal connections between these variables cannot, of course, be determined from the correlations between them. It is possible, for example, that individuals who adhere to a traditional sex-role ideology perceive exaggerated personality differences between the sexes as justification for their beliefs (and, conversely, that those with a feminist ideology underestimate the differences) or that those who perceive the sexes as differing markedly derive their ideology from this perception. Ellis and Bentler report, however, that those who are more traditional in their sex-role attitudes tend to be more conservative in their general political outlook, a finding that gives some credence to the former interpretation.

In contrast, correlations between the students' scores on the Attitudes toward Women Scale and their self-report scores on the three PAQ scales were unimpressive. The relationships did tend to be in predictable directions—men who were more traditional in their attitudes tending to be more masculine on the M and M-F scales and traditional women tending to be more feminine on the F scale and less masculine on the M and M-F scales. The magnitudes of the correlations were low, however, and not uniformly significant. Our suspicion, voiced earlier, that the psychological characteristics associated with masculinity and femininity are not strongly related to role-related phenomena was thus confirmed in this instance.

Still further confirmation of our suggestion that the association among masculine and feminine personality traits, attitudes toward sex roles, and role behaviors is low is found in sets of data involving the widely used California Personality Inventory Femininity Scale (CPI Fe Scale; Gough 1968). Our inspection of the items indicated that twelve refer to sex-typed interests—six of them masculine (e.g., "I think I would like the work of a building contractor") and six feminine (e.g., "I think I would like the work of a dress designer"). Of the remaining twenty-four items, some are not easily classified (e.g., "I prefer a shower to a bathtub"), but a number can be considered to be related to personality characteristics. When we examined the content of the latter, we could find no example of a statement that clearly reflected a feminine attribute, as defined by the F scale items on the PAQ, although a number appeared to be related to attributes appearing on the M scale (e.g., "I am very slow in making up my mind") or the M-F scale ("I am inclined to take things hard").

We have found that the correlations between Fe scores and AWS scores in female and male college students are essentially orthogonal (unpublished data). Even more informative data were obtained by Joy Stapp and Allen Kanner[1] (unpublished), who administered the Fe scale and the short form of the PAQ (see Chapter 3) to a sample of thirty-one male and forty-four female students at the University of California, Berkeley. Positive but nonsignificant correlations were

---

1. We wish to thank Dr. Joy Stapp and Mr. Allen Kanner for making the data of their study available to us. Their results are reported here and later in this chapter in a discussion of the Bem Sex Role Inventory.

found between Fe scores and F scores on the PAQ (.04 for males, .13 for females). Ironically, in view of the title of the CPI scale, significant correlations *were* found between the Fe scale and the PAQ M scale (−.49 and −.42 for males and females, respectively) and between the Fe and M-F scales (−.64 and −.40). Item analyses indicated that the significant correlations were determined almost exclusively by the items reflecting PAQ-related personality characteristics, significant biseral r's between the M scale, the M-F scale, or both being found in ten items for males and nine items for females. (In three instances in males and two in females, a significant item correlation was found with F, but in no instance was the highest correlation found with this scale.) The twelve items related to sex-typed interests showed only a minimal relationship to the PAQ scales. Of the seventy-two correlations involving these items, most were close to zero and only six (five of them in the predicted direction) were significant. None of the six, however, involved the same sex on the same item.

Similar evidence suggesting that conventional masculinity-femininity scales heavily weighted with items referring to sex-typed interests and similar role phenomena are not highly related to measures of psychological masculinity and femininity has been found by Wakefield, Sasek, Friedman, and Bowden (1976; Wakefield, personal communication). Correlations were obtained between the Bem (1974) M and F scales and three such masculinity-femininity measures, drawn from the Minnesota Multiphasic Personality Inventory (Hathaway & McKinley 1967), California Personality Inventory (Gough 1957), and Omnibus Personality Inventory (Heist & Yonge 1968). Although these measures tended to be significantly related to each other, nonsignificant correlations were found in both sexes between each of them and the Bem scales with the exception of M and the CPI scale. Modest but significant correlations were found, however, between the Bem scales and the bipolar Need for Heterosexuality scale from the Adjective Check List (Gough & Heilbrun 1965). The latter, it is important to note, is composed of trait names.

RELATIONSHIPS WITH SELF-ESTEEM

Still another measure for which data were obtained in our initial study of the PAQ was the Texas Social Behavior Inventory (TSBI; Helmreich, Stapp, & Ervin 1974), a self-report scale designed to measure social competence and self-esteem. Scores on this scale were highly correlated with M scale scores, not merely in the samples of male students but also in females. (Substantial positive correlations were also found in both sexes between Self-esteem and M-F scores.) The correlations between F scale scores and Self-esteem were lower than those for the M scale but were also highly significant and positive, not only in women but also in men. The finding that masculinity in males and femininity in females are related to feelings of self-esteem and social competence was easily predictable. However, the relationships between the latter and cross-sex characteristics—femininity in males and masculinity in females—contradict the common assumption that only sex-appropriate behaviors and attributes are associated with indices of psychological well-being. Foreshadowing of these results, however, can be seen in studies such as Heilbrun's (1968). Heilbrun reported that an unselected group of female undergraduates, compared to a group of females who were clients of a university psychological counseling center, tended to have higher Adjective Check List (Gough & Heilbrun 1965) scores on clusters of adjectives that reflected agentic (masculine) as well as communal (feminine) characteristics.

The positive correlation of both M and F scores with our Self-esteem measure led us to seek a method of combining scores on the two scales to determine how they jointly relate to Self-esteem. Calculation of a multiple correlation coefficient did little to account for variance in Self-esteem, beyond that determined by the M scores alone. This result suggested that the combination of M and F, while it might be additive, was not linear. Rather than seeking a sophisticated mathematical solution, we adopted a simple classificatory scheme that both has turned out to be extremely useful and has subsequently been employed extensively for descriptive purposes. This procedure essentially involves combining the data on each scale for both sexes and finding the median for the total group. Using M and F scores, individuals are then classified into one of four groups, depending on their position above or below the median on the two scales. These four groups have been labeled *Androgynous* (high on both M and F), *Masculine* (the "conventional" male, high on M and low on F, or the cross-sex female), *Feminine* (the "conventional" female, low on M but high on F, or the cross-sex male), and *Undifferentiated* (low on both M and F).

Before discussing the relationship between Self-esteem scores and these joint M and F categories, we will interject a description of the distribution of males and females across the four groups. In both sexes, the cross-sex category (Feminine for males, Masculine for females) contained a markedly lower proportion of individuals than the other three, while the sex-traditional category (Masculine for males, Feminine for females) tended to contain the largest proportion of individuals. Substantial numbers of both sexes, however, fell into the two extreme categories; in fact, the proportion classified as Androgynous (high M and F) in one sample of males outstripped that of the sex-traditional category.

Calculation of the mean Self-esteem scores for males and females in each of the four categorical groups revealed highly significant differences among them, both sexes showing the same order. Undifferentiated students were lowest in mean Self-esteem, Feminine next, then Masculine and, highest of all, Androgynous. These data suggest that in both sexes M and F combine additively to determine Self-esteem. While the ordering follows quite directly from the correlational data, it was nonetheless contrary to conventional wisdom to find that "masculine" women, a group with stereotypically cross-sex characteristics, report themselves higher in self-esteem and social competence than traditional, "feminine" women, high on expressive, communal characteristics but relatively low on instrumental, agentic ones. A comparison of the means of the Feminine males and Feminine females on Self-esteem also revealed an unexpected finding, namely that these cross-sex males were no lower in Self-esteem than the "traditional" females.

Self-esteem, the Personal Attributes Questionnaire, and Other Measures of Masculinity and Femininity

The relationships with Self-esteem reported above have been partially replicated in groups of college students by Bem (1977) and by Wetter (1975), both of whom used a different measure of masculinity and femininity from the PAQ. Because of the potential implications of the failure of these investigators to duplicate our results fully, detailed consideration will be given each of their studies and the measures they employed.

In her investigation, Bem also used the Texas Social Behavior Inventory (Helmreich et al. 1974) to measure self-esteem but employed the Bem Sex Role Inventory (1974) to measure masculinity and femininity. Bem reported that both M and F scores contributed to Self-esteem in females but that only M scores were related to this measure in males. Further, the relationship with M appeared to be substantially lower in both sexes than we have consistently found with the PAQ. While the BSRI and the PAQ contain many similar items, data obtained from college students by Stapp and Kanner (unpublished) indicate that the correlations between the parallel scales on the two instruments are less than their individual reliabilities. (The correlations of the two M scales were .75 and .73 for males and females, respectively, of the two F scales, .57 and .59.) Two differences between the scales may account for the lowered correlations. First, in Bem's inventory, respondents are given a trait description (e.g., independent) and asked to rate how characteristic it is of them. The PAQ, however, consists of bipolar scales (e.g., independent-dependent), respondents being asked to specify the point on the bipolar scale most descriptive of themselves. Although the impact of using bipolar rather than unipolar scales is unknown, this factor could conceivably lower the correlations between the two measures.

Second, items assigned to Bem's M scale are trait descriptions that had been judged to be more desirable for men than for women; those assigned to the F scale are traits that had been judged to be more desirable for women than for men. The social desirability ratings for the PAQ, on the other hand, were obtained by asking subjects to specify where on each bipolar scale the ideal member of each sex fell. Items assigned to the M and F scales were those judged to be socially desirable for *both* sexes (i.e., the mean ratings for the ideal man and woman, although often statistically different, were nonetheless both on the same side of the scale midpoint). Items on which the mean ratings of the ideal male and female fell toward the *opposite* poles were assigned to a separate (M-F) scale. Inspection of the content of the BSRI and the PAQ indicates that, for trait descriptions common to both instruments, those belonging to our M-F scale are to be found on both the M and F scales of the BSRI (particularly on M) while other M and F items on the BSRI, not found on the PAQ, might well have been assigned to an M-F scale had our selection criterion been used. This impression was supported by an analysis of the Stapp-Kanner data in which part-whole correlations were obtained between scores on each of the three PAQ scales and each of the BSRI items. On nine of the sixty BSRI items, the highest correlation was with the M-F scale while, for a number of others, the correlation with M-F scores was very similar in value to the correlation with M or with F scores. In this connection, it is instructive to recall that the correlations between M and F we have found in college students have been uniformly positive, while the correlations between M-F and F have been uniformly negative. On the other hand, the correlations between M and F reported by Bem (1974) for the BSRI have tended to be slightly *negative*. This pattern of low positive correlations between the PAQ M and F scales and low negative correlations between the BSRI scales was also found in both sexes by Stapp and Kanner. The presence of what we would classify as M-F items on Bem's scales may thus largely be responsible both for the difference in the signs of the correlations between the two sets of M and F scales and for the imperfect relationships between the parallel scales on the BSRI and the PAQ.

The division of the items on the PAQ into three scales and on the BSRI into two has a number of additional implications, the following being most relevant to the Self-esteem findings. First, our data have consistently indicated that M-F scores have a markedly lower correlation with Self-esteem than M scores. Inclusion of M-F items on an M scale could therefore be expected to reduce the magnitude of the correlation with our Self-esteem measure. Second, when we computed correlations between Self-esteem scores and responses to individual PAQ items, we discovered that, while all F items—scored in a feminine direction—were positively correlated with Self-esteem, M-F items—scored in a masculine direction—were also positively related to Self-esteem, *even when they describe expressive, feminine characteristics.* Thus inclusion of items on an F scale that would be classified as M-F by our conceptual definition would reduce the correlation with Self-esteem even more markedly, since the scale would contain items both positively and negatively related to the criterion variable. The possibility exists, then, that the presence of items on the BSRI M and F scales that would not clearly meet our criterion for inclusion on these scales may sometimes cause somewhat different results to be obtained with the PAQ and the BSRI, not only in their relationships to self-esteem but also in their relationships with other variables.

In the second study attempting to replicate our findings on the relationships between self-esteem and masculinity and femininity, Wetter

(1975) used two novel instruments. The self-esteem measure was specifically devised for his study and the masculinity and femininity measures were scales derived from Jackson's (1967) Personality Research Form (PRF ANDRO scale) by Berzins, Welling, and Wetter (1975). The Personality Research Form does not ask respondents to assess themselves on trait descriptions but contains such items as "I think it would be best to marry someone who is more mature and less dependent than I." Although items for the PRF ANDRO scales were chosen as illustrations of the masculine and feminine attributes found on Bem's (1974) inventory, their content suggests that the scales tap a broader range of role-related behaviors and attitudes than the latter. The correlations reported by Berzins, Welling, and Wetter between the PRF ANDRO and the Bem scales range from .50 to .65, thus further suggesting that, while there is substantial overlap between the measures, they are not interchangeable.

Wetter classified his subjects (college students) on their joint masculinity and femininity scores, using the median split method. The differences among the four resulting groups in mean Self-esteem scores tended to mirror our results. The magnitude of the relationships was less than we had found in our samples, however, the Undifferentiated and Feminine groups in particular not consistently differing in their mean scores on Wetter's self-esteem measure. The possibility raised by these results is that the kinds of items about sex-role behaviors and preferences included on the PRF ANDRO measure not only fail to be strongly related to the personality dimensions of masculinity and femininity, as the previously cited Kanner and Stapp data suggest, but also do not necessarily enter into the same relationships with other variables (such as self-esteem) as the latter.

MASCULINITY, FEMININITY, AND BEHAVIOR

Informative data have been reported by Bem[2] (1977) from a series of experimental studies in which subjects were classified by the median split method on the basis of their masculinity and femininity scores on the BSRI and the behavior of the four groups compared. In the first experimental situation, originally reported in Bem (1975), sub-

---

2. In combining masculinity and femininity scores, Bem (1974) originally proposed what was in essence a balance model, individuals being defined as Androgynous whose scores on the two scales were essentially equal, independent of their absolute level; Masculine individuals as those whose masculinity scores exceeded their femininity scores; and Feminine individuals as those whose femininity scores exceeded their masculinity scores. This method of combining scores, essentially based on subtraction, has the effect of lumping together in the Androgynous category individuals we would classify as Undifferentiated and as Androgynous. In the paper cited above, Bem reanalyzed her previously reported experimental data (Bem 1975; Bem & Lenney 1976) using our four-way scheme and, on the basis of these results, suggested the greater utility of this "additive" method of combining scale scores as opposed to a subtractive one.

jects were given the opportunity to play with a kitten. Bem reasoned that individuals high in femininity, being more nurturant, would both initiate more interactions with the kitten and enjoy them more. The results from male subjects generally confirmed this expectation. In females, however, both M and F scores were related to the subjects' behavior, so that both Androgynous and Masculine women responded more to the kitten than women in the Feminine and Undifferentiated categories. In addition, Androgynous subjects of both sexes were most responsive and Undifferentiated subjects the least. (As an aside, we should note that play often involves agentic—including aggressive— elements [e.g., Aldis 1975]. Playing with a kitten may have elicited the expression of "masculine" characteristics as well as of nurturant, feminine characteristics.)

In a second experiment, subjects were placed in a social conformity situation in which they were falsely told that cartoons had been rated as funny or unfunny by other subjects when the reverse was actually true. Here Bem's expectation was that high M individuals, being more independent, would show less conformity in their cartoon ratings than individuals scoring low in M. In both sexes, this prediction was confirmed, Androgynous and Masculine subjects conforming less than Feminine and Undifferentiated subjects.

Still further behavioral data have been reported by Bem, Martyna, and Watson (1976) in a pair of investigations designed to explore expressiveness. In the first of these studies, female and male students were selected to represent in equal numbers Masculine, Feminine, and Androgynous individuals by means of her subtractive method of scoring the BSRI. (By this method, Androgynous individuals include those we would categorize as Undifferentiated; see Footnote 2.) In the experimental situation, each subject was given the opportunity to interact with a baby. Analysis of the subjects' nurturant behaviors toward the infant revealed no significant differences related to these three BSRI categories but, when the subjects were reassigned by the four-way median split method, Androgynous and Feminine students of both sexes were found to be significantly more responsive than the Masculine and Undifferentiated students. In the second study, students selected as in the first study were placed in a same-sex dyadic situation in which one was to act as a relatively passive listener while the other (who was actually a confederate of the experimenter) talked about himself or herself. The talker spoke of being a transfer student who felt lonely and socially isolated and was pleased to have the opportunity to talk to another student. The amount of verbal and nonverbal nurturant behavior exhibited by each listener was determined. Statistical analyses indicated that, for both methods of classifying subjects, Masculine (high M, low F) students were the deviant group, being significantly less nurturant in their behavior toward the talker than those in the other categories. (The method of selecting and initially classifying subjects probably resulted in a very limited number of Undifferentiated individuals being chosen, so that the meaningfulness of the data from this group is problematic.)

A final set of data that should be mentioned again involves self-report, but of an objective, factual nature. In his doctoral dissertation (1976) one of our students, William Beane, gathered life history data from a group of academic male scientists, as well as their responses to the PAQ. (Reference to other aspects of this study will be made in later chapters.) Those classified as Androgynous or Masculine (i.e., those high on M) listed more academic, extracurricular, and athletic honors received during adolescence and reported higher estimates of dating frequency than those classified as Feminine or Undifferentiated.

This series of studies yields encouraging evidence that a self-report measure of clusters of masculine and feminine attributes such as the Bem Sex Role Inventory and the Personal Attributes Questionnaire is related to observable behaviors and not merely to other self-report measures. The studies further suggest that the four-fold classification scheme for combining M and F scores is a useful one.[3] Considerable caution should be exercised, however, in designing behavioral studies aimed at establishing the concurrent validity of M and F scales in time-limited situations involving a narrow range of responses. The degree to which individuals exhibit agentic or communal behaviors, we again emphasize, is determined by a multiplicity of self- and situational variables. The predictability of individuals' display of agentic and communal behaviors from their M and F scores is likely to be particularly low in settings in which the individuals perceive strong pressures for sex-role conformity. Our speculations about the loose associations among gender-related phenomena also suggest that the existence of relationships between M and F scores and sex-typed behaviors of a different sort from the acting out of the types of predispositions tapped by these scales cannot automatically be assumed.

Overview of the Investigation

The relationships that have emerged from our research, supplemented by the data of other investigators, suggest that the psychological dimensions of masculinity and femininity, considered singly and in combination, have important consequences for other significant areas of functioning in both men and women. The demonstration that masculine and feminine characteristics form separate dimensions that vary relatively independently of each other also has profound implications for the ways we think about men and women and about sex-role differentiations.

3. The utility of this method of approach in instances in which the scales are each positively correlated to the criterion measure is not always apparent from the abbreviated discussion above. For example, Bem's analyses involved determining both multiple regressions of masculinity and femininity scores on the various dependent variables and the differences among the means of the four groups on these variables. As we have found in our Self-esteem data, the two scale scores did not combine linearly, so that the four-way classification scheme yielded more useful information than multiple regression.

The findings we have reviewed, however, have almost exclusively been obtained from college students in the United States, individuals who tend to be homogeneous in age and socioeconomic background, most coming from homes in which the parents are upper-middle-class and college-trained. Better-educated individuals are likely to have more egalitarian attitudes toward the sexes and, as parents, are less likely to impose rigid sex-role standards in rearing their children (e.g., Holter 1970; Scanzoni 1975). It is also possible that the educational, vocational, and interpersonal activities of well-educated, middle-class individuals in the American culture are particularly likely to demand both agentic and communal attributes for their successful execution. The acquisition and exhibition of these two sets of characteristics may therefore be reinforced in middle-class individuals of both sexes and may contribute to their feelings of social competence and self-esteem to a greater degree than in individuals from other cultural or socioeconomic groups.

The potential implications of the data made it crucial to determine not only whether the basic patterns of relationships found in our initial investigation could be replicated in other samples of college students but also whether they would be found in other populations. In the investigations to be reported here, our central efforts were focused on gathering data from a large number of junior and senior students enrolled in public high schools, a population both younger and considerably more diverse in a number of demographic characteristics than college students. These students were administered the Personal Attributes Questionnaire, the TSBI Self-esteem measure, and the Attitudes toward Women Scale, and the associations among these measures and their relationships to such demographic variables as the students' socioeconomic backgrounds were explored.

The work of anthropologists has stressed the intimate connections among masculine sex roles, achievement orientation, and the inculcation of achievement motives in males. The research of psychologists has also suggested that the nature of achievement motivation is related to gender. Female achievement behaviors were found by early investigators to be so inconsistent and resistant to theoretical analysis that subsequent investigators have tended to confine their studies to males (e.g., McClelland, Atkinson, Clark, & Lowell 1953) or have proposed different measures of achievement motivation for the two sexes (e.g., Mehrabian 1968, 1969). Factors unique to women that inhibit achievement behaviors have also been suggested (e.g., Horner 1968). The scope of our investigation was therefore expanded to include a study of achievement motivation and its relationship to the psychological dimensions of masculinity and femininity. For this purpose we devised an objective measure—the Work and Family Orientation (WOFO) Questionnaire—to be administered to the high school students. This self-report questionnaire, which during the course of our investigations has undergone several revisions, was designed in the hope that a multifactor instrument would emerge that, in conjunction with other measures, could be used to predict the achievement behaviors and aspirations of not only males but also females. A survey of the achievement motivation literature relevant to this inquiry will be found in Chapter 6.

In the second major extension of our previous work, some of the familial antecedents of masculinity and femininity were also explored. In addition to rating themselves on the M and F scales of the Personal Attributes Questionnaire, students also assessed each of their parents on the same characteristics so that parent-child resemblances could be determined. Information was also sought from the students on their parents' child-rearing attitudes and behaviors, and the interrelationships between these data and the measures of masculinity and femininity in students and in their parents were determined. The relationships of these parent variables with other student variables, most notably their achievement motivation and self-esteem, were also explored. The prior literature bearing on the influence of these parental factors will be presented in Chapter 9.

While high school students constituted the core sample of our investigation, we sought to verify and extend some of the findings obtained with these students by obtaining data from still other populations. In several instances, we took advantage of the cooperation of colleagues to gain information about individuals from unique populations, including students from foreign countries and such highly selected groups as academic scientists. Each of these samples was given one or more of the instruments administered to the high school students, occasionally supplemented by additional measures.

In the following chapter, we present a detailed description of our major psychometric instruments.

3. Measuring Instruments

The test battery for the high school sample, reproduced in Appendix A, consisted of a Family Information Sheet, on which respondents supplied demographic data about themselves and their family, and two test books made up of six objective questionnaires. In the first booklet were the Personal Attributes Questionnaire (PAQ), the Texas Social Behavior Inventory (TSBI), the Work and Family Orientation Questionnaire (WOFO), and the Attitudes toward Women Scale (AWS), the scales all inquiring about the respondents' characteristics and attitudes. In the second booklet were questionnaires seeking information about the respondents' family: the Parental Attributes Questionnaire and the Parental Attitudes Questionnaire. Brief descriptions of the instruments and their development are given below.

In other samples, given all or part of the test battery, supplementary measures were occasionally obtained. These will not be described here but at the place where data from these non–high school samples are discussed.

Family Information Sheet

The Family Information Sheet, reproduced in Appendix A, Table I, asked respondents to supply data about their sex and birth date; the adult(s) in their home responsible for their upbringing (natural mother and/or father, stepmother or father, foster mother or father, etc.) during three age periods: birth to five years, six to ten years, and eleven years and beyond; the employment status, occupation, and education of their father and mother (or their surrogates); the family's religion and ethnic background; and the age and sex of the respondents' siblings.

Personal Attributes Questionnaire

The instrument used to assess masculinity and femininity was the short form of the Personal Attributes Questionnaire (Spence, Helmreich, & Stapp 1974, 1975). This version (reproduced in Appendix A) is composed of twenty-four bipolar items describing personal characteristics, on each of which respondents are to rate themselves on a five-point scale. The questionnaire is divided into three eight-item scales, labeled Masculinity (M), Femininity (F), and Masculinity-

Femininity (M-F).[1] Each item is scored from 0 to 4, a high score on items assigned to the M and M-F scales indicating an extreme masculine response and a high score on F scale items indicating an extreme feminine response. Total scores are obtained on each scale by adding the individual's scores on the eight items. The range of possible values is thus 0 to 32 for each scale.

The method used to combine scale scores so that individuals can be jointly described on M and F or on all three scales is described in a later section (p. 35).

DEVELOPMENT OF THE PAQ

We briefly described the development of the PAQ in Chapter 2. The steps in the derivation of the three PAQ scales are so essential to an understanding of the concepts of masculinity and femininity as we have defined them that we will present a more detailed description of them here.

The full version of the PAQ contains 55 bipolar items drawn from a pool of over 130 items that had largely been put together by Rosenkrantz, Vogel, Bee, Broverman, and Broverman (1968) from nominations by students of characteristics differentiating men and women. The primary purpose of these investigators was to demonstrate the existence of "sex-role stereotypes" by having subjects rate the typical adult male and the typical adult female on each item. Ratings of the ideal individual (sex unspecified) were also obtained. In a replication and extension of their study, with larger samples, we first administered the entire pool of items to groups of introductory psychology students with instructions to rate on each item either the typical adult male and the typical adult female, the typical college student of each sex, or the ideal individual of each sex. Following these ratings, the students were asked to rate themselves on each item.

The fifty-five items we selected for the PAQ were drawn from among those for which both sexes exhibited a consistent stereotype about sex differences. That is, the mean ratings of the typical member of each sex given by female and by male respondents differed significantly for these items, whether the typical adult or the typical student was being rated. Comparison of the mean self-ratings of the women and men indicated that, on all fifty-five items, the sexes also turned out to differ significantly in the direction of the stereotype in their self-report. Thus the PAQ is made up of items describing characteristics that are not only commonly believed to differentiate the sexes but on which men and women tend to report themselves as differing.

The ideal ratings on these fifty-five items were also in the direction

---

1. In earlier publications (Spence et al. 1974, 1975), we called this scale "Sex-specific" but have now adopted the designation "Masculinity-Femininity" because it better communicates the scale's bipolar nature in contrast to the Masculinity and Femininity scales.

of the stereotype—that is, for each item the mean rating of the ideal woman and the ideal man lay on the same side of the scale midpoint as the mean rating of the typical member of that sex, although often closer to the extreme pole. From these latter data it may be inferred that the stereotypic characteristics included on the PAQ are favorably regarded, socially desirable attributes.

The ideal ratings were used to divide the PAQ items into three scales: Masculine, Feminine, and Masculine-Feminine. Masculine items were defined as characteristics socially desirable in both sexes but believed to occur to a greater degree in males. An item was considered to meet this definition if the mean ratings of both the ideal man and the ideal woman fell on the same side of the scale midpoint and toward the stereotypically masculine pole. Twenty-three items exhibited this pattern and were therefore assigned to the Masculinity (M) scale. Feminine items were similarly defined as socially desirable characteristics said to occur to a greater degree in females. Mean ratings of both the ideal man and woman fell on the stereotypically feminine side of the midpoint for eighteen items, which were thus assigned to the Femininity (F) scale. For items assigned to the third scale, the mean ratings of the ideal man and woman lay on the *opposite* sides of the midpoint, suggesting that what was socially desirable for one sex was not socially desirable for the other. The thirteen items exhibiting this pattern were assigned to a separate scale, identified as the Masculinity-Femininity (M-F) scale. One item could not be classified.

In the PAQ, the respondents are asked to rate themselves on each of the bipolar items on a five-point scale and separate scores are determined for each individual on the three scales. In the initial sample of individuals (college students) to whom the PAQ was given, part-whole correlations were computed between each of the item scores and each of the three scale scores (M, F, and M-F). The correlations of the items with the scale to which each had been assigned were found to be higher than their correlations with the other two scales. The results of this analysis thus justified empirically the division of the items into three self-report scales, a division initially made on the basis of the patterning of ratings of the ideal member of each sex. Comparisons of the mean self-ratings of the male and female members of the initial sample revealed a significant difference in the expected direction for every item as well as for the three scale scores, thus permitting the PAQ to be used as a measure of masculinity and femininity.

Conceptual justification for the division of the items into the three scales was found by inspecting item content. As would have been predicted by Bakan (1966) and other theorists, the items on the M scale were found to refer largely to instrumental, agentic characteristics, while items on the F scale refer largely to expressive, communal attributes. The content of the M-F scale is mixed, containing items that could be classified as agentic, as communal, or as a combination of both. The items included on the short, eight-item version of the scale may be described as falling into two major groups. The first group is

composed of two items referring to instrumental, agentic characteristics (aggressiveness and dominance), the second of items referring
to a cluster of characteristics suggesting emotional vulnerability and
the need for emotional support (e.g., cries easily, strong need for
security, feelings easily hurt).

Items on the M-F scale might have been reassigned to the M or F
scales, where possible, on the basis of agentic or communal content
or might have been dropped altogether from the PAQ, leaving only
the M and F scales. Several reasons dictated their retention as a separate scale. First, reassignment would do violence to our definition of
masculinity and femininity as attributes more characteristic of one
sex than the other but socially desirable in both. That is, the data
suggested that for these items what is socially desirable differs in the
two sexes, thus making it impossible to assign the items to either the
M or F scales. Second, analyses of the data, such as the part-whole
correlations reported above, suggested that the M-F items are more
related to each other than to either the F or M scales. Still further
analyses, some of which are reported below, indicate that M-F scale
scores add information not available from the M and F scales alone.

SOCIAL DESIRABILITY AND INTELLIGENCE

Since PAQ attributes are socially desirable, an initial threat to the
instrument's validity was the possibility that scores might be distorted
by respondents' bias toward selecting socially desirable answers. This
relationship was explored in college students using the Marlowe-
Crowne Social Desirability (SD) scale (Crowne & Marlowe 1961) as
the index of social desirability. The correlations between the SD scale
and the three PAQ scales in male and female students ranged between .08 and .36 (Spence, Helmreich, & Stapp 1975). While several
of the correlations reached statistical significance, their magnitude
was unimpressive. Further, when partial correlations controlling for
SD scores were computed between the PAQ scales and a measure of
self-esteem (TSBI; see below), the previously established relationships between the PAQ and Self-esteem measures remained unchanged. Even more convincing data may be found in the pages that
follow. The patterns of differences in PAQ scores between samples
drawn from different populations of individuals and the relationships
found between PAQ scores and several behavioral indices are not ex-
plicable on the basis of social desirability, thus suggesting that individual differences in PAQ scale scores are not seriously contaminated
by this type of response bias.

Still another exogenous variable to be considered is intelligence,
since brighter individuals might acquire desirable characteristics in
greater abundance or be more adept at presenting themselves in a
favorable light than those of lesser ability. Using the Scholastic Aptitude Test Verbal and Quantitative scores as a measure of intelligence,
we recently examined the relationships between V and Q scores and
the three PAQ scales in a sample of approximately five hundred col-

lege students. These proved to be essentially orthogonal, the correlations ranging from .02 with M to −.12 with F.

DEVELOPMENT OF THE SHORT FORM

For the short form of the PAQ, used with very occasional exception in the samples whose data are to be reported here, eight items were chosen from each of the original scales, primarily on the basis of the magnitude of the part-whole correlation between the item and the scale to which it belonged. For one sample of college students given the full PAQ, the correlations between the full scale scores and the eight-item version were .93, .93, and .91 for M, F, and M-F respectively. Cronbach alphas for a sample of students given the short form were .85, .82, and .78 for M, F, and M-F respectively. Thus, despite their brevity, the scales are satisfactorily reliable.

MEDIAN SPLIT METHOD FOR JOINT CLASSIFICATION ON M, F, AND M-F

In instances in which more than one of the individual scales on the PAQ are found to be correlated with other variables, a method of combining scale scores is necessary if the nature of the conjoint relationship is to be determined. The approach we have adopted for purposes of both description and prediction is first to determine for a total sample (females and males combined) or a normative group the median scores on the M and F scales. Then the individuals are classified by means of a 2 by 2 table according to their position above or below the median on the two scales. The four cells and the identifying label we have given to each one are shown in Table 3-1. The four-way classification may be expanded into an eight-way classification by dividing individuals in each of the four cells into those falling above and those falling below the overall median on the M-F scale.

We have established two sets of normative values for the purpose of classifying subjects on the short form of the PAQ. The first is based on the rounded mean of the medians of the males and the females in the high school sample, to be described. (The mean of the medians for the two sexes was used rather than the median of the total sample because of unequal numbers of males and females.) The values thus established (all out of a possible 32) are 20 for the M scale, 23 for

Table 3-1. *Scheme for Classifying Individuals on Masculinity and Femininity Scores by a Median Split*

| | | Masculinity | |
		Above median	Below median
Femininity	Above median	Androgynous	Feminine
	Below median	Masculine	Undifferentiated

the F scale, and 15 for the M-F scale, individuals obtaining these scores or above being classified as above the median and those obtaining lesser scores being classified as below the median.

A second set of norms was established in a similar manner, using the data from 715 college students. The medians for the F and M-F scales turned out to be the same as for high school students; those for the M scale turned out to be one point higher. The values are thus 21, 23, and 15 for M, F, and M-F respectively. Although strict comparability across samples is compromised by the use of different norms, we concluded that relationships within a given type of population might be more clearly revealed if values established for that population were employed.

A TECHNICAL NOTE ON THE COMBINATION OF PAQ SCORES

Since not only the PAQ scales but also almost all the other measures we have employed yield continuous scores, we have uniformly calculated Pearson r's to determine the magnitude and the direction of the relationship of each PAQ scale to other variables of interest. We have also routinely tested the relationships for curvilinearity and, with rare exceptions (which will be specifically noted), have found them to be linear.

Multiple regression is one of the techniques that can be used to determine the joint relationship between the PAQ scales and some other variable in an attempt to increase the predictability of the latter. Our initial decision to use a categorical system for combining PAQ scores was based on our finding that linear regression did not notably improve the prediction of Self-esteem scores when M and F scores were entered stepwise into the regression equation, despite the fact that both were linearly and significantly related to each other and to Self-esteem. Multiple regression has also failed to bring about marked changes in the amount of variance accounted for in a number of subsequent analyses, indicating that the ineffectiveness of the multiple regression technique was not unique to Self-esteem.

A complex description of the joint relationship of the PAQ scales to other variables is possible to achieve using dummy weights in regression, but the categorization method we have developed has turned out to be both easier to communicate conceptually and more parsimonious computationally. There are, however, a number of drawbacks associated with the use of our categorization scheme.

The first is the loss of useful data on individual variability when respondents are classified into broad categories. When accuracy of prediction (as opposed to descriptive clarity) is a goal, a multiple r to determine whether the variance accounted for can be increased, relative to any PAQ scale taken singly, should routinely be calculated. Accuracy can also be increased by use of more refined categorizations, such as four-way splits of both M and F based on quartiles. We have tested such schemes, relating the resulting categories to Self-esteem. These breakdowns on Self-esteem (and subsequently on other variables, each monotonically and positively correlated to M and F) indicated that no new conceptual information about the nature of the relationship was revealed. For heuristic purposes we have therefore chosen to employ the simplest meaningful classification system in describing the combination of PAQ scale scores. Should the relationship between PAQ scores and other variables of interest not be monotonic, however, a more refined classification than a median split may be required to reveal the joint relationships.

A second drawback in the use of the categorical method has to do with the classification of cases whose scores fall at or near the median. The joint distribution for females and males on each of the PAQ scales is essentially normal. Particularly since the possible range of scores on each of the eight-item scales is relatively small, a considerable number of respondents can be expected to be closely clustered around the median. (For example, in the case of our high school sample, the percentage of individuals falling within ±1 point of the median was 26 for M, 27 for F, and 25 for M-F.) A shift of even one point on one scale in an individual's score can therefore result in a shift in category assignment for a substantial number of respondents and can thus significantly alter the distribution of individuals in the four- and eight-category schemata. However, in the populations for which we have multiple samples, the stability of means and medians has been great, and marked differences have not been found between populations of nonselected individuals (e.g., college vs. high school students).

Nevertheless, when relatively small samples are drawn, some variation in the sample median and the resultant categorical distribution is to be expected. One solution, of course, is to recompute the median splits for each sample (assuming it consists of both sexes), particularly if the sample is drawn from a unique population, and to make the categorizations according to ad hoc norms. However, we have used the general norms developed in our research with high school and college populations to classify individuals from other populations, even at the risk of some random distortion in the categorical distributions, because of our interest in making cross-group comparisons to determine if theoretically meaningful differences in the pattern of distributions are present. The sensitivity of the categorization method to random variations suggests, however, that cross-group differences should be interpreted cautiously unless sample sizes are large.

The particular norms used should be dictated by the research questions of interest. In some cases, such as investigations using a relatively small random sample of college students, the general college norms we have developed with large samples would probably be most appropriate. In other cases, the computation of categorical scores using norms both from the research population and from our college or high school population might be desirable. For example, a cross-cultural investigator might wish to compute norms for the society being studied and also to examine the distribution produced by U.S. norms. Similarities and differences in the pattern of scores on other measures, such as Self-esteem, could then be examined.

In summary, the median split technique provides data subject to some statistical distortion. The method should be used with particular sensitivity to whether the research questions deal primarily with between-group or within-group comparisons, and results from its use should be interpreted with caution, especially when between-group comparisons are being made. The same caveats hold when degree of concordance of categorization is being sought for test-retest data or in comparisons of two masculinity-femininity measures (e.g., the PAQ and the Bem Sex Role Inventory). Even when test-retest correlations on the individual scales or correlations across different instruments are high, the degree of agreement in categorizing individuals may be relatively modest because of the influence of small random shifts in scores close to the median.

Texas Social Behavior Inventory

The short, sixteen-item form of the Texas Social Behavior Inventory (Helmreich & Stapp 1974) was used to measure self-esteem (see Appendix A, Table III). The TSBI is composed of statements designed to assess the individual's self-confidence and competence in social situations. For each item respondents rate themselves on a five-point scale, varying from "not at all characteristic of me" to "very much characteristic of me." Responses are scored 0 to 4, high scores indicating high self-esteem, and summed to yield individuals' overall scores. The range of possible scores is thus 0 to 64.

Oblique factor analyses of the full (32-item) scale have revealed three factors that may be labeled self-confidence, social dominance, and social competence (Helmreich, Stapp, & Ervin 1974). Generally, however, the scale appears to assess a quite unitary concept of social self-esteem. Correlations of the TSBI with the Marlowe-Crowne SD scale in a sample of college students have been found to be relatively low (.12 in women and .29 in men; Spence, Helmreich, & Stapp 1975).

The correlation between the short and long forms for a sample of college students given the latter was found to be .96. For a sample of college students given the sixteen-item version, the Cronbach alpha was .91. Evidence for the construct validity of the TSBI is to be found in such studies as experimental investigations of interpersonal attraction, in which predictions of the differential reactions of individuals high and low in self-esteem to competent men (e.g., Helmreich, Aronson, & LeFan 1970) were successfully verified.

Attitudes toward Women Scale

A short, fifteen-item version of the Attitudes toward Women Scale (Spence & Helmreich 1972b; Spence, Helmreich, & Stapp 1973) was employed (see Appendix A, Table IV). This scale contains statements describing the rights, roles, and privileges women ought to have or be permitted and requires respondents to indicate their agreement with each statement on a four-point scale ranging from "agree strongly" to "disagree strongly." Items are scored 0 to 3, high scores indicating a profeminist, egalitarian attitude. Possible total scores thus run from 0 to 45.

The fifteen-item version has been found to have a correlation of .91 with the original fifty-five item AWS in a sample of college students. The Cronbach alpha of the fifteen-item form has been found to be .89, again in a sample of college students.

Extensive data concerning score differences between various groups in expected directions provide evidence for the construct validity of the AWS. For example, the present writers have found that women score higher (are more profeminist) than men and that college students score higher than their same-sex parent (Spence & Helmreich 1972b); that undergraduate students in introductory psychology score lower than graduate students in psychology but higher than engineering majors; that high-scoring, profeminist students differ in their reactions to competent women, and so on.

Work and Family Orientation Questionnaire

The Work and Family Orientation Questionnaire was developed especially for the present project as a measure of achievement motivation and aspiration.

The initial version of the Work and Family Orientation Questionnaire (WOFO-1), which was given to the bulk of the samples, contains twenty-two items. The final three items inquire about the least amount of education that would satisfy the respondent, the relative importance of marriage in comparison to vocation in determining life satisfaction, and the number of children ideally desired. Each of these items is independently scored. The remaining nineteen items consist of statements concerning work- and achievement-related situations to which individuals respond on a five-point scale ranging from "strongly agree" to "strongly disagree." These items are in part original and in part derived from items on scales developed by Mehrabian (1969). It was also our intent to develop scales tapping several possible facets of achievement motivation rather than a single, global measure.

The data from high school students tested during 1974–75 were factor analyzed independently by sex, using the principal components solution with oblique rotation in SPSS (Nie, Hull, Jenkins, Steinbrenner, & Bent 1975). From the resultant factor solutions, six scales were formed, labeled Work Orientation, Mastery, Competitiveness, Effort, Job Concerns, and Spouse Career Aspirations. (More detail about the procedures used to form the scales is found in Chapter 7.) The composition of the instrument, factor pattern matrices, scale composition and reliabilities, and scale intercorrelations are given in Appendix A (Tables V–VIII).

Examination of the factor structure of the original instrument (WOFO-1) suggested that the important theoretical concept of competitiveness was poorly measured and needed further explication. Because of this deficiency and the inappropriateness of several items in the original scale for an adult population, a revised measure (WOFO-2) was developed. In this form, the items dealing with the pay and prestige of jobs for self and spouse were dropped, while five new items dealing with mastery and competition were added. The resultant fourteen-item scale was administered to the high school students tested in 1975–76, as well as to several samples of older individuals whose data will subsequently be reported.

Factor analyses of this scale were conducted using the same solution applied to WOFO-1. From this factor analysis, four scales were derived which we have labeled Work Orientation, Mastery, Competitiveness, and Personal Unconcern. Composition of the instrument, the factor pattern matrix, scale composition and reliabilities, and scale intercorrelations are given in Appendix A (Tables IX–XI). A further development of the instrument (WOFO-3) will be described in later chapters.

Parental Attitudes Questionnaire

The Parental Attitudes Questionnaire, shown in Appendix A, Table XII, was also devised for the present project. The first section of the questionnaire consists of fifty-eight items, inquiring about parents' attitudes and behaviors or the family atmosphere. (Respondents were instructed to interpret "parent" broadly, to include a stepparent, foster parent, or other adult guardian responsible for their upbringing all or most of their lives.) The first eight items contain statements about both parents or the family as a whole. These are followed by twenty-five statements about the mother and a parallel set of statements about the father. Each item is accompanied by a five-point scale, ranging from "very characteristic" to "very uncharacteristic."

The last section contains five items, designed to determine the parent to whom the respondent feels closest or most resembles in ideals and personality, as well as the degree of parental agreement about child rearing. These items, each accompanied by five response alternatives, were scored separately. Except for the question about child rearing, the purpose of these items was to provide a measure of mother vs. father identification. A number of investigators (e.g., Heilbrun 1973) have operationalized the identification concept in terms of the parent whose actual or perceived characteristics the child more closely resembles. In the present investigation, students were asked by means of these items to specify directly the parent whom they resemble more or to whom they are closer, thus providing a global measure of identification independent of the similarity between the students' self-ratings on the characteristics included on the Personal Attributes Questionnaire and their perception of their parents on the same characteristics.

In devising the questionnaire we consulted parent interview schedules and objective questionnaires used in prior investigations of parent-child relations. We were influenced in particular by the findings of such investigators as Baumrind (1971) and Coopersmith (1967)—working with the parents of young children—and Heilbrun (1973)—working with perceptions of parents by adolescents and young adults. Their investigations suggest that such parental behaviors as degree of affection; use of praise, criticism, and punishment as disciplinary techniques; use of reasoning; degree of encouragement of independence; strictness of rules; and consistency of rule enforcement have an important impact on family closeness and harmony and on the development in children of the types of characteristics under investigation here. In addition to items relating to these variables, our interests also lead us to include several items concerning the parents' attitudes toward "women's liberation" and sex-role training. No effort was made to assess the parents' cognitive training of their children or the educational or occupational goals they set for them. In pilot work with college students, a preliminary questionnaire containing over one hundred items was administered. Largely because of the limited amount of time available from respondents to be given the full test battery, the original version was cut drastically in length, the items showing the most promise of being related to students' masculinity and femininity and self-esteem being retained.

In the high school sample whose data are to be reported, students were identified whose homes had been intact since birth. The responses of these students to the initial fifty-eight items of the Parental Attitudes Questionnaire were factor analyzed for each sex by alpha factor analysis with the equimax rotation technique. Nine factors emerged in each sex: seven were highly comparable and two had less similarity. Based on the results of these analyses, seven scales common to each sex were constructed, items with factor loadings of .30 or more on a given factor in both sexes being assigned to the scale representing that factor. For the remaining two factors for each sex, separate male and female scales were developed, using the .30 factor loading as a criterion for item selection. Thus there were eleven scales—seven common to both sexes, two derived from the data from males, and two derived from the data from females. A label and a brief description of each scale are given in Table 3-2, both labels and descriptions reflecting high scores on the scales.

Separate scores were computed on all eleven scales for each respondent. Each item was scored from 0 to 4, and item scores were summed to obtain the scale score.

Factor or other similar analyses reported in prior investigations typically reveal that two basic dimensions underlie parental behaviors, these commonly identified as acceptance vs. rejection and restrictiveness vs. permissiveness (e.g., Schaefer 1959). Parallel results emerged in the high school sample from second-order factor analyses based on

Table 3-2. *Parental Behavior Scales from the Parental Attitude Questionnaire*

Common to both sexes
  1. Father Positivity (N = 11). Father encouraging and supportive, consistent, physically affectionate, praises, uses reason.
  2. Mother Positivity (N = 8). Mother nonpunitive and noncritical, encourages discussion, interested, consistent, few arguments.
  3. Father Democracy (N = 8). Father uses reason, not strict, encourages discussion, allows questioning, noncritical.
  4. Mother Democracy (N = 8). Mother encouraging, uses reason, does not insist on her own way, mother and father encourage questioning of rules.
  5. Rule Enforcement (N = 6). Many family rules, mother strict, mother and father care about rule enforcement.
  6. Family Protectiveness (N = 3). Mother and father cautious about child for fear of hurt, knew what child was up to.
  7. Sex-Role Enforcement (N = 4). Father and mother unsympathetic to "women's lib," minded child playing with opposite-sex toys.

Specific to each sex
  8. Male Family Harmony (N = 7). Family close, does things together, both parents affectionate, father encouraging; respondent will bring up children same way.
  9. Female Family Harmony and Mother Supportiveness (N = 16). Family close, parents will be pleased by child having a career, encourage child to stick up for rights; mother affectionate, praising, interested, encouraging, uses reason; respondent will bring up children same way.
  10. Male Achievement Standards (N = 9). Parents pleased by successful career; father sets high standards, uses discussion, is approving; mother encourages to do best, is interested, praises child for doing well.
  11. Female Standards (N = 5). Child has a daily schedule, mother strict and critical, mother and father set high standards.

N = number of items

the scale scores derived from the original factor analyses and computed by the principal axis technique with varimax rotation. (The results are reported in Table XV, Appendix A.) Three similar factors were found in each sex which may be labeled Mother and Family Acceptance, Father Acceptance, and Strictness of Family Rules and Standards. For both sexes, the scales loading highest on the Mother-Family Acceptance factor were Mother Positivity, Mother Democracy, and Family Harmony (Male scale for males, Female scale for females). For males, the Male Achievement Standards scale also loaded heavily, and Father Positivity moderately, on the Mother-Family Acceptance factor, but in females the loadings on the parallel scales (Father Positivity, Female Standards) were relatively low. The scales contributing most to the Father Acceptance factor in both sexes were Father Positivity and Father Democracy; in males, Family Harmony also contributed moderately to this factor. Scales loading highest on the third factor—Strictness of Family Rules and Standards—were the same or parallel for each sex: Rule Enforcement, Family Protectiveness, and Male Achievement Standards or Female Standards. The Sex-Role Enforcement scale, it is interesting to note, did not contribute significantly to any of these factors in either sex.

Items on the questionnaire and the results of the factor analyses are shown in Appendix A (Tables XII–XIII). Also reported (Table XIV) are Cronbach alphas for the scales and the correlations among them.

Parental Attributes Questionnaire

The respondents in the high school sample were presented with the sixteen items making up the Masculinity and Femininity scales on the Personal Attributes Questionnaire and asked to rate their mother on each of these characteristics, as they perceived her. (If they had been brought up most of their life by a stepmother, foster mother, or other female guardian, they were to answer for her instead.) They were then asked to rate their father or father surrogate on each item. The Parental Attributes Questionnaire is presented in Appendix A, Table XVI. The eight M-F items on the Personal Attributes Questionnaire on which high school students rated themselves were omitted from the parent questionnaires because of time limitations. A Parental Attributes Questionnaire containing all three PAQ scales, however, was employed with a sample of college students. (Self-report data on these scales were also obtained from the mothers and fathers of many of these college students.)

4. Sample Characteristics and Testing Procedures

High School Students

SAMPLE CHARACTERISTICS

The core sample of the project was composed of juniors and seniors enrolled in five New England public high schools. Students in three of these schools were tested during the 1974–75 academic year. In one of these schools, located in a community in the greater Boston area, the participating students were predominantly from Catholic families of Italian extraction who were of middle- to upper-middle-class socioeconomic status, as determined by the occupation and education of the father or other head of household. The second school, also located in the greater Boston area, served a more heavily blue-collar community that was predominantly Irish Catholic in ethnic-religious identification. The third school was a regional high school outside Worcester, Massachusetts, whose students more frequently came from Protestant middle-class families.

Students from the other two schools were tested during the 1975–76 academic year. One of these schools was located in a coastal city in Massachusetts, the other in a suburb of New Haven, Connecticut, both serving predominantly middle-class families. A broad range of socioeconomic and religious backgrounds, however, was found at every school. In one of the schools, all junior and senior English classes participated in the study and, in the others, junior-senior classes in social science.

Students in all schools were given the same test battery, except for the Work and Family Orientation Questionnaire (WOFO). Students in the first three schools in which testing was conducted were given the initial version of this questionnaire (WOFO-1), and those in the two schools tested in the subsequent year were given a later revision of the questionnaire (WOFO-2).

Although the students from the five schools differed in a number of identifiable demographic characteristics, there was no indication that other factors associated with the school in which they were enrolled interacted with the variables on which the students were being tested. Statistical analyses were therefore conducted without regard to the particular school which students attended.

As will be described in more detail later, the students were all tested during regular class sessions, the test battery being administered by their class teacher. It did not prove feasible to obtain data on the number of students in each class who, for whatever reason, chose not to participate, but our impression was that the participation rate was close to 90%, with more females cooperating than males. Of those who did take part, not all were able to complete the entire test battery in the time available, however, or to supply usable data on all the questionnaires they attempted. These partial protocols were not ignored. Rather, in each analysis, the results from all students who supplied usable data on the relevant measure or measures were retained. The largest single group, obtained for students answering the Personal Attributes Questionnaire (PAQ), numbered 1,769 (756 males and 1,013 females).

The smallest subsample consisted of 374 males and 589 females and was composed of students who met the following criteria: (a) came from intact homes, (b) could be classified as to socioeconomic level, (c) with occasional exception on a particular measure, supplied usable data on the entire test battery, and (d) were white. (The latter restriction was imposed because of possible differences between white and nonwhite populations and the small number of the latter in the total sample.) This group provided data in the analyses that attempted to uncover the pattern of relationships between the students' masculinity and femininity and their perceptions of their parents' masculinity and femininity and their parents' behavior toward them. Because of the highly selected nature of this sample, the major analyses performed on all students for whom directly relevant data were available were repeated for members of this restricted group. The basic relationships occurring in the larger sample were in all cases replicated in the smaller one and, for this reason, will not routinely be reported in later chapters.

Demographic data. In racial composition, the total sample of students was almost exclusively white, 97% of the students identifying themselves as belonging to this racial group. The nonwhite students were fairly evenly distributed over socioeconomic groups. No formal attempt was made to classify the students on ethnicity since the open-ended question in which they were to supply this information (a format used because of community sensitivities) produced answers of various kinds and, frequently, no ethnically relevant answer at all.

Over 90% of the students came from intact homes, that is, homes in which both the natural (or adoptive) mother and father had resided during all three age periods about which the students were queried. Of the remaining students, a number had a stepparent and a natural parent in the home, at least during the age period of eleven years and beyond. Forty-nine students indicated that during this period only the mother was present, and thirty-three reported some other type of adult guardianship (father only, grandparent[s], foster parents, etc.). Because of the difficulties associated with assigning families whose head of household was female to a socioeconomic level and because of the relatively small numbers of homes involved, all analyses to be reported that include socioeconomic class as a factor were based on students coming from homes in which the head of the household was male (natural father, stepfather, male guardian, etc.). Informal inspection of the occupational and educational data reported for women who were heads of households suggested that they did not come disproportionately from one social class.

Table 4-1 shows the breakdown of the sample in which there was a male head of household into four socioeconomic levels and, within each of the levels, the family's religious affiliation. Socioeconomic status was determined by a composite index based on the head of household's education and occupation.

Although the four socioeconomic groups have been labeled Upper, Upper middle, Lower middle, and Lower, respectively, it should be understood that, in comparison with the population as a whole, the distribution is truncated at both extremes. In the families identified as Upper class, the fathers' occupations were predominantly in professional or middle-management business categories, so that the label as used here does not represent extreme wealth or the upper reaches of social position. The homes identified as Lower class were very stable, almost 89% of them being intact and 99% of the male heads of households being reported as employed. Sixty percent of the mothers in these families were reported as high school graduates, and an additional 19% had had some kind of training beyond high school. (For Lower-class fathers, the comparable figures were 47% and 30%.) "Lower" class is thus being used only in a relative sense, "blue collar" or "working class" being more accurate.

Inspection of Table 4–1 reveals that religious affiliation was associated with socioeconomic level. The percentage of Catholic families increased linearly with class, 40% of the Upper-class students reporting this affiliation as opposed to 79% of the Lower-class students. Conversely, the percentage of Protestant families decreased linearly with social class (e.g., 34% of Upper class vs. 19% of Lower class), as did the percentage of Jewish families (e.g., 17% of the Upper class vs. 0% in the Lower).

Further description of the sample may be found in Appendix B, which contains the distributions for each socioeconomic class of mothers' and fathers' education, the percentage of intact homes at each of the three age periods, the number of children in the family, and the fathers' and mothers' employment status. Little or no difference among classes was noted in racial composition, the percentage

Table 4-1. *Distribution of High School Sample among the Four Socioeconomic Groups and Percentage within Each Group in Each Category of Religious Preference*

Class	N	Catholic	Protestant	Jewish	None	Other	% of total
Upper	185	40	34	17	9	0	14
Upper middle	520	58	31	7	3	1	39
Lower middle	496	62	29	7	1	1	37
Lower	144	79	19	0	2	0	11
% of total		59	29	8	3	1	100

of fathers who were employed, or the percentage of intact families, but the rest of the variables showed not unanticipated associations with class.

ADMINISTRATION OF THE TEST BATTERY

In all the high schools in which testing was conducted, the cooperation of faculty members of a specific academic department was obtained. The teachers agreed to administer the various questionnaires to members of their junior-senior classes on two successive days in the regular classroom setting. With rare exception, testing was done by all teachers on the same days. On the first day, students were given a brief explanation of the study and instructions on how to fill out a machine-scorable answer sheet and were then asked to fill out the Family Information Sheet. In most classes, the two test booklets containing the six major questionnaires were administered on the second day. However, in some classes, the first test booklet was administered following the Family Information Sheet on the first day, the second booklet the next day.

Students were given a very general explanation of the purpose of the study by their teacher and were told that they would be questioned about what they themselves were like, their opinions on several topics, and their perceptions of their families. It was explained that students from a variety of schools were being surveyed so that an accurate picture of student views could be obtained.

Teachers also instructed the students that participation was voluntary and that, while they were urged to answer all questions if they chose to take part, they were free to stop at any time. (Nonparticipating students did, however, remain in their seats until the end of each session.) Confidentiality of their answers was stressed and, to guarantee this, students were asked to identify themselves on their answer sheets by a code name or by their telephone number. This identifying code was used only to match answer sheets.

The first test booklet contained the Personal Attributes Questionnaire, the Work and Family Orientation Questionnaire, the Attitudes toward Women Scale (AWS), and the Texas Social Behavior Inventory (TSBI), each accompanied by its own brief explanation and instructions. The seventy-seven items making up these scales were numbered consecutively, however, and students recorded their responses on a machine-scorable answer sheet. The second booklet, supplied with a second answer sheet, contained the Parental Attitudes Questionnaire, followed by the Parental Attributes Questionnaire for the mother and for the father, the three scales totaling ninety-five items. At the conclusion of each class session, the test booklets and answer sheets were collected by the teacher and returned to one of the investigators or one of their assistants, available at the school during the test days to distribute materials and to answer teacher and student questions.

Students and teachers were also promised that after the data were analyzed they would be given a report of the results. A semitechnical report stressing the major trends in the data was prepared, and copies were sent to the participating school close to the end of the school year in which testing took place.

Supplementary Samples

Data will be reported in later chapters from a number of samples given one or more of the instruments administered to the high school students, occasionally supplemented by measures not obtained from the latter. Several of the largest samples were composed of students in introductory psychology at the University of Texas at Austin tested during the years 1974 to 1976. Students ordinarily were administered the instruments during a regular class period early in the semester or in special group testing sessions in which they participated to fill a course research requirement. In previous research we have found that a very substantial proportion of the students in this population come from white, upper-middle- and upper-class Protestant homes. Because of the homogeneity of these samples, no attempt was made to break them down on the basis of demographic factors.

Other samples include such groups as Ph.D. scientists and female varsity athletes at the same institution, as well as students from countries other than the United States. The composition of these groups will be described in more detail when their data are presented. The primary purpose of testing these supplementary samples was to determine whether some of the relationships found in high school students and in our earlier studies of college students would be replicated in other types of populations as well as to explore further some of the implications of our major findings.

5. Interrelationships among the Personal Attributes, Self-esteem, and Attitudes toward Women Measures

Correlations among the Measures

In our original study with college students (Spence, Helmreich, & Stapp 1975), differences were found between the means of males and females on the three Personal Attributes Questionnaire (PAQ) scale scores—males scoring significantly lower on the F scale and higher on the M and M-F scales (scored in a masculine direction) than females. It was this demonstration of significant sex differences on the scale that justified identification of the several clusters of attributes with the concepts of masculinity and femininity.

Of more critical interest, the correlations of the M and F scales were significantly positive in both sexes, thus refuting a bipolar interpretation of masculinity and femininity that regards the two clusters of attributes essentially as opposites. The M-F scale did support the implications of the bipolar conception, however, this scale being moderately correlated in a positive direction with M scores and in a negative direction with F scores.

These same relationships have been explored in two subsequent samples of college students. The students, 715 in number, were drawn from introductory psychology classes over two successive semesters. Both samples were tested with the short forms of the several scales, as described in Chapter 3. Significant differences (p's < .01) between the means of men and women on the three PAQ scales were again found in both samples. The mean of these sample means for each sex is reported for the three scales at the bottom of Table 5-1. The mean of the means is also reported for the Self-esteem measure (TSBI) and the Attitudes toward Women Scale (AWS). In both samples, the difference between the means of the two sexes was not significant for Self-esteem but was significant (p's < .01) for the AWS, women being more profeminist than men. These latter findings also confirmed our earlier results.

The pattern of correlations among the PAQ scales was also replicated, M and F showing a positive correlation, M-F showing a positive correlation with M and a negative correlation with F. The data suggest, however, that the magnitude of the correlation found between M and F in our initial samples (Spence, Helmreich, & Stapp 1975) was somewhat inflated, especially in males. In these subse-

Table 5-1. *Matrix of Mean Correlations, Based on the Data from Two Samples of College Students, among the PAQ Scales, Self-esteem, and AWS*

	M	F	M-F	Self-esteem	AWS
Masculinity (M)					
Men	1.00	.22	.55	.72	−.13
Women	1.00	.09	.56	.70	.07
Femininity (F)					
Men		1.00	−.17	.23	.03
Women		1.00	−.24	.22	−.16
Masc-Fem (M-F)					
Men			1.00	.48	.00
Women			1.00	.46	.21
Self-esteem					
Men				1.00	−.08
Women				1.00	.02

Means and SD	$\bar{X}$	SD	$\bar{X}$	SD	$\bar{X}$	SD	$\bar{X}$	SD	$\bar{X}$	SD
Men										
Sample 1	22.28	4.28	22.56	3.64	16.87	4.20	39.27	8.07	25.87	7.27
Sample 2	21.09	4.07	22.29	3.62	16.50	4.04	38.48	7.35	26.48	9.14
Mean of means	21.69	4.18	22.43	3.73	16.69	4.12	38.88	7.27	26.18	8.21
Women										
Sample 1	19.62	4.28	24.36	3.68	12.60	4.51	38.58	7.79	29.22	9.56
Sample 2	19.45	4.36	24.37	3.67	12.43	3.99	38.89	7.92	29.95	9.59
Mean of means	19.54	4.32	24.37	3.68	12.52	4.25	38.74	7.86	29.59	9.58

Note: For $df = 713$, $r_{.05} = .07$.

quent samples, the r's were lower, although they were still positive and significantly different from zero. The mean correlations of the two samples are reported in Table 5-1.[1]

Also shown in the table are the mean correlations between these scales and the Attitudes toward Women and the Self-esteem measures. Our earlier finding of a high positive correlation in both sexes between Self-esteem and the M scale and a more modest but significant correlation between Self-esteem and the F and M-F scales was again replicated in both samples.

Finally, attention should be called to the correlations with the Attitudes toward Women Scale. In the initial sample, the correlations of the AWS with the other measures were low and only occasionally significant. In Table 5-1 the presence of low and not uniformly significant correlations is again observed. For those correlations greater than zero, the pattern tends to be a mirror image with respect to di-

1. With samples of the size employed in the present investigation, very low correlations (often less than ±.10) were significantly different from zero. Rather than indicating in this and subsequent tables which of the correlations reached significance, the convention was adopted, for the guidance of the reader, of reporting at the bottom of the table the approximate value of r required for significance at the .05 level for the comparison contained in the table that involved the smallest number of subjects.

rection in the two sexes—profeminist attitudes being negatively associated in males and positively associated in females with high M and M-F and the reverse occurring with high F. The data thus support our earlier contention that the association between abstract attitudes toward appropriate *role behaviors* for men and women and the *psychological attributes* of masculinity and femininity is slight.

HIGH SCHOOL SAMPLE

In Table 5-2, the same data are reported for the sample of male and female high school students. Although these students were younger than the college samples, lived in a different part of the country, and were more heterogeneous in such other demographic characteristics as socioeconomic class, the intercorrelations among the M, F, and M-F scales and the correlations of each of these scales with the Self-esteem measure are similar to those for the college samples. The direction of the correlations between the PAQ scales and the AWS was again opposite in the two sexes. The magnitudes of the correlations continued to be low although, in females, all three *r*'s were significant.

Separate correlation matrices were also obtained for the male and female high school students within each socioeconomic group. These data will not be reported, since the magnitudes of the correlations among the measures were similar across classes in both females and males, and no systematic trends associated with class could be detected. Our fears that our initial PAQ findings might be confined largely to middle-class students thus proved groundless.

Although no class differences in the interrelationships of the scales were found, minor differences in mean scores were observed. Inspec-

Table 5-2. *Matrix of Correlations among the PAQ Scales, Self-esteem, and AWS for High School Students*

	M	F	M-F	Self-esteem	AWS
Masculinity (M)					
Men	1.00	.11	.44	.64	−.02
Women	1.00	.11	.48	.66	.09
Femininity (F)					
Men		1.00	−.20	.26	.14
Women		1.00	−.31	.24	−.10
Masc-Fem (M-F)					
Men			1.00	.42	−.06
Women			1.00	.41	.16
Self-esteem					
Men				1.00	.01
Women				1.00	.04

Means and SD	X̄	SD	X̄	SD	X̄	SD	X̄	SD	X̄	SD
Men	21.51	4.31	20.79	4.00	17.66	3.96	38.76	8.56	23.34	8.16
Women	19.31	4.49	24.05	3.90	13.21	4.38	38.76	9.07	30.55	8.76

Note: For $df = 750$, $r_{.05} = .07$.

tion of Table 5-3, which presents the means of the socioeconomic groups on each measure, indicates that there was a slight tendency for the Lower-class or the Lower- and Lower-middle-class students of both sexes to be lower on M and F than the other groups and for the Lower-class females to be lower on M-F. Mean Self-esteem also tended not to be as high in students from these socioeconomic groups. Despite the consistent trends, however, simple analyses of variance yielded no significant differences among the four classes.

On the other hand, Table 5-3 suggests that the socioeconomic groups did differ in their scores on the Attitudes toward Women Scale, the Upper-class students expressing the most liberal attitudes and the Lower-class students the most traditional attitudes toward women's roles. Religious affiliation, it will be recalled, varied across the four socioeconomic groups. Since this variable could be expected to be related to attitudes toward women, the AWS data were subjected to a two-way analysis of variance in which both religion and class were taken into account. The main effects for religion as well as for class were significant (p's $< .001$), the students expressing no religious preference reporting the most profeminist attitudes, followed in order by the Jewish, Protestant, and Catholic students. The interaction between the two variables was not significant ($p > .05$), however, suggesting that class differences in AWS scores cannot be completely accounted for by differential proportions of the several religious groups in the socioeconomic groups.

Joint Classification on PAQ Scales

SAMPLE DISTRIBUTIONS

Some of the most revealing relationships between the PAQ scales and other variables were obtained by classifying individuals on their joint

Table 5-3. *Means and Standard Deviations of PAQ Scales, Self-esteem, and AWS Broken Down by Social Class for the High School Sample*

	N	M		F		M-F		Self-esteem		AWS	
		$\overline{X}$	SD	$\overline{X}$	SD	$\overline{X}$	SD	$\overline{X}$	SD	$\overline{X}$	SD
Upper											
Males	75	22.7	4.7	21.0	4.3	17.8	4.5	39.2	10.0	24.8	8.1
Females	98	19.4	4.6	23.9	4.0	13.0	4.3	39.7	9.9	34.0	8.5
Upper middle											
Males	193	22.0	4.3	20.7	4.0	18.1	4.0	39.7	8.1	23.7	8.4
Females	281	19.8	4.3	23.8	3.9	13.4	4.4	39.4	9.0	31.2	8.3
Lower middle											
Males	189	21.5	3.9	21.2	4.0	17.7	3.8	38.1	8.7	23.0	7.6
Females	266	19.4	4.4	24.5	3.8	13.3	4.4	38.6	8.5	29.4	8.9
Lower											
Males	41	21.2	4.4	20.1	3.2	17.2	3.7	38.1	8.3	19.6	6.6
Females	85	18.0	4.6	24.0	4.4	12.2	3.9	37.3	8.8	27.5	9.1

PAQ scores by the median split method, rather than by considering individual scale scores. As was outlined in Chapter 3, this method involves first classifying individuals as falling above or below the median of their normative group (both sexes combined) on the M scale and the F scale. The four resulting cells are identified as Androgynous (above the median on both M and F), Masculine (above on M, below on F), Feminine (below on M, above on F), and Undifferentiated (below on both). This four-way classification scheme may be further elaborated by dividing individuals falling into each cell into those scoring above and those scoring below the overall median on M-F.

COLLEGE STUDENTS

The two groups of college students whose data were described earlier were combined to form a single sample of 715 men and women, each of whom was classified into one of four categories on the basis of their M and F scores. The percentage of each sex falling into each category is shown in Table 5-4. The results are in essential agreement with our initial study (Spence, Helmreich, & Stapp 1975). Males most frequently fell into the Masculine category (high M, low F) and least frequently into the cross-sex Feminine category (low M, high F); the females' pattern was the expected mirror image, the most frequent category being Feminine and the least frequent Masculine. In both sexes, substantial percentages fell into the two extreme categories—Androgynous (high M and F) and Undifferentiated (low M and F).

Each of the four masculinity and femininity groups shown in Table 5-4 for each sex is further broken down into the percentage of the total group who scored above and below the overall median on M-F. For example, 3% of the males were classified as Feminine, high M-F, and 5% as Feminine, low M-F (for a total of 8% in the Feminine category). Thus, of the Feminine males only 38% (3%/8%) fall above the overall median on M-F; the rest fall below. In the other three categories of males, this ratio is reversed—84% of the Androg-

Table 5-4. *Percentage of College Students Falling into Each of the Four and Each of the Eight Categories Based on Median Splits on M, F, and M-F*

				Males				Females		
				Masculinity (M)						
			Above		Below		Above		Below	
Femininity (F)	Above	M-F Above	27	Andro 32	3	Fem 8	13	Andro 27	6	Fem 32
		M-F Below	5		5		14		26	
	Below	M-F Above	31	Masc 34	18	Undiff 25	10	Masc 14	11	Undiff 28
		M-F Below	3		7		4		17	

ynous, 91% of the Masculine, and 72% of the Undifferentiated men being above the median on M-F. In females, both Feminine and Undifferentiated women tend more frequently to be low in M-F (only 19% and 39%, respectively, falling above the median). For Androgynous women the split is almost equal (48% above) and, for Masculine women, the split is weighted toward high M-F (71% above).

Before leaving this table, attention is called to those Undifferentiated individuals high in the masculine characteristics on the M-F scale. At first blush, this combination of attributes seems contradictory. These individuals, although describing themselves as low in desirable instrumental attributes, are not only relatively low in their altruistic concern for others but are also relatively insensitive to others' reactions toward them. We suspect that individuals described as having "passive-aggressive" personalities are frequently found among the individuals exhibiting this pattern of attributes.

HIGH SCHOOL STUDENTS

The same kind of four-way and eight-way breakdown is shown for the high school sample in Table 5-5. The data once more essentially replicate the major features found in the college samples. Considering first the four-way classification on M and F, males and females are found most frequently in the traditional category for their sex and least frequently in the cross-sex category. When the four categories are split into high and low M-F groups, males tend predominantly to be above the median and females to be below the median in all groups except Feminine males and Masculine females, these two groups showing the reverse pattern. Although cross-group comparisons must be made with particular caution because of the difference in the value of the M scale median used to classify college and high school students, it is interesting to note in Tables 5-4 and 5-5 that, in high school females, a greater percentage was classified as Androgynous and a lesser percentage as Undifferentiated than in college women.

Table 5-5. *Percentage of Students in High School Sample Falling into Each of the Four and Each of the Eight Categories Based on Median Splits on M, F, and M-F*

			Males				Females			
			Above		Below		Above		Below	
Above	M-F	Above	19	Andro	2	Fem	11	Andro	3	Fem
				25		8		35		32
		Below	6		6		24		29	
Below	M-F	Above	36	Masc	15	Undiff	8	Masc	5	Undiff
				44		23		14		18
		Below	8		8		6		13	

(Femininity (F) on vertical axis; Masculinity (M) heading spans Males and Females)

Male high school students, however, fell more frequently in the Masculine category and less frequently in the Androgynous category than college men.

A similar four-way classification for each socioeconomic group also produced instructive results. (A further breakdown on M-F was not attempted because of the small N's in many of the cells.) The results, shown in Table 5-6, indicate that in both sexes lower-class status is associated with an elevation in the Undifferentiated category and a corresponding depression in the Androgynous and cross-sex categories. Chi squares of the matrix were of borderline significance (p's $< .20$) for both sexes.

Relationships of PAQ Categories to Self-esteem Scores

COLLEGE STUDENTS

We have already reported that, in both the high school and the college student populations, highly stable correlations were found between TSBI Self-esteem scores and each of the three PAQ scales, with the relationship between Self-esteem and M scores being particularly striking in its magnitude. The presence of these positive correlations suggested that combining PAQ scores would increase the predictability of Self-esteem scores, an inference not fully supported in our orignal study by calculation of a multiple r. This failure was a major factor in leading us to adopt the alternate approach of classifying individuals by the median split method. Classification of students on M and F scores resulted in the expected differences among categorical groups—the order of the mean Self-esteem scores, from lowest to highest, being Undifferentiated, Feminine, Masculine, and Androgynous in both sexes. The mean differences between adjacent categories were both large and statistically significant, an outcome suggesting that the combination between M and F in determining Self-esteem is additive although apparently not linear.

In seeking to replicate these findings in our group of 715 college students, we determined the mean Self-esteem scores for the men and women falling into each of the four categories based on M and F

Table 5-6. *Percentage of High School Students Falling into Each of the Four M and F Categories within Each Socioeconomic Class*

	Males				Females			
	Undiff	Fem	Masc	Andro	Undiff	Fem	Masc	Andro
Upper	17	9	44	30	20	31	12	36
Upper middle	20	6	49	25	17	29	18	36
Lower middle	22	8	41	29	15	34	14	37
Lower	35	4	48	13	24	40	9	28

scores. In order to determine the contribution of M-F (an analysis not undertaken in our initial study), each of the four cells was subdivided into individuals who were above and below the overall median on the M-F scale. The mean Self-esteem scores for women and men in both the four and the eight groups are shown in Table 5-7. The four groups are listed in the expected order of mean Self-esteem and, within each group, the mean for the individuals below the M-F median is shown before the mean of those above the median. Immediately apparent from the table is confirmation in both sexes of our earlier finding about the order of the four basic groups. (The differences were also highly significant.) Within each group, M-F also showed the anticipated relationship with Self-esteem: in each instance, the mean Self-esteem score of those scoring above the median was higher than that of those scoring below the median. A plot of the eight means, however, is saw-toothed rather than linear. For example, while the Undifferentiated students of both sexes have a lower mean on Self-esteem than the Feminine students, the mean of Undifferentiated students who are above the median on M-F is slightly higher than that of Feminine students who are below the median on M-F.

HIGH SCHOOL STUDENTS

A parallel analysis of the data for the high school sample is reported in Table 5-8. The most striking outcome of this analysis is its similarity to what was found in college students. Thus within each sex the order of mean Self-esteem scores from low to high is Undifferentiated, Feminine, Masculine, and Androgynous, with a jagged pattern of means resulting when the four-way split is amplified to eight-way to take M-F into account.

RELATIONSHIP OF PAQ CATEGORIES TO ATTITUDES TOWARD WOMEN

The correlations between the Attitudes toward Women Scale and the PAQ scales have been uniformly found to be low but consistent in their pattern of signs. It was therefore decided to examine the mean

Table 5-7. *Mean Self-esteem Scores for College Students Classified by Median Split Method on M, F, and M-F*

	Undiff		Fem		Masc		Andro	
	Lo M-F	Hi M-F	Lo M-F	Hi M-F	Lo M-F	Hi M-F	Lo M-F	Hi M-F
Males	28.7	35.2	34.5	38.0	38.0	40.5	38.9	43.8
	33.2		35.9		40.1		42.5	
Females	33.0	35.6	35.2	40.0	41.4	43.6	42.9	44.9
	34.5		37.3		42.0		43.4	

Table 5-8. *Mean Self-esteem Scores for High School Students Classified by Median Split Method on M, F, and M-F*

	Undiff		Fem		Masc		Andro	
	Lo M-F	Hi M-F	Lo M-F	Hi M-F	Lo M-F	Hi M-F	Lo M-F	Hi M-F
Males	30.8	32.7	32.7	36.8	35.5	41.2	39.2	45.3
	32.0		34.0		40.2		43.8	
Females	29.8	36.4	35.1	38.2	40.6	43.2	43.1	46.3
	31.4		35.4		42.2		44.1	

AWS scores for male and female students in each of the four M and F categories. These data are reported for both college and high school samples in Table 5-9. Separate analyses of variance for the two sexes in each group revealed significant ($p < .05$) differences among the PAQ groups in all comparisons. In both the high school and the college samples, these results came about primarily because of the higher means in the cross-sex categories (Masculine females and Feminine males). Thus individuals who conspicuously violate traditional expectations by being high in the psychological attributes stereotypically associated with the other sex and low in the attributes associated with their own sex tend to be more egalitarian in their attitudes than their contemporaries.

The PAQ and Empathy

Several of our colleagues have recently conducted a study in which the PAQ and a slightly modified version of Mehrabian and Epstein's (1972) Empathy scale were administered to 102 male and 113 female undergraduates at the University of Texas (Foushee, Davis, & Archer 1977).[2] Because of its novel findings, we report it here.

Table 5-9. *Mean AWS Scores in Each of the Four M and F Categories for College and High School Samples*

	Undiff	Fem	Masc	Andro
	College students			
	Undiff	Fem	Masc	Andro
Males	25.3	29.2	25.8	25.8
Females	30.2	28.4	32.6	29.5
	High school students			
Males	22.5	26.7	23.0	23.7
Females	30.1	29.7	33.5	30.4

2. We are grateful to Clay Foushee, Mark Davis, and Dr. Richard Archer, all of the University of Texas at Austin, for making their data available.

In devising their scale, Mehrabian and Epstein defined empathy as heightened responsiveness to another's emotional experience, a definition that should be distinguished from an earlier view of empathy as cognitive role taking or predictive accuracy (e.g., Dymond 1949). The scale consists of thirty-three statements, each accompanied by a nine-point scale, such as "I cannot continue to feel OK if people around me are depressed," "I become very involved when I watch a movie," and "It makes me sad to see a lonely stranger in a group."

According to our conceptualization of masculinity and femininity, the PAQ scales should be related to the ability of an individual to empathize, in the sense of participating in the feelings of others. Scores on the F scale, defined as communion, should be related to Empathy in a positive direction, while scores on the M-F scale, with its emphasis on emotional vulnerability, might be expected to be negatively related. That is, individuals classified as feminine by virtue of scoring low on the M-F scale should exhibit more empathic reactions than high-scoring, masculine individuals. Prediction for the agentic orientation we have defined as masculinity is less clear, but the positive correlations between the M and M-F scales suggest that the relationship between M and Empathy might be negative although not of the same magnitude as that with M-F. Finally, the significant difference between the sexes on the three PAQ scales suggests that females, as a group, should show greater empathy than males.

The F and M-F scales of the PAQ were indeed significantly ($p < .01$) related to Empathy in the expected directions, F correlating .46 in females and .26 in males. The correlations with M-F were even higher, $-.54$ in females and $-.35$ in males. Also as anticipated, M showed negative but lower correlations with Empathy in both sexes (male $r = -.09$, n.s.; female $r = -.21$, $p < .05$).

The finding that all three PAQ scales are related to Empathy suggests that use of the eight-way classification to provide another view of the relationship between masculinity and femininity and empathy would be instructive. However, the samples were too small to permit this breakdown. Instead, two four-way classifications were made—the first based on M and F and the second on M-F and F. For each four-way classification, a 2 (male vs. female) by 4 (PAQ classification) analysis of variance of Empathy scores was conducted. In both analyses, significant main effects (p's $< .001$) were found for both sex and PAQ categories. The interactions did not approach significance. The most striking differences in Empathy scores among PAQ categories appeared in the classification based on F and M-F. Examining the latter category means for Empathy, presented in Table 5-10, it is apparent that the significant PAQ effect is largely caused by one group in each sex. In males there is a depression of Empathy scores among those high in M-F and low in F ("Masculine" males), while in females there is a substantial elevation of scores among those low in M-F and high in F ("Feminine" females).

To explore further the relationships between the attributes comprising the PAQ and this conceptualization of empathy, the correlations between each item of the PAQ and the Empathy scale were com-

Table 5-10. *Means and Standard Deviations of Empathy Scores Broken Down by Four-Way Classification on M-F and F*

	Lo M-F/Lo F	Lo M-F/Hi F	Hi M-F/Lo F	Hi M-F/Hi F
Males				
Mean	26.91	25.10	13.14	20.13
SD	19.12	17.50	19.51	17.50
Females				
Mean	33.88	53.58	25.46	33.48
SD	16.21	19.84	20.22	23.71

puted for each sex. These correlations ranged in absolute magnitude from .07 to .59 in females and from .02 to .33 in males. The content of the PAQ items relating most strongly to Empathy scores provides some insight into the nature of empathy as operationalized by Mehrabian and Epstein. The largest correlations are with items that convey a sense of emotionality and emotional vulnerability, for example, "excitable in major crisis" (M-F), "feelings easily hurt" (M-F), "needs approval" (M-F), "cries easily" (M-F), and "emotional" (F). It is noteworthy that those items of the PAQ which appear to have the most face-valid relationship with at least the classic concept of empathy ("aware of others' feelings," "understanding," "able to devote self to others") tended to relate less strongly in both sexes than those dealing with pure emotionality and susceptibility to emotional hurt.

These results also clarify the nature of the M-F scale, this clarification in turn helping to explain some of the relationships into which M-F enters. The M-F scale contains items describing two agentic characteristics—aggression and dominance—and a series of predominantly expressive "feminine" items (scored in a reverse, masculine direction) describing susceptibility to emotional hurt and the need for emotional support. This constellation of characteristics—aggression and dominance and *lack* of emotional vulnerability—has a substantial positive correlation with the agentic characteristics contained on the M scale and with Self-esteem. The constellation is more modestly related to the F scale, a scale containing items describing interpersonal awareness and concern for others. Thus those with a strong interpersonal orientation tend to be only somewhat less "tough" and more emotionally vulnerable than those whose interpersonal orientation is relatively weak. Interpersonal awareness and emotional vulnerability appear to have opposite but intuitively reasonable relationships with Self-esteem. Thus the seeming paradox that *high* femininity as defined by high F scores and *low* femininity as defined by high M-F scores are both positively related to the Self-esteem measure is resolved.

Special attention should be called to the fact that these data on the associations between the Empathy scale and the PAQ differ in pattern from those for the variables we have considered thus far. Masculinity (M) has, in general, proved to be the dominant variable in most relationships with the PAQ. In this case, however, both F and M-F proved to be the major contributors. Further, the direction of the relationships of the individual scales was negative in the case of M and M-F and positive in the case of F. We will later encounter other instances where relationships with masculinity and femininity are not linear and not additive, but this example serves to counter the notion that a uniform order of relationship between PAQ categories and other measures is to be expected.

Cross-cultural Studies

Differential socialization practices and sex-role expectations may contribute heavily, if not exclusively, to the development of the clusters of psychological characteristics that both stereotypically and actually differentiate the sexes in a given culture and thus define for that culture "masculine" and "feminine" attributes. Although observation suggests that in a wide variety of cultures agentic, instrumental characteristics are regarded as "masculine" and communal, expressive characteristics as "feminine," the anthropological evidence reviewed earlier indicates that these distinctions are not universal. Our findings of sex differences on our M, F, and M-F scales may thus be restricted to certain societies and cultures.

In those societies in which psychological masculinity and femininity can be equated with the agentic-communal distinction, the distinction may be even more rigidly sex-linked than in our own, males being more actively discouraged from developing and expressing "feminine" characteristics or females from developing "masculine" ones. The pattern of intercorrelation among the M, F, and M-F scales and their relationship to such other variables as self-esteem and attitudes toward women may therefore also vary across cultures.

The systematic conduct of cross-cultural research has been beyond our resources but, with the cooperation of colleagues, we have been able to examine PAQ data that provide provocative information from students in several other countries. One sample consisted of ninety-five male and eighty-nine female Lebanese students fluent in English and enrolled at the American University in Beirut.[3] The means for each sex on the M, F, and M-F scales and the correlations among the scales are shown in Table 5-11. Scores on the Attitudes toward Women Scale were also available from these students, and the correlations of this measure with the PAQ are also reported.

The data in Table 5-11 reveal several departures from those found with students in the United States. The sexes differ significantly ($p < .001$) on the F and M-F scales and on the AWS. However, although the means differ in the expected direction, the difference on the M scale between the sexes does not approach significance ($F < 1$).

3. We appreciate the assistance of Dr. Joel Saegert, formerly of the American University in Beirut, now of the University of Denver, who coordinated the data collection.

Table 5-11. *Means and Intercorrelations among the Three PAQ Scales and AWS for Lebanese College Students*

	X̄	SD	M	F	M-F
Males					
M	21.10	4.24	1.00		
F	22.35	4.90	−.13	1.00	
M-F	16.89	4.49	.43	−.31	1.00
AWS	28.36	7.53	−.18	.14	.11
Females					
M	20.69	4.20	1.00		
F	23.69	3.23	.00	1.00	
M-F	13.91	4.48	.39	−.28	1.00
AWS	35.18	5.85	−.13	−.12	.08

Note: For $df = 90$, $r_{.05} = .20$.

We can only speculate on this result, but it seems likely that women attending a coeducational university in a Middle Eastern country might come from less traditional homes and might be more instrumentally oriented and more similar to men than women in the general Lebanese population. In this connection it should be noted that the mean AWS score for these women is markedly higher than that for their American counterparts (35.18 vs. 29.59). It should also be noted that students at the American University are primarily Christians and Druses and not Moslems. As a result, they are quite probably an idiosyncratic sample.

The pattern of the correlations of the PAQ scales is in general similar to those for American students, M and F being nonsignificantly related (although for men the correlation is slightly negative) and M-F significantly related in a positive direction to M and in a negative direction to F. Low relationships of these scales with the AWS are also found, none of the r's being significant.

To gain some sense of the joint distribution of Masculinity and Femininity and a comparison with the distribution in American students, the Lebanese were classified using the U.S. college student medians. The percentages of females and males in each of the four categories are given in Table 5-12. Compared with the U.S. college data, more Lebanese males are classified as Feminine and fewer females as Undifferentiated.

One must interpret these cross-cultural data tentatively, but it does seem safe to say that, for this upper-middle-class sample, the results do not depart radically from the data obtained from American students and that the similarities outweigh the differences.

Results from a sample of twenty-eight elementary and thirty-three secondary school males and forty-four elementary and forty-three secondary school female students from Ramat Gan, Israel, are given in Table 5-13. Since the two age groups yielded similar results, the combined results are presented. The students, varying in age between twelve and eighteen years, were given a Hebrew version of the PAQ

Table 5-12. *Percentage of Lebanese College Students in the Four M and F Categories*

	PAQ category			
	Undiff	Fem	Masc	Andro
Males	22	24	26	28
Females	17	33	17	33

translated and backtranslated from the English form.[4] The sexes are significantly different (*p*'s < .01) on the F and M-F scales; however, as in the Lebanese sample, the difference between means on the M scale, while in the anticipated direction, is not significant. Both females and males scored lower on F than their U.S. and Lebanese counterparts, while females scored higher on M and M-F. The intercorrelations among the PAQ scales replicate the American pattern, with M and F showing lower (and nonsignificant) positive correlations and M-F showing significant relationships in opposite directions with M and F.

A four-way classification on M and F was next computed using the U.S. high school norms, the results being shown in Table 5-14. The most striking departures from American students are found in two cells: the percentage of Masculine females is greatly elevated over the U.S. high school samples, while a similar elevation is found in the percentage of Undifferentiated males. Explanations of the latter are not easily summoned, but the greater frequency of Masculine Israeli girls might be attributed jointly to the political and economic circumstances in that country and the systematic, although not completely successful (e.g., Mednick 1975), attempts to create a nonsexist society.

A final cross-national sample of 115 male and 173 female Brazilian

Table 5-13. *Means and Intercorrelations among the Three PAQ Scales for Israeli Students*

	X̄	SD	M	F	M-F
Males					
M	21.53	4.91	1.00		
F	19.97	4.49	.03	1.00	
M-F	17.42	3.45	.57	−.11	1.00
Females					
M	20.73	4.49	1.00		
F	22.25	4.72	.08	1.00	
M-F	15.8	3.69	.38	−.25	1.00

4. We appreciate the assistance of Avi and Debbie Blattstein of the Department of Educational Psychology, the University of Texas at Austin, who translated and administered the PAQ. We are also grateful to Dr. Joseph Gamzu of the University of Texas for assistance in translation.

Table 5-14. *Percentage of Israeli Students in the*
Four M and F Categories

	PAQ category			
	Undiff	Fem	Masc	Andro
Males	39	10	32	19
Females	25	15	32	28

college students was tested with Portuguese translations of the PAQ, the AWS, and the TSBI.[5] Table 5-15 gives the means and intercorrelations of these measures, which differ considerably from the other samples. Masculinity, on which the sexes do not differ significantly, is markedly lower than in the U.S. college sample, as is Self-esteem. The sexes do differ significantly in the expected direction on the F and M-F scales and the AWS (p's $< .01$). The means for F are similar to those of the U.S. sample, while both M-F and AWS scores are depressed.

The intercorrelations among the measures again diverge sharply from the other samples. In males, M is unrelated to M-F, while Self-esteem is orthogonal to all three PAQ scales. The PAQ correlations in women are more similar to the American pattern, but the correlations of these scales with Self-esteem are, like those of the males, nonsignificant. The AWS yields only one significant correlation: a negative relationship with Self-esteem in males.

The four-way M and F classification using U.S. college norms (shown in Table 5-16) produces a distribution for females close to that of U.S. college women, with the largest percentage being found

Table 5-15. *Means and Intercorrelations among the Three PAQ Scales,*
Self-esteem, and AWS for Brazilian College Students

	X̄	SD	M	F	M-F	Self-esteem	AWS
Males							
M	18.98	3.91	1.00				
F	21.61	4.41	.28	1.00			
M-F	13.71	3.20	.06	−.25	1.00		
Self-esteem	35.30	6.67	.00	.00	.06	1.00	
AWS	20.70	4.80	.08	.03	.06	−.25	1.00
Females							
M	18.53	4.62	1.00				
F	23.27	4.31	.17	1.00			
M-F	12.57	3.49	.27	−.34	1.00		
Self-esteem	35.19	6.39	.11	.16	−.14	1.00	
AWS	22.89	3.82	−.04	.03	−.06	−.08	1.00

Note: For $df = 113$, $r_{.05} = .18$.

5. We wish to thank Dr. Edward Conolley, Sherman Oaks, California, who made these data available to us.

Table 5-16. *Percentage of Brazilian Students in the Four M and F Categories*

	PAQ category			
	Undiff	Fem	Masc	Andro
Males	37	29	12	22
Females	30	36	10	24

in the Feminine category and the smallest in the cross-sex, Masculine category. Brazilian males, however, exhibit a markedly different pattern. The smallest group is the Masculine, with only 12% of the males thus assigned. The percentages scored as Undifferentiated or Feminine are greatly inflated.

Observation suggests that the elevation of "feminine" characteristics in males and the depression of "masculine" characteristics in both sexes in this sample of students are not unrepresentative of Brazilian culture. Different socialization emphases with respect to socially desirable characteristics may, in turn, result in a quite different constellation of variables contributing to social competence and self-esteem than in other cultures. Viewing these findings from a great cultural and physical distance, however, we are unable to speculate more concretely about the causes of the several discrepancies between these Brazilian students and their counterparts in this country or even to determine their representativeness.

Indeed, all these cross-cultural data should be seen as very crude and tentative explorations of the theoretical constructs of masculinity and femininity in non-U.S. settings. Overall, however, there are enough parallels in the data we have obtained, particularly in the intercorrelations among the PAQ scales, that support our basic conceptualization of masculinity and femininity to suggest that further comparative work can provide valuable information on the organization and implementation of these clusters of attributes.

Unique Populations

The consistency of interrelationships of the PAQ scales in the U.S. samples, as well as the strong relationship between the PAQ and Self-esteem, led us to seek data from unique samples where the distributions of Masculinity and Femininity might be expected to differ from those in the general population. Data from special groups, in addition to being of interest in their own right, also provide an opportunity for conceptual validation of the PAQ through demonstrating its ability to discriminate between the general population and selected subgroups.

The groups we have studied to date have been made available through the assistance of students and colleagues at the University of Texas at Austin who have been studying them as part of other research.[6] They include 110 male and female homosexuals; 161 male and female academic scientists and engineers all holding the Ph.D.; and 41 female varsity athletes. These three groups are each distinguishable from the general population on at least one measurable dimension—sexual orientation in the homosexuals, educational attainment in the scientists, and successful varsity competition in the female athletes. The data are of special interest because of the societal stereotypes concerning masculinity and femininity that have been applied to homosexuals and to female scientists and athletes.

MALE AND FEMALE HOMOSEXUALS

The popular image of the male homosexual as tending to be feminine and the lesbian as tending to be masculine has found some support in the research literature (e.g., Manosevitz 1971; Thompson, Schwartz, McCandless, & Edwards 1973). Indeed, as Constantinople (1973) has noted, the ability to distinguish between hetero- and homosexual orientation has frequently been a criterion for the inclusion of items in M-F scales and for scale validation.

The literature relating cross-sex typing with homosexuality is by no means unanimous, however. For example, Aaronson and Grumpelt (1961) found a number of masculine-oriented male homosexuals using the MMPI Masculinity-Femininity scale; while Brown (1957, 1958) has argued that sex-role inversion and homosexuality must be differentiated. Hooker (1965) has also criticized the dichotomous masculine-feminine conceptualization as inadequate for homosexuals.

In a study exploring the implications of psychological masculinity and femininity for homosexuality, Ward (1974) administered the PAQ, the TSBI Self-esteem measure, and the AWS to fifty-six male and fifty-four female self-designated homosexuals. (The long forms of the latter two measures were employed, so that the means obtained for the sample cannot be compared directly with those of other groups reported here.) The test battery also included ad hoc questions on partner preference as well as questions on personal adjustment, including participation in psychotherapy. The respondents were recruited through contact in gay bars and through gay activist organizations. It should be noted at the outset that this, like most research samples of homosexuals, can by no means be assumed to be a representative cross section of the American gay population. The sample ranged in age from 16 to 47 with a mean of 26.2 years; 32% of the sample were college students.

6. We appreciate the assistance of Mr. Steven Ward, who collected the homosexual data as part of an undergraduate honors thesis (unpublished, 1974); Dr. William Beane, now at the University of Indiana at South Bend, who gathered the scientist data as part of a doctoral dissertation (1976); and Dr. Waneen Spirduso, Department of Health, Physical Education, and Recreation, who permitted our participation in her extended study of female athletes.

Analyses were performed that compared not only the male and female homosexuals but also the gay sample with the unselected college samples reported by Spence, Helmreich, & Stapp (1975). Gay males and females differed significantly ($p < .01$) from the same-sex college students on all three scales of the PAQ. Male homosexuals, contrasted with college males, scored significantly lower on the M and M-F scales and higher on the F scale, while the lesbian sample, contrasted with college females, scored higher on M and M-F and lower on F. Within the gay sample, females scored significantly higher than males on the M and M-F scales, reversing the usual sex differences, while the sexes did not significantly differ on the F scale. Homosexual males did not differ from the unselected sample of college males in their mean on the Self-esteem measure, but lesbians had significantly higher Self-esteem scores than college females. Finally, female and male homosexuals did not differ significantly in their endorsement of sexual equality on the AWS, and both were significantly more liberal ($p < .001$) than college students. Means, standard deviations, and intercorrelations of these measures are given in Table 5-17.

The pattern of intercorrelations is highly similar to that of the college and high school population, the single exception being that in men the usual negative relationship between M-F and F is reversed; although the correlation is not significant, men scoring higher on F tended to score higher rather than lower on the M-F scale. It is of particular interest that, despite the significant differences between the homo- and heterosexual groups and between male and female homosexuals on the PAQ scales, the internal relationships of these scales and their correlation with Self-esteem remain basically unchanged.

On the other hand, when the homosexual sample was classified into the four masculinity and femininity categories, using the M and F medians from college students, striking differences were found, as

Table 5-17. *Means, Standard Deviations, and Intercorrelations of the PAQ, TSBI, and AWS in Homosexuals*

	$\overline{X}$	SD	M	F	M-F	Self-esteem	AWS
Males							
M	19.32	4.32	1.00				
F	23.41	3.87	.21	1.00			
M-F	13.79	4.15	.66	.09	1.00		
Self-esteem	81.20	17.52	.74	.34	.41	1.00	
AWS	67.04	8.41	—.16	—.02	—.35	—.09	1.00
Females							
M	21.65	5.07	1.00				
F	22.54	4.09	.36	1.00			
M-F	15.61	4.44	.53	—.17	1.00		
Self-esteem	87.22	18.47	.65	.13	.50	1.00	
AWS	69.17	8.33	.01	—.21	.16	.05	1.00

Note: The long forms of both the TSBI (Helmreich, Stapp, & Ervin 1974) and AWS (Spence & Helmreich 1972a) were administered.
For $df = 50$, $r_{.05} = .27$.

shown in Table 5-18. As the consensus of the literature suggests, a dramatic reduction in the number of conventionally classified individuals is found (only 9% of the males are Masculine and only 13% of the females are Feminine), but the redistribution into the other categories differs greatly between the sexes. Of the homosexual males, 50% were Undifferentiated, while 23% were classified as Feminine and 18% were designated Androgynous. Among lesbians, the largest group was Androgynous (33%), but the percentages classified as Undifferentiated (32%) and Masculine (22%) were also elevated. To summarize, the percentage of gay males classified as Undifferentiated or Feminine is far greater than in the college population, 73% falling into these two groups. The low percentage of lesbians classified as Feminine is offset by large increases in the number designated as Masculine or Undifferentiated, with a smaller increase in the Androgynous category.

The results for Self-esteem are not perfectly parallel to those for college students in that the difference between those high and low in masculinity (Androgynous and Masculine vs. Feminine and Undifferentiated) is more accentuated, with the two high masculine categories having markedly higher Self-esteem. Indeed, among lesbians, the Masculine group had slightly (and nonsignificantly) higher Self-esteem than the Androgynous. Reinforcing these Self-esteem data were the reports of the respondents about their involvement in psychotherapy. Androgynous and Masculine individuals of both sexes reported seeking psychotherapy less frequently than those in the Feminine and Undifferentiated groups.

While it would be presumptuous to formulate any theories of homosexuality or of its concomitants from these data, they do suggest that the dualistic formulation of masculinity and femininity we have proposed may differentiate epidemiologically between homosexual and heterosexual populations. They also suggest that the causal factors determining sexual orientation may be different among those falling into the four categories we have defined. One clear implication is that research in homosexuality might be less ambiguous if attempts to isolate etiological forces were examined in terms of both the psychological masculinity and femininity of the individual subject.

Table 5-18. *Percentages of Homosexuals in the Four M and F Categories and Self-esteem Means by Category*

| | PAQ category | | | |
	Undiff	Fem	Masc	Andro
Males				
Percent	50	23	9	18
Mean Self-esteem	76.9	77.5	92.0	92.7
Females				
Percent	32	13	22	33
Mean Self-esteem	70.5	81.0	99.2	97.4

FEMALE VARSITY ATHLETES

The opportunity to examine the societal stereotype of the "masculinized" female athlete made the study of a group of varsity women athletes particularly attractive. The forty-one members of seven varsity women's teams at the University of Texas at Austin volunteered to complete the PAQ during a session in which they were participating in physical tests. (The women were also given the Work and Family Orientation Questionnaire; data from this instrument will be reported in Chapter 7.) The PAQ scale means, standard deviations, and intercorrelations are given in Table 5-19. As the data indicate, relative to college women, the athletes score somewhat higher on the M and M-F scales and lower on the F scale. The pattern of intercorrelations, however, is highly similar to that of the general college population.

The combined distribution of M and F scores is very different from that of all college women when the athletes are categorized by our general college norms, as is shown at the bottom of Table 5-19. The largest group is composed of those women classified as Androgynous, while the smallest is in the Feminine category. The Masculine category is greatly inflated while the Undifferentiated is somewhat reduced. The validity of the instrumental-expressive dualism we have proposed is strongly supported by the higher M scores observed among these athletes. The notion that instrumentality need not be achieved at the expense of expressivity is demonstrated in the fact that almost 40% of these women were Androgynous, high in both dimensions. The demonstration is particularly impressive in this specific group of women who have all taken on "masculine" roles in their devotion to competitive sports.

MALE AND FEMALE SCIENTISTS

The group of academic scientists given the PAQ provided interesting comparisons with college students on several dimensions. One was

Table 5-19. *Means, Standard Deviations, and Intercorrelations of the PAQ Scales and Percentages in the Four Categories for Female Varsity Athletes*

	$\overline{X}$	SD	M	F	M-F
M	21.58	3.85	1.00		
F	22.68	3.74	.25	1.00	
M-F	17.77	3.74	.55	—.08	1.00

	PAQ category		
Undiff	Fem	Masc	Andro
20	10	31	39

Note: For $df = 39$, $r_{.05} = .30$.

that these were members of an older population who had demonstrated a considerable level of instrumental orientation (i.e., obtaining a doctorate and a faculty position at a major university). A more specific interest was the relative masculinity and femininity of female scientists who have embraced roles that continue to be sought or attained less frequently by women than by men. Means, standard deviations, and scale intercorrelations on the PAQ for the 143 male and 18 female scientists are presented in Table 5-20.

In the case of male scientists, the pattern and magnitude of correlations are almost identical to those of college males. However, their mean scores on both M and M-F are higher than those of the college group. Female scientists also show elevated M and M-F scores when contrasted with college women.[7] The mean differences in scale scores between male and female scientists are in the same direction as the scores for the college population (M and M-F higher in males, F higher in females), with the F and M-F differences being significant (p's $<$ .01). The difference on M, however, fails to reach significance.

When the four category distributions are computed using college student norms, the distribution for male scientists, as may be seen in Table 5-21, is similar to that of college males, the major difference being a reduction in the proportions of Feminine and Undifferentiated individuals and a consequent increase in the proportion of those in the Masculine and Androgynous categories. As with college males, the largest group is Masculine, followed in descending frequency by Androgynous, Undifferentiated, and Feminine.

The results for female scientists (see Table 5-21) show a very different distribution from that of college women. The largest group is Androgynous, with 46% of the women falling in this classification. The proportion of female scientists in the Masculine category (23%)

Table 5-20. *Means, Standard Deviations, and Intercorrelations of the PAQ Scales for 143 Male and 18 Female Scientists*

	$\overline{X}$	SD	M	F	M-F
Males					
M	23.23	4.75	1.00		
F	20.84	4.29	.20	1.00	
M-F	17.23	4.30	.61	−.22	1.00
Females					
M	22.0	4.97	1.00		
F	23.38	3.56	.41	1.00	
M-F	15.00	4.51	.89	−.44	1.00

Note: For $df = 141$, $r_{.05} = .15$; for $df = 16$, $r_{.05} = .47$.

7. The scientists' PAQ data should also be compared with the data obtained from fathers and mothers of college students, reported in detail in Chapter 10. The fathers were very similar in their means to the male scientists and, like the latter, scored higher on M than the college men. However, the mothers' means on M and M-F were lower than those of the female scientists and comparable to the female students.

Table 5-21. *Distributions of Scientists across the Four M and F Categories*

| | PAQ category | | | |
	Undiff	Fem	Masc	Andro
Males	20	5	43	32
Females	8	23	23	46

is also markedly higher than in the college sample. The greatest reduction is in the Undifferentiated classification, with only 8% falling into this group.

The pattern of these results is consistent with our theoretical expectations. Male scientists, who are following a demanding and traditionally masculine profession, are predictably similar to college males, although somewhat higher in masculinity. In the case of female scientists, it is not surprising that their agentic characteristics should be elevated, as expressed in the increased percentage of Androgynous and Masculine women. The female scientists are rather similar to the female varsity athletes, particularly in the high incidence of Androgyny. We will examine other data from the scientist sample in the discussion of achievement motivation in Chapter 7.

Summary

We will attempt below to extract the major results from the bewildering mass of data reported in this chapter and to summarize them briefly.

1. The PAQ data obtained from college students replicated in all essential details our previous findings with this population. Males scored significantly higher on the M and M-F scales than females and significantly lower on F. The intercorrelations between M and F support the implications of a dualistic model, low but significantly *positive* relationships being found between these scales in both sexes. The M-F scale, scored in a masculine direction, is more bipolar, exhibiting a substantial *positive* correlation with M and a more modest but still significant *negative* correlation with F in both women and men.

When students were classified into one of the four masculinity and femininity categories by the median split method, the greatest percentage in each sex was shown to be conventionally typed (Masculine males, Feminine females) and the lowest percentage cross-typed. When these categories were further subdivided into those above and those below the overall median on M-F, the majority of females were below the median and the majority of males were above the median in all categories except the cross-typed.

2. Highly similar results were found in a sample of high school stu-

dents who, like the college students, were largely white but were considerably more heterogeneous in ethnic and socioeconomic background. The similarity extended to median values on the three PAQ scales, the medians for M-F and F being the same in the high school as in the college sample, the median for M being one point lower.

3. When the high school students were broken down into four socioeconomic groups, comparisons revealed only minor differences between them on the PAQ, a somewhat lower percentage of Androgynous individuals and a somewhat higher percentage of Undifferentiated individuals being found in lower-class groups than in upper-class groups. While these differences were found in both sexes, they were only of borderline significance. Significant differences were found between the socioeconomic groups, however, in attitudes toward women, the lower class being most traditional and the upper class most egalitarian.

4. In both high school and college samples, significant positive correlations were found in both females and males between the TSBI Self-esteem measure and the M, M-F, and F scales, the magnitudes of the correlations being in the order in which the scales are listed. Highly significant differences were found in both sexes among the mean Self-esteem scores for the four categories, the highest self-esteem being reported by the Androgynous students, followed by the Masculine, Feminine, and Undifferentiated. These results also confirm our previous findings. When the four-way classification for each sex was expanded to an eight-way classification to include M-F, high M-F students had higher means than low M-F students in each of the four categories, but the progression of the eight groups was in each instance saw-toothed rather than linear.

5. In both college and high school students, correlations between scores on the AWS and PAQ scales tended to be in predictable directions for both sexes but were low and not always significant. A comparison of mean scores in the four categorical groups indicated that cross-sex members of both sexes tended to be more profeminist than those in the other categories. Overall, the results confirmed our hypothesis that masculine and feminine attributes are not strongly related to abstract attitudes about acceptable sex roles for women.

6. Inspection of the content of the M-F scale reveals that it contains two major types of items: the masculine, agentic characteristics of aggression and dominance and a series of feminine, expressive items describing emotional vulnerability and the need for emotional support. Analyses of data from the Mehrabian and Epstein (1972) Empathy scale—a questionnaire measuring heightened responsiveness to another's emotional experience—revealed that empathy was most highly related, in both sexes, to the latter group of M-F items and less strongly related to the expressive items on the F scale. These data helped clarify not only the nature of the M-F scale but also the positive rela-

tionship between Self-esteem and both high masculinity on M-F and high femininity on F. It appears that concern with interpersonal relationships per se tends to result in *higher* self-esteem and social competence, while a low degree of aggression and dominance, coupled with emotional vulnerability (and strong empathic reactions to others' emotionality), is associated with *lower* self-regard.

7. Analyses of PAQ data from Lebanese, Israeli, and Brazilian students simultaneously revealed both considerable cross-national stability and cultural differences. In all three samples, significant differences between the sexes in the predicted direction were found in mean F and M-F scores, but only nonsignificant trends were found in M. Classification of the students from each country into the four masculinity and femininity categories, using the relevant high school or college norms for the U.S. samples, yielded distributions that frequently differed from those obtained from North American students although, with one exception (Israeli girls), the smallest percentage was found in the cross-sex category. The patterns of intercorrelations between the PAQ scales, however, were similar to those found in American students, again with a single exception. In Brazilian males, no significant correlation was found between M and M-F. The Brazilian students of both sexes also differed from their counterparts in the United States in their failure to exhibit significant correlations between Self-esteem and any of the PAQ scales.

8. Data were sought from several unique populations in which the distributions across the masculinity and femininity categories might be expected to differ from those found in college students. In a sample of homosexuals, males scored significantly lower than unselected male college students on M and M-F and higher on F, differences that resulted in a marked elevation in the percentage categorized as Undifferentiated and as Feminine on the basis of student norms. Lesbians scored higher on M and M-F, resulting in an elevation in the Androgynous and, even more particularly, the Masculine category. Intercorrelations between the scales and between each of the scales and Self-esteem were basically the same for both male and female homosexuals as in unselected college students.

Female varsity athletes scored somewhat higher than unselected females on M and M-F and somewhat lower on F. The largest percentage of these women were classified as Androgynous (college norms) and the next largest percentage as Masculine. Similar data were obtained from female Ph.D. scientists, these women scoring higher on M and M-F than female college students and falling most frequently in the Androgynous category. Male scientists also scored higher than college males on M and M-F and showed a marked elevation in the Masculine category. Taken together, these data provide substantial evidence that self-reported masculinity and femininity have important implications for significant real-life behaviors.

6. Achievement Motivation: Background Literature

Males have been described as having a greater set toward achievement than females, a difference frequently characterized as reflecting the agentic, instrumental orientation of men as opposed to the communal, expressive orientation of women. Many of the attributes that reflect agency and are found on our M and M-F scales—such as competitive, dominant, or active—indeed seem to specify characteristics that reflect achievement motivation. Because of these conceptual resemblances, the investigation of achievement motivation became an important component of our study of masculinity and femininity. Even more particularly, we were hopeful that a multifactored instrument could be devised that might be useful in predicting real-life achievement behaviors and might, by taking masculinity and femininity into account, clarify some of the sex differences in achievement needs that have been suggested by prior investigations.

The vast literature on achievement motivation has been reviewed elsewhere (see, e.g., recent discussions by Weiner 1970, 1972; Atkinson & Raynor 1974; Mednick, Tangri, & Hoffman 1975; Revelle & Michaels 1976). As much of our empirical efforts represents a fresh start, we will provide only a brief summary of relevant portions of current theories of achievement motivation and focus more of our discussion on empirical and theoretical issues that bear most directly on our concerns.

Although early work by the appropriately named German psychologist, N. Ach (1910), and by Lewin (1926) dealt with aspects of the motive to achieve, the definition of achievement motivation as a research area stems primarily from the work of Murray (1938). Murray defined personality in terms of needs that act in conjunction with "presses" from the perceived and objective environment to determine behavior. Included in his definitions of the need to achieve are tendencies "to do things as rapidly and/or well as possible. . . . To master, manipulate and organize physical objects, human beings or ideas. . . . To overcome obstacles and attain a high standard . . . to excel one's self. To rival and surpass others" (1938, p. 164). This definition clearly lays out the instrumental orientation we have been exploring.

The study of achievement motivation was greatly stimulated by the work of McClelland and his colleagues. In his general theory of motivation, McClelland (1951) had defined motives as tendencies that are learned and that both energize and direct behavior toward specific goals. In the landmark work in the field, McClelland, Atkinson, Clark, and Lowell (1953) looked particularly at individual differences in achievement motivation and presented an assessment technique that has dominated the field for more than twenty years. In the system

developed by McClelland et al., using Murray's Thematic Apperception Test (TAT, 1938), fantasy material elicited by stimulus pictures
is coded for achievement imagery. If a TAT story is judged to contain
achievement imagery, it is scored for each of ten subcategories of
achievement, and the sum of all subcategory scores represents the
strength of the individual's achievement needs. While the system
takes into account different components of achievement, as does Murray's definition, the achievement score assigned to any individual is a
global one, and no attempt is made to examine interrelationships of
components or their individual relationships to criteria of achievement.

An extensive literature has developed exploring the validity and
implications of the concept of achievement motivation as defined by
McClelland et al. Although the relationships are often quite modest
in magnitude, the corpus of research taken as a whole provides considerable evidence for the validity of the formulations and for the
existence of stable, measurable, individual differences. Environmental
influences on the expression of imagery have been studied by taking
protocols under varying stimulus conditions (Veroff 1957; Walker &
Atkinson 1958; Atkinson & McClelland 1948; Clark 1952) or by in-
structional sets such as describing the achievement measure as an
intelligence test (McClelland et al. 1953). The relationship of individual differences in measures of achievement motivation to systematic variation in criterion measures has also been examined. These
validity studies include such dependent variables as intensity and
quality of performance, Zeigarnik effects, choice of work partners,
and delay of gratification (McClelland et al. 1953; Atkinson 1958).

Theoretical Conceptions of Achievement Motivation

The development of theory has proceeded in tandem with empirical
research and has, in fact, outstripped methodological developments.
The first formal statement of a theory of achievement motivation was
advanced by Atkinson (1957), who proposed a mathematically pre-
cise model with the projective assessment of a global construct of
achievement motivation as its cornerstone. The basic theory, along
with its revisions (Atkinson 1964; Atkinson & Feather 1966), predicts
individual behavior in a given situation rather than long-term, task-
oriented strivings. It may be useful to summarize this theory before
turning to the issues related to masculinity and femininity.

Atkinson's theory of achievement motivation defined the primary
determinants of achievement behavior and specified a mathematical
relationship between the components. The basic theoretical statement
and its revisions are straightforward and deal with the behavior of
individuals in the psychological present, that is, as noted above,
achievement activities in immediate situations.

The theory assumes that what is called resultant achievement motivation consists of the algebraic sum of the tendency to engage in an

achievement-oriented activity and the tendency to avoid engaging in a task that might result in failure. Both these tendencies are defined as functions of three variables present in varying amounts in all individuals. The tendency to achieve success (T_S) is composed of (1) the motive to achieve success (M_S), conceived as a relatively stable personality disposition, measured most often by the TAT; (2) the subjective probability that performance will be followed by success (P_S); and (3) the incentive value of success (I_S). The relationship among the variables is multiplicative.

The relationship between the probability of success and the incentive value of success is expressed as $I_S = 1 - P_S$, based on the argument of Lewin, Dembo, Festinger, and Sears (1944) that the attractiveness of success increases as tasks become more difficult. The implications of these definitions are that T_S is most strongly aroused by tasks having an intermediate probability of success and that, when P_S is held constant, individuals with a stronger motive for success show a stronger tendency to achieve.

The tendency to avoid failure (T_{AF}) is conceived as an inhibitory force that acts to block the expression of achievement-related activities. The three components of this tendency are defined as the motive to avoid failure (M_{AF}), the probability of failure (P_F), and the incentive value of failure (I_F).

The motive to avoid failure is defined as a disposition apart from the motive for success and in operationalization of the theory, M_S and M_{AF} are measured separately by different instruments. In contrast to the projective measurement of M_S, M_{AF} has most commonly been assessed by objective tests, the most widely used being the Manifest Anxiety Scale (Taylor 1953), the Mandler-Sarason Test Anxiety Questionnaire (Mandler & Sarason 1952), and the Alpert-Haber Achievement Anxiety Test (Alpert & Haber 1960). Heckhausen (1963), however, has also developed a projective technique for scoring fear of failure from the same TAT pictures used to measure M_S.

The probability of failure is defined as the subjective probability that performance will be followed by failure. The tendencies to seek success and avoid failure are combined mathematically to express resultant achievement motivation (T_A).

ELABORATIONS OF THE THEORY

The model defined above implies that individuals in whom the motive to avoid failure is stronger than the motive to achieve success (i.e., whose T_A is negative) should avoid all achievement-related activities. Experimental data and common sense indicate that many individuals in this category nonetheless do indulge in achievement-oriented activities both in the laboratory and in the real world. To account for this observational discrepancy, the concept of *extrinsic motivation* was added to the model (e.g., Atkinson 1974). The term "extrinsic" refers to sources of motivation that can overcome a resultant inhibitory tendency, such as the interest value of a task and tendencies to seek approval or to comply with authority. Thus, the expression of achievement behavior can be defined as the sum of T_S, T_{AF}, and extrinsic motivation.

A number of other additions and modifications have been made to the basic theory in an attempt to improve its ability to account for behavioral variance in both laboratory and naturalistic settings. One qualification of the theory has been the recognition that individual differences in level of ability or competence may influence the perception of external cues defining level of difficulty and hence may mediate subjective probabilities of success and failure (Moulton 1967; Shrable & Moulton 1968).

Another important addition to the theory comes from the work of Raynor (1968, 1969, 1974), who considers the impact of long-term, future goals on achievement behavior. To account for the influence of such goals on present behavior, Raynor adds the concept of *contingent motivation*, aroused when the individual feels that "immediate success is necessary in order to guarantee the opportunity to strive for some number of future successes, while immediate failure means future failure by guaranteeing loss of the opportunity to continue in that path" (1974, p. 128). Conversely, if immediate success does not influence the opportunity to strive for future goals and immediate failure does not guarantee future failure, the situation is defined as noncontingent. Raynor hypothesizes that individuals evaluate situations in terms of their contingent or noncontingent relationship to future goals and that these contingencies and associated subjective probabilities influence achievement-related behavior.

In an experimental test of these notions, Raynor (1970) found that ratings of the perceived instrumentality of grades in a course for future careers interacted with resultant achievement motivation in predicting final course grades. When perceived instrumentality was low, grades of high and low resultant achievement groups did not differ; when instrumentality was high, high achievement groups made higher grades.

The issues raised by Raynor's insistence on the importance of fitting a present activity into perspective with the individual's long-term goals have broad implications both for understanding the body of extant research data and for the design of future research. In our attempt to relate masculinity and femininity to achievement strivings in both sexes, the issue is of paramount importance. In commenting on the validity of laboratory investigations of achievement behavior, Raynor remarks that "attempts to create 'ego-involvement' of subjects in laboratory experiments are successful to the extent to which they involve use of the subject's life goals, or those aspects of motivation related to them" (1974, p. 154).

Other approaches to increasing the predictive validity of the static model of achievement motivation have rejected the unitary construct of the motive to achieve success and have focused on developing multidimensional measures of the construct. We will consider these efforts in a later section.

In the area of stable individual differences, Horner (1968) has proposed fear of success as another dispositional component to supplement the two originally defined concepts—motive for success (M_S) and motive to avoid failure (M_{AF}). She sees this additional disposition as especially useful in accounting for sex differences in behavior in competitive, achievement situations. Horner has argued that, particularly in women, success in competitive situations may lead to negative consequences (i.e., social rejection) and that appreciation of these consequences may lead to the acquisition of a stable disposition to fear success, the results of this disposition being the inhibition of achievement strivings. Horner developed a TAT-like projective technique for measuring this disposition, employing instead of a pictorial a verbal cue with a same-sex protagonist—"At the end of the first term, John (Anne) finds himself (herself) at the top of his (her) medical school class." Using a simple, present-absent categorization of the imagery elicited by the cue, she found that women more frequently than men gave responses with fear of success imagery and that undergraduate women in an honors program (assumed to have high ability and a history of success) showed somewhat more fear of success than nonhonors women. Horner also provided some experimental evidence suggesting that women high in fear of success may perform better in noncompetitive settings than in mixed-sex, competitive settings. The concept of fear of success has aroused considerable empirical interest and theoretical controversy, and we will return to it in the next section.

INDIVIDUAL DIFFERENCES IN ACHIEVEMENT MOTIVATION

The effects of social class and religion. Among the more consistent findings in the achievement literature are those showing class differences. Higher levels of dispositional, achievement motivation are associated with higher socioeconomic status (Rosen 1956, 1962; Douvan & Adelson 1958; Veroff, Atkinson, Feld, & Gurin 1960; Littig & Yericaris 1965; Carney & McKeachie 1963). A series of cross-cultural studies conducted by Rosen (1962, 1972, 1973) in Brazil has also tended to support the same linear relationship. These class differences in achievement motivation are generally attributed to consistent class differences in child-rearing practices and are assumed to stem from greater emphasis on achievement, mastery training, and self-direction in the middle than in the lower classes (Rosen 1956; Kohn 1959). (The relation of parental attitudes and behavior to the development of achievement motivation will be discussed in Chapter 9.)

Some evidence has also been found for religious differences in achievement motivation. Using data from interviews of a representative sample of the U.S. population, Veroff, Feld, and Gurin (1962) found the highest achievement motivation among Jewish males, followed by Catholic males and, finally, Protestants. In general, however, class differences are stronger than those across religious lines.

Sex differences. The greatest confusion in the understanding of achievement motivation has been created by data concerning sex differences. The basic problem arises when the inconsistencies among three sources of data are confronted: (1) expression of need to achieve under neutral (baseline) conditions, (2) the effect of arousal manipulations on expressed achievement needs, and (3) performance measures. In the initial research of McClelland et al. (1953), most of the data were gathered from males, but comparisons of male and female responses were reported. The disturbing finding in these studies was that, while women tended to show higher achievement scores on the TAT measure, they did not show increases in achievement scores when given achievement-arousing instructions. Other investigators have also reported that, unlike men, women produce equally high achievement scores under neutral and achievement sets (Veroff, Wilcox, & Atkinson 1953; Alper & Greenberger 1967). Research into sex differences in the achievement motivation of children has produced generally inconsistent results, with girls scoring higher on some indices and lower on others and with the pattern of sex differences varying at different ages (Veroff 1969; Veroff et al. 1975). On the other hand, data contrasting the school performance of girls and boys have rather consistently shown girls receiving higher grades in the absence of measurable differences in ability (e.g., Monday et al. 1967; Achenbach 1970). One outcome of the empirical muddle surrounding sex differences was a general hiatus in research on the topic. As Alper (1974) points out, major investigators concentrated on work with males, Atkinson (1958) devoting one footnote to female achievement motivation and Heckhausen (1967) only 9 of 215 pages.

Paralleling increased concerns with the rights and roles of women, research on the nature of the inconsistencies between the sexes has recently become popular (see, e.g., Mednick, Tangri, & Hoffman 1975). Much of the research, both old and new, has centered on the isolation of factors influencing the achievement scores of women, especially in response to TAT stimuli.

The sex of TAT stimulus figures has been noted as an influence on the expression of achievement imagery of women. Although the data are not unequivocal, several investigators have found women's scores higher in response to male cues (Cowan & Goldberg 1967; Veroff, Wilcox, & Atkinson 1953). French and Lesser (1964) found, however, that under intellectual arousal male figures elicited more achievement imagery but, when arousal concerned women's roles, female figures produced higher scores. The latter data stress the importance of the value system invoked in determining the strength of responses elicited.

A number of investigators have suggested that women differ from men in the needs served by achieving behavior. Both Crandall (1967) and, more recently, Hoffman (1975) have suggested that women's achievement motivation is more bound to affiliative needs. In arguing that women work for love and approval rather than for mastery, Hoffman suggests that, because of inadequate encouragement for independence, women feel that safety and effectiveness lie in affective ties. These arguments stress a quite different underlying mechanism for equivalent achievement in women and men.

Other differences between the sexes have been found in attributions concerning performance. Crandall (1967) reported that males and females are equally accurate in assessing their ability but tend to err in opposite directions. That is, males tend to overestimate their own competence while females underestimate. Deaux and Emswiller (1974) found that males were expected to do better at tasks labeled "masculine" while females were expected to do somewhat better at "feminine" tasks. However, when expectancies for "masculine" and "feminine" tasks were averaged, males were expected to outperform females. Similarly, women have been shown to be less likely to attribute successful performance to their own abilities than men (McMahan 1971; Frieze 1973). Women's attributions for performance tend more to emphasize luck (Feather 1969) or luck and effort (Bar-Tal & Frieze 1973; Frieze 1973).

Much of the theoretical and empirical discussion about social concerns over achievement and attributions about performance has centered on Horner's (1968) construct of fear of success. To many workers in the area of achievement, this proposed disposition has appeared to capture the essence of the conflict between social acceptance and competitive achievement striving. Therefore, it seems appropriate to consider the fear of success concept in greater detail.

Fear of success revisited. After much research and speculation, the status of the motive to avoid success is equivocal (Tressemer 1974; Zuckerman & Wheeler 1975). The problems associated with the concept are emphasized by the inconsistencies in data across studies and failures to replicate Horner's original findings. One of the basic premises, of course, was the presence of a stronger fear of success motive in women than men. However, of sixteen studies reviewed by Zuckerman and Wheeler, nine showed more fear of success imagery in women while seven reported more such imagery in males. Horner, of course, argued that the motive is aroused in competitive achievement situations and collected her original data at a competitive, major university. Hoffman (1974), however, failed to replicate Horner's sex differences in the same university setting.

Inconclusive results have also been obtained relating age to fear of success imagery. Monahan, Kuhn, and Shaver (1974) reported that the frequency of fear of success imagery declined with age among ten- to sixteen-year-old girls, while no age relationship was found in boys. Tangri (1969) found that senior college women provided more fear of success imagery than juniors. However, Moore (1972) uncovered no relationship between age and the amount of imagery among female graduate students.

Investigations of the relationship between fear of success and measures of sex-role orientation have similarly produced contradictory results. Alper (1974) reported that, in some samples, women with more traditional attitudes toward sex roles showed relatively high fear of success. Other studies (Peplau 1973; Wellens 1973) failed to demonstrate a relationship with sex-role attitude measures. Heilbrun, Kleemeier, and Piccola (1974), on the other hand, found in college women that high fear of success was associated with less traditional attitudes about women's roles and a more masculine role orientation.

Still another area of contradiction is seen in studies relating measured fear of success to academic performance and measures of resultant achievement motivation. Although some studies have found more fear of success among female honors students (Horner 1968) or honors students of both sexes (Hoffman 1974), others have found *no* relationship (Peplau 1973) or a complex relationship mediated by parental identification (Heilbrun et al. 1974). The correlations obtained with both the TAT measure and Mehrabian's (1968) achievement scale have been nonsignificant or weakly significant. It is unclear whether, as Horner (1968) contends, fear of success inhibits the expression of achievement imagery or whether a direct (but weak) relationship exists between fear of success and achievement motivation.

Addressing the inconsistencies in the fear of success literature, Zuckerman and Wheeler (1975) suggest that a major problem in the research is unreliability of measurement of the concept. Most studies, following Horner's lead, have used only a single cue to elicit imagery. When investigators have used multiple cues, the correspondence of fear of success scores across cues has been low (Morgan & Mausner 1973; Spence 1974).

Several investigators have considered the possibility that the fear of success may reflect cultural values rather than stable individual dispositions (Spence 1974; Zuckerman & Wheeler 1975; Monahan, Kuhn, & Shaver 1974). For example, Spence, presenting data from TAT stories and questionnaires elicited by multiple cues, argues that what is being measured is the individual's contemporary attitudes toward specific areas of achievement in women and men and their perceptions of the consequences of achievement. This contention is reinforced by the large differences found when the story cue changed from single to married and from male to female. While these beliefs about the sanctions associated with various role enactments are doubtless influenced by personality characteristics, the elevation of the measure to the category of stable disposition seems unwarranted. We have argued earlier that dispositional attributes, role enactments, and role attitudes are not necessarily strongly correlated. To the extent that this is true, the distinction between attitudes and dispositions is central. In summary, research on fear of success has produced inconsistent findings. We will argue later that a distinct factor concerning negative aspects of achievement can be isolated. However, the majority of the data obtained with Horner's TAT-like measure might better be regarded as situation-specific assessments of attitudes concerning appropriate achievement activities.

Objective Measures of the Disposition to Achieve

Researchers in the tradition of McClelland, Atkinson, and their colleagues have been single-minded in their devotion to a unitary, fantasy-based measure of the motive to achieve success and in their rejection of other attempts to measure achievement motivation by objective measures (see, e.g., Atkinson & Raynor 1974, p. 190). The result, in practice, has been a curious marriage of measures and methods with the motive to achieve success measured projectively and the motive to avoid failure customarily assessed by objective instruments.

Workers in this tradition have not, as we have noted, attempted to break the motive for success into its constituent parts and to look at them independently, although the motive is constructed from subcategories. One possible reason is the low reliability of the individual fantasy components; another is doubtless the theoretical elegance of a unitary motive.

Other investigators, dissatisfied with the projective measurement of the motive, have engaged in the development and validation of objective measures of achievement (e.g., Mehrabian 1968, 1969; Raven, Molloy, & Corcoran 1972; Herrenkohl 1972; Veroff, McClelland, & Ruhland 1975). Both projective and objective measures have demonstrated modest predictive validity in contrived, time-limited laboratory studies and in predicting broader real-life criteria of achievement behaviors such as undergraduate grades (cf. Raynor & Rubin 1971; Brown 1974; Lesser et al. 1963; Rosen 1956). The correlations between objective and projective measures have proved, however, to be disastrously low. Weinstein (1969), for example, reported an average r of only .08 between eight projective and objective measures. This lack of congruence could stem in part from unreliability of measurement and in part from lumping somewhat correlated but possibly interacting components together to represent a single loose construct called achievement motivation.

Rationale of the Work and Family Orientation Questionnaire

As described in Chapter 2, using scales devised by Mehrabian (1968, 1969) as a departure point, we undertook the development of an objective questionnaire to employ with the core sample of high school students. A key factor in our decision to employ an objective instrument rather than the TAT was a practical one. Because of time constraints, it was necessary to employ a simply administered measure that could be completed in a brief interval. The size of the samples also dictated the use of a machine-scorable instrument. We were also convinced that achievement motivation is more usefully conceived as a multifaceted rather than a unitary phenomenon and attempted to devise items that would tap its several possible components.

The results of factor analytic studies, several appearing after the initiation of our research, support the validity of this contention.

Weinstein (1969), for example, employed factor analysis on a matrix of eight measures of achievement motivation (projective and objective) and twelve measures of risk taking, all given to male undergraduates, and concluded that both achievement motivation and risk taking are multidimensional in nature. Mitchell (1961), working with data from female undergraduates, factor analyzed a set of projective, objective, and self-descriptive measures of achievement motivation. Including individual items from a number of tests in his factor analyses, Mitchell found that items often operate independently of one another and that discrete and face-valid factors emerge. Among the factors specified were self-satisfaction, wish fulfillment, nonacademic achievement motivation, external pressure to achievement, and generalized motivation.

A highly informative study was also conducted by Veroff, McClelland, and Ruhland (1975) using three types of instruments to assess achievement motivation: objective questions, projective questions, and behavioral assessment from choices of behaviors to be performed. An important aspect of the study was the fact that the subjects were a cross-sectional sample of urban adults, including blacks and whites as well as members of both sexes. Factor analyses were initially computed for each race and sex group separately; however, when these analyses indicated a homogeneity of structure across all subjects, a single factor analysis of the complete sample was computed.

The results of the analysis isolated six major factors. These were *assertive competence motivation*, defined as "the desire to see one's self successfully performing valued achievement activity in the society" (p. 182); *task competence motivation*, defined as motivation to achieve the demands of a task; *fear of failure*, defined conventionally; *social comparison motivation*, defined as the need to evaluate performance in terms of others; *future achievement orientation*, defined by long-term goals; and *hope of success*, which the authors contend comes closest to Atkinson's originally defined achievement motive.

No race differences were found, but a pattern of interesting sex differences did emerge. Women were lower in assertive competence motivation but were higher in hope of success and lower in fear of failure. Veroff et al. interpreted these results as follows:

> ... women are explicitly taught to value achievement only under circumscribed settings. They do not especially learn to value assertive competence above other goals but they do learn to value task competence. Furthermore, if women are put in a constrained setting where achievement is clearly relevant, they evidently anticipate gratification in successful performance more than men do and are not as inhibited by potential failure as men are. (1975, pp. 187–188)

Jackson, Ahmed, and Heapy (1976) also questioned the notion of a unitary construct of achievement motivation and postulated six facets of achievement motivation. Factor analysis of data from five sources (self-rating, personal description, interaction simulation, adjective check list, and personality questionnaire) yielded the six hypothesized factors: Status with Experts, Acquisitiveness, Achievement via Independence, Status with Peers, Competitiveness, and Excellence. A second-order factor analysis was also performed to explore the possibility that a single broad, second-order dimension might account for most of the variance of the primary factors, as a unitary construct would imply. However, the analysis yielded three second-order factors rather than one. The first second-order factor combined Acquisitiveness, Achievement via Independence, and Competitiveness; the second emphasized Status with Experts and Status with Peers. The third linked Excellence with Achievement via Independence. The authors argued that the existence of these distinct second-order factors makes it inappropriate and an oversimplification to "refer to an individual as possessing high n-Ach without further specification of its kind and quality" (1976, p. 17).

Taken as a whole, these studies thus suggest that the notion of a unitary construct of achievement motivation may be too simplistic to account for broad patterns of behavior in real-life settings. They also suggest that important components of achievement motivation related to masculinity and femininity which may operate independently include orientation toward work, striving for excellence, the desire to surpass others, and concern with the reactions of others toward achievement.

It was also our hope in devising our objective measure—the Work and Family Orientation Questionnaire (WOFO)—that a single set of achievement motivation scales could be developed that would be useful in analyzing data from both sexes. Development of unisexual scales is predicated on the assumption that the nature of achievement motivation is essentially the same in both males and females. If this assumption were correct, one would anticipate that the factor analytic structure produced by the data of each sex would be similar. As reported above, this was indeed the result found with an adult sample by Veroff et al. (1975).

In this connection, it has been shown that the sexes differ in the activities in which they typically elect to express their achievement needs. Some of the difficulties surrounding the attempt to find an empirical or conceptual model that will predict the achievement behaviors of both females and males may thus be caused by the failure to consider sex differences in mode of expression. Women with traditional, family-oriented interests, for example, may satisfy their achievement needs directly through domestic activities or community service or vicariously through the career achievements of their husbands or the accomplishments of their children. The results of a study by Veroff and Feld (1970) support this contention. These investigators report that highly educated women also high in achievement needs feel particularly restricted by marriage and make child *rearing* an achievement goal, while less educated women report that *having* children seems to satisfy achievement needs. In order to determine the relationship between achievement factors and goals, a series of items relating to aspirations for one's spouse (items that we anticipated would yield more informative data for females than males), personal educational aspirations, and the relative importance of career vs. marriage was included on the versions of the WOFO given to high school and college students. (It was, in fact, these items that led us to identify the instrument to respondents as the Work and Family Orientation Questionnaire.)

While Veroff et al. (1975) have reported a similar factor structure in women and men for their achievement measures, other investigators (e.g., Mehrabian 1968, 1969) have found it necessary to develop nonidentical scales for the two sexes. Thus a strong alternate possibility was that the factor structure of our instrument would differ for males and females. This outcome seemed particularly likely in adolescent groups that included a large proportion of noncareer-oriented girls.

Bronfenbrenner (1974) has emphasized the confusion of many adolescents regarding life goals and their attainment. Confusion may be particularly marked in girls who have not thought beyond becoming a wife and mother. Articulation of achievement needs, as they have typically been conceived, may therefore be inhibited or delayed in girls oriented primarily toward these familial goals.

As will be seen in the following chapters, analyses of the data obtained from the Work and Family Orientation Questionnaire gave some support for the latter possibility but nonetheless permitted a useful unisexual instrument to be developed.

7. Achievement Factors and Their Correlates

In Chapter 3 we briefly described the development of two versions of the Work and Family Orientation Questionnaire (WOFO) and the scales into which they were broken down. Results obtained from the high school students will be presented first.

High School Sample

The questionnaire given to high school students included three items relating to vocational and marital goals. The first item asked respondents to indicate the *least* amount of education that would satisfy them. The second asked the importance to life satisfaction of marriage in comparison with a job, while the third asked the number of children the respondent would ideally like to have. Responses of the total high school sample for each question broken down by sex and social class are presented in Table 7-1.

The breakdown for educational aspiration is consistent and intuitively reasonable. Desire for higher education is linearly related to social class with, for example, 34% of Upper-class males and only 9% of Lower-class males planning on a graduate degree. Overall, males have somewhat higher educational aspirations than females.

The relative importance of marriage vs. career shows less marked differences. More Upper-class respondents of both sexes and more males than females reported feeling that marriage is unimportant. Somewhat to our surprise, more males (17%) than females (14%) indicated that marriage is the most important goal. This discrepancy is largely caused by a high percentage of Lower-class males (26%) reporting this attitude, a result that may reflect their expectations that their life's work will provide little satisfaction.

Differences were also found among PAQ categories, particularly in those who chose the alternative specifying that marriage was most important. About 25% of the Androgynous and Feminine boys selected this alternative, in contrast to about 15% of the Masculine and Undifferentiated boys. Among girls, twice as many in the Masculine category specified that marriage was unimportant (12%) or less important (13%) than those in the other categories.

Responses to the item inquiring about number of children desired

Table 7-1. *Percentage of High School Students Giving Each Response to Items on Educational Aspiration, Marriage, and Family Size (Work and Family Orientation Questionnaire)*

A. Least amount of education to satisfy

Social class	Males					Females				
	High school	Vocat train (post H.S.)	Some college	College degree	Post-grad degree	High school	Vocat train (post H.S.)	Some college	College degree	Post-grad degree
Upper	7	8	7	45	34	6	7	13	57	17
Upper middle	12	13	8	53	14	12	15	13	49	10
Lower middle	19	18	8	42	13	21	21	10	38	9
Lower	28	22	13	28	9	30	24	4	29	12
Total	15	15	8	46	16	17	17	11	44	11

B. Importance of marriage vs. job for life satisfaction

Marriage is

Social class	Males					Females				
	Most impt	More impt	Equally impt	Less impt	Unimpt	Most impt	More impt	Equally impt	Less impt	Unimpt
Upper	17	32	26	10	14	4	46	34	7	10
Upper middle	19	37	27	6	11	12	47	28	5	7
Lower middle	13	40	24	10	12	17	44	27	6	5
Lower	26	28	32	4	9	19	46	26	4	4
Total	17	36	26	8	12	14	46	28	6	6

C. Number of children ideally desired

Social class	Males					Females				
	0	1	2	3	4+	0	1	2	3	4+
Upper	9	6	39	32	13	11	5	39	26	20
Upper middle	9	6	49	25	11	8	5	39	26	21
Lower middle	11	9	43	24	13	6	6	36	26	25
Lower	7	4	48	22	20	3	7	35	28	28
Total	10	7	45	25	13	7	6	38	26	23

were first related to religious affiliation. The results of this analysis were in the expected direction: 18% of Catholic males and 29% of Catholic females hoped for four or more children, for example, while for Protestants and Jewish respondents the corresponding percentages were 9% for males and 17% for females. The differences between religious groups were not strong, however. Therefore it was not surprising that no consistent class differences were found. The modal number of children desired for both sexes was two, with a higher percentage of females (23%) than males (13%) looking forward to four or more offspring. Ten percent of the males and 7% of the females expressed a desire for no children. Even among Catholics, 9% of the males and 6% of the females indicated no interest in children.

No significant differences related to categories of the Personal Attributes Questionnaire (PAQ) were found in boys, but Masculine girls were more likely than those in other categories to want no children or only one child (14% and 9% respectively vs. 7% and 5% for the total group).

The Attitudes toward Women Scale (AWS) scores of those desiring the various numbers of children were also compared by a 2 (sex) by 5 (number of children desired) analysis of variance. In addition to the previously noted sex difference (females were more profeminist), a significant main effect for number of children was found ($p < .01$). This was reflected in a linear trend in both sexes: the more profeminist the respondent, the fewer children sought.

We will report further analyses using the educational aspiration variable later. First, however, the procedures used to derive scales will be described in the section below. The outcome of these derivations is then summarized in the section that follows.

DERIVATION OF THE ACHIEVEMENT SCALES

Our theoretical notions about the nature of achievement motivation suggested that achievement needs have conceptually separable components. The procedures used to develop such a measure were not quite as straightforward as our brief descriptions in Chapter 3 implied, so that further elaboration of the analytical steps leading to the scales will be undertaken at this point.

The nineteen Likert-scaled items of the initial version of the instrument (WOFO-1) were approached through separate factor analyses of the data from female and male high school students. Since we were convinced that achievement motivation would more usefully be conceptualized as consisting of several correlated rather than orthogonal components, we used oblique rotational procedures instead of a varimax solution. These analyses, shown in Tables VI and VII of Appendix A, yielded rather different structures for males and females. Six conceptually clear factors emerged for males. The factor analysis of female responses gave five factors and a much less coherent structure. This outcome has occurred in other studies, and one approach to such sex differences has been to develop separate achievement scales for men and women (e.g., Mehrabian 1968). A more fruitful approach, we believed, would be to develop scales from the conceptually cleaner factor analysis of male responses and to use these scales for analyses between and within the sexes, providing the reliabilities of the male-derived scales are satisfactory in both sexes.

As we shall see, analyses using the male-derived scales exhibit strong and consistent relationships in each sex. This desirable outcome does not, however, explain the observed lack of congruence in the factor analyses of the two sexes. One possible explanation is that the sexes differ fundamentally in the possession and interrelation of the attributes, so that even when the same behaviors are under investigation (e.g., academic achievement) structurally different achievement needs account for these behaviors in the two sexes (French & Lesser 1964). Another possibility is that the sexes differ primarily in the *incidence* of particular types of achievement-related aspirations. Society places pressures on males for vocational achievement and for obtaining the requisite training; thus adolescent males, whether or not their own achievement needs are high, are able to interpret achievement-oriented items in these terms. For young females whose aspirations are more purely domestic, the items and issues contained in the usual achievement test may have little meaning or relevance. In samples in which such females form a sizable proportion of those tested, noncomparable factor structures based on the responses of the two sexes would not be unexpected. If this hypothesis is correct, women whose aspirations include stereotypically masculine goals should produce results similar to those of males.

As one test of this possibility, we classified respondents on the basis of answers to the previously discussed item dealing with educational aspirations. The categories in Table 7-1 were combined to give two groups: those whose minimum aspiration was a college or professional degree and those with more modest goals.

As noted, a higher percentage of males than females aspire to a college degree or beyond (62% vs. 55% respectively). It is also likely, of course, that a lower percentage of women than men with high educational aspirations have a strong career interest. Nevertheless, as a rough test of the differential aspirations hypothesis, we performed the same factor analysis of the WOFO-1, using as our sample only those women with college or professional degree aspirations. The results were dramatic: females with higher educational aspirations produce a factor structure remarkably similar to that of the unselected sample of males. The major difference in pattern is that females lump job aspirations for themselves with those for spouses while males maintain this distinction. These results imply that the observed differences between the sexes are probably more a function of focus of aspiration than of more fundamental psychological differences between the sexes.

This finding strongly suggests that researchers should attempt to ascertain subjects' aspirations when investigating the relationships between achievement measures and criteria, especially in women where more diversity is expected. This emphasis on direction of aspiration parallels the argument of Bem and Allen (1974) that the salience of a personality trait must be assessed in order to isolate transsituational consistencies in its expression. These results also suggested that use of the male-derived achievement motivation scales may yield similar relationships to other characteristics and achievement-related behaviors in both sexes. We proceeded on this assumption, developing achievement scales based on the factor analysis of the male sample given WOFO-1. These scales are described below.

ACHIEVEMENT SCALES ON WOFO-1

To obtain conceptually clear measures that could be applied to a variety of samples, we adopted the policy of constructing unit-weighted scales from the male factor matrix. Items with loadings greater than ±.30 were reversed if necessary and summed to yield six scales scored in the direction of high needs for attainment. The labels given each of these six scales and an exemplary item are (1) *Work Orientation* ("Once I undertake a task, I dislike goofing up and not doing the best job I can"); (2) *Mastery* ("I would rather do something at which I feel confident and relaxed than something which is challenging and difficult"); (3) *Competitiveness* ("I really enjoy working in situations involving skill and competition"); (4) *Effort* ("I wouldn't mind spending more than 40 hours a week working at a job that interested me, even if I didn't get paid more for the overtime"); (5) *Job Concerns* ("It is important to my future satisfaction in life to have a job or career which pays well"); and (6) *Spouse Career Aspirations* ("Assuming that I get married, I would like my husband or my wife to have a job or career which pays well").

The composition of the derived scales, interrelations, and reliabilities for each sex are shown in Appendix A, Table VI to Table VIII. The two items of the Competitiveness scale are essentially orthogonal (r's of .12 and .04 for males and females), which is particularly regrettable because of the theoretical interest of the concept. (This outcome led us in a revision of the scale, WOFO-2, to attempt to measure competitiveness more adequately. Data obtained from WOFO-2 will be reported in a later section.)

The intercorrelations of the scales for each sex are reported in Appendix A, Table VIII. The correlations among the four scales dealing with instrumental activity (Work, Mastery, Competitiveness, and Effort) are all positive and range from .05 to .32. Work, Mastery, and Effort are most tightly bound, with Competitiveness tending to show weaker relationships. The correlations of the two vocational scales (Job and Spouse) with the other four are weaker and occasionally negative. However, concern with personal pay and recognition is quite strongly correlated with desire for similar attainment by the spouse. This association is particularly true in females, where the correlation is .61.

In the next section, we will examine sex and class differences in achievement orientation as measured by these scales and will then turn to the correlates of achievement needs.

SEX AND CLASS DIFFERENCES IN ACHIEVEMENT MOTIVATION

The six achievement scales were individually compared by 2 (sex) by 4 (social class) analyses of variance. Means and standard deviations are found in Table 7-2, along with the p values found in the ANOVAs. Significant sex differences were found on four of the six scales—Mastery, Competitiveness, Job, and Spouse—with males scoring higher except for Spouse, where females predictably report more desire for their spouses' vocational success than do males.

Significant differences as a function of social class were found only in Mastery and Effort. In both cases Upper-class students scored highest, while Lower-class students tended to score lowest.

The sex by social class interaction was not significant for any of the scales. The interactions for Competitiveness and Effort did, however, approach significance ($p<.10$). For both variables the effect is caused by shifts in the pattern of means in the Lower class. In the case of Competitiveness, Lower-class males score as markedly more competitive than those in the other classes, while Lower-class females rate themselves as much less competitive than other females. The trend on Effort again comes primarily from the Lower-class students, males reporting themselves as less motivated to work hard than the other groups and females more closely resembling the Middle-class students in their scores.

Overall, the main effects for sex and class are in the expected direction, and the presence of interactions of only borderline significance suggests that analyses conducted with the population as a whole will present a veridical picture of achievement relationships. We will return to the issue of sex differences in achievement motivation later in this chapter, after examining the pattern of correlations of other measures with the WOFO scales.

CORRELATES OF ACHIEVEMENT MOTIVATION

The correlations of the PAQ, Self-esteem, and AWS measures with the six WOFO-1 achievement scales for each sex are presented in Table 7-3. Considering first the PAQ scales, the strongest relationships in both sexes are between M and Work, Mastery, and Competitiveness; all correlations are significantly positive and in excess of .20. That the instrumental focus of masculinity results in a significant positive relationship with the agentic components of achievement motivation is quite to be expected. Weaker relationships were found between the M-F scale and the achievement measures. The strongest correlations found for M-F are with Mastery in both females and males and Competitiveness in females.

The Job and Spouse scales show small and nonsignificant relation-

Table 7-2. *Means and Standard Deviations of WOFO-I Achievement Scales Broken Down by Class and Sex for High School Students*

Social class	Work		Mastery		Comp		Effort		Job		Spouse	
	$\overline{X}$	SD	$\overline{X}$	SD	$\overline{X}$	SD	$\overline{X}$	SD	$\overline{X}$	SD	$\overline{X}$	SD
Upper												
Males	8.59	1.97	12.67	3.29	4.22	1.74	5.52	1.70	8.69	3.08	4.39	2.04
Females	8.58	2.12	12.52	3.63	4.18	1.79	5.89	1.76	7.39	3.27	5.49	1.90
Upper middle												
Males	8.52	2.17	12.41	3.48	4.31	1.72	4.88	1.98	8.69	2.68	4.26	2.08
Females	8.56	1.95	12.30	3.14	4.17	1.68	5.16	1.89	7.72	3.03	5.30	1.90
Lower middle												
Males	8.50	2.11	12.44	3.60	4.30	1.73	4.92	2.12	8.78	2.66	4.21	1.95
Females	8.41	1.99	12.16	3.34	4.08	1.84	4.72	2.09	7.72	2.85	5.11	1.86
Lower												
Males	8.40	2.03	11.54	3.05	4.77	1.95	4.20	1.91	9.33	2.40	4.69	1.90
Females	8.05	2.11	11.60	3.70	3.72	1.94	5.00	1.91	8.21	2.71	5.40	1.64
ANOVA	p		p		p		p		p		p	
Sex	NS		$<.05$		$<.05$		NS		$<.01$		$<.01$	
Class	NS		$<.01$		NS		$<.01$		NS		NS	
Sex x Class	NS		NS		$<.10$		$<.10$		NS		NS	

ships with all three PAQ scales. No consistent relationships with F were found. The largest correlation was between this measure and Work in females, a significant but unimpressive .15.

Self-esteem is positively related to all six scales, the largest correlation (.32) being with Mastery in both males and females. Again, this pattern of relationships is consistent and, in view of the correlations found with M, unsurprising.

Correlations of the AWS with the scales show several interesting though modest relationships. A profemininist attitude is positively associated with Work, Mastery, and Effort and negatively but weakly related to Competitiveness in both sexes. The Job scale is significantly related to the AWS in males ($r = -.28$) in the direction that males concerned with obtaining high-paying and prestigious jobs are less sympathetic to equality of rights and roles for women. To our surprise, the same relationship occurs in females, although more weakly ($r = -.16$).

The pattern of correlations between the PAQ, Self-esteem, and AWS measures and the achievement scales is theoretically consistent, although the magnitude of significant correlations is not large. However, as the exposition progresses, it will be seen that the strength of the lawful relationships between masculinity and femininity and achievement needs is far greater than is suggested by the size of overall correlations.

ACHIEVEMENT MOTIVATION AS A FUNCTION OF PAQ CATEGORY AND SEX

Having found previously that a categorical, median split classification of individuals on the Masculinity and Femininity scales of the

Table 7-3. *Correlations of WOFO-1 Achievement Scales with PAQ Scales, Self-esteem, and AWS for High School Students*

	Work	Mastery	Comp	Effort	Job	Spouse
Masc (M)						
Males	.20	.26	.21	.04	.10	.00
Females	.27	.38	.36	.13	.08	.00
Fem (F)						
Males	.08	.14	.05	.13	.02	−.04
Females	.15	.04	−.02	.12	.00	.05
Masc-Fem (M-F)						
Males	.07	.17	.00	.01	−.02	.00
Females	.12	.22	.18	.04	.02	−.10
Self-esteem						
Males	.10	.32	.14	.06	.11	.06
Females	.20	.32	.26	.15	.11	.10
AWS						
Males	.08	.12	−.04	.15	−.28	.10
Females	.14	.14	−.05	.18	−.16	−.18

Note: For $df = 600$, $r_{.05} = .08$.

PAQ clarified the relationship of these concepts to Self-esteem, we expected a similar breakdown to provide revealing information on the relationship of these variables to the various components of achievement motivation specified by the WOFO. Accordingly, the six achievement scales were subjected to 2 (sex) by 4 (PAQ category) analyses of variance, the results of which are given in Table 7-4. These data suggest that most of the differences between males and females reported in Table 7-3 are, in fact, associated with differences between PAQ categories. Thus, when scores on the six achievement scales are related to the masculinity and femininity categories, the only significant main effects for sex are found on the two variables dealing with self and spouse's jobs. For these two variables, the results show that males are more concerned with having prestigious and well-paying jobs and females are more concerned with having their spouses in the best possible positions.

On the other hand, significant main effects for PAQ categories were found for five of the six achievement scales (the exception being desire for spouse's career). In general, the largest distinction is between the categories high and low in M (Androgynous and Masculine vs. Feminine and Undifferentiated). However, F also contributes to achievement differences. Overall, Androgynous individuals show the highest motivation, followed by Masculine, then Feminine, then Undifferentiated individuals. The exceptions to this generalization are, however, of interest. For males, the highest mean for Effort is found among those classified as Feminine; otherwise the order is Androgynous, Masculine, and Undifferentiated. The other exception to the order of means is on the Job scale, where Feminine males express the *lowest* desire for prestigious and well-paying jobs (falling lower even than Undifferentiated males).

In women, the only exception to the descending Androgynous, Masculine, Feminine, Undifferentiated order is for Competitiveness. Masculine women score as most competitive, followed in the usual order by the other three groups. For women, the desire to be best and to win over others may be suppressed to some degree by the possession of feminine, expressive characteristics.

Significant sex by PAQ classification interactions are found for the Work and Competitiveness scales. In both instances, Androgynous and Masculine females score higher than their male contemporaries, while Feminine and Undifferentiated females score lower. For Effort and Mastery, where the interaction results are less sharp but approach significance ($p < .20 > .10$), the results tend to parallel this general pattern.

EDUCATIONAL ASPIRATION AND ACHIEVEMENT MOTIVATION

To evaluate further the contention that sex differences in achievement motivation are primarily a function of masculinity and femininity, a more extensive evaluation of the differences between males and females with high educational aspirations and those with more

Table 7-4. Means and Standard Deviations of WOFO-1 Achievement Scales Broken Down by Sex and PAQ Category for High School Students

PAQ category	Work		Mastery		Comp		Effort		Job		Spouse	
	$\bar{X}$	SD	$\bar{X}$	SD	$\bar{X}$	SD	$\bar{X}$	SD	$\bar{X}$	SD	$\bar{X}$	SD
Andro												
Males	8.73	1.90	13.38	3.18	4.58	1.55	5.05	2.09	8.81	2.74	4.23	1.87
Females	8.87	1.88	13.25	3.00	4.58	1.74	5.20	2.02	7.86	2.84	5.35	1.79
Masc												
Males	8.43	2.13	12.49	3.52	4.42	1.64	4.60	1.96	8.58	2.67	4.21	1.82
Females	8.81	2.10	13.24	3.35	4.86	1.80	4.99	2.20	7.68	2.93	4.86	1.81
Fem												
Males	8.28	2.20	11.66	3.52	3.86	2.03	5.20	2.18	7.98	3.16	4.02	1.75
Females	8.10	2.02	11.12	3.46	3.63	1.93	4.98	2.04	7.26	2.98	5.14	1.93
Undiff												
Males	8.03	2.26	11.16	3.26	3.83	1.77	3.68	1.92	8.28	2.46	4.15	1.80
Females	7.49	1.94	10.94	3.23	3.55	1.91	3.77	1.94	7.70	2.79	5.23	1.65
ANOVA	p		p		p		p		p		p	
Sex	NS		NS		NS		NS		$<.001$		$<.001$	
PAQ	$<.001$		$<.001$		$<.001$		$<.002$		$<.016$		NS	
Sex x PAQ	$<.034$		$<.16$		$<.050$		$<.141$		NS		NS	

modest goals was conducted. It will be recalled that the factor analysis of the achievement scales for women with high expressed desire for education resulted in a factor structure parallel to that for males. Two approaches were taken to these data: the first consisted of contrasting the high and the low aspiration groups by analysis of variance, the second of comparing the patterns of correlations between personal attributes and the achievement scales for the total population and the two subgroups.

For each achievement scale 2 (sex) by 4 (social class) by 2 (educational aspiration) analyses of variance were computed. Significant main effects (p's < .001) for aspiration were found on the Work, Mastery, and Effort scales, with high aspiration individuals having higher scores, but no significant main effects were found for Competitiveness, Job, or Spouse. Educational aspirations did not enter into significant interactions on any scale.

The change in the factor structure of WOFO-1 found when responses of women with high aspirations were analyzed separately suggested that differences in the strength of correlations with other attributes might also be found if high and low aspiration groups were analyzed separately. Accordingly, separate correlation matrices were computed between the achievement scales and the PAQ, Self-esteem, and AWS measures for each sex and each aspiration group. No major changes were found for the low aspiration groups, but differences did appear in the matrices for high aspiration males and females. These correlations are presented in Appendix C, Table I. Particularly noticeable are elevated correlations of Mastery with M (r's = .39 and .42 in males and females respectively) and with Self-esteem (r's of .43 and .38). The relationships of F scores remain similar and the correlations with the AWS and the Job and Spouse scales are essentially unchanged.

As a further test of the influence of aspiration on achievement motivation, 2 (sex) by 4 (PAQ category) by 2 (aspiration) analyses of variance were also computed. Other than the three previously mentioned level of aspiration main effects on Work, Mastery, and Effort, the patterns of means were essentially unchanged. Aspiration did not enter into significant interactions on any achievement scale. Thus, both overall and within a given level of aspiration, the relationships between PAQ category, sex, and achievement motivation are stable and in the pattern we have previously discussed.

It is possible, however, that educational aspirations may influence the relationship between masculinity, femininity, and achievement motivation in a different way. That is, individuals at different levels of masculinity and femininity may differentially exhibit high educational aspirations. For example, a higher percentage of Masculine than Undifferentiated males may be likely to aspire to college or professional degrees. However, social class confounds this relationship because the distribution of PAQ categories differs somewhat as a function of social class and because the normative expectation for higher education of Upper-class individuals is to receive at least an undergraduate degree, while in the Lower class a high school diploma is the typical goal. Examination of the relations between PAQ categories and aspirations in the two middle classes, where expectations are somewhat less environmentally determined, can provide some information on this phenomenon. Accordingly, crosstabulations of aspiration by sex were computed for the Upper middle and Lower middle classes and are reported in Table 7-5.

As the table indicates, there are significant class differences in aspiration. For males, 64% of the Upper middle class have high aspirations, in contrast to 54% of the Lower middle class. For females the corresponding figures are 55% for the Upper middle and 47% for the Lower middle. As noted earlier, a higher percentage of males overall have high educational aspirations.

In both the Upper and Lower middle classes a significant separation between PAQ categories and aspirations is found, with a higher percentage of Androgynous and Masculine individuals having high aspirations. Females provide a more interesting pattern of results than males, dividing significantly into three distinct groups. Masculine females are most likely to have high aspirations, followed at some distance by Androgynous and finally by Feminine and Undifferentiated females.

Overall, aspiration appears to serve as a moderator variable for many relationships among achievement-related variables. The results obtained reinforce Raynor's (1974) specification of the importance of understanding long-term individual goals when studying achievement phenomena.

Achievement Motivation (WOFO-2) in Other Groups

It will be recalled from Chapter 3 that a revision of the achievement instrument was undertaken in which items related to competition were

Table 7-5. *Percentage of Upper-Middle- and Lower-Middle-Class High School Students in Each PAQ Category with High and Low Educational Aspirations*

| | Males | | | | | Females | | | | |
	Undiff	Fem	Masc	Andro	N	Undiff	Fem	Masc	Andro	N
				Upper middle class						
Low aspiration	46	44	33	31	64	56	58	24	38	99
High aspiration	54	56	67	69	113	44	42	76	62	121
				Lower middle class						
Low aspiration	52	67	44	38	77	66	61	38	47	115
High aspiration	47	33	55	62	89	34	39	62	53	102

added and items related to jobs for self and spouse were dropped. The resulting fourteen-item scale (WOFO-2) was administered to several groups: 120 male and 237 female high school students in the two schools tested last (see Chapter 3), 220 male and 275 female students in introductory psychology at the University of Texas at Austin, and two additional samples from the same institution whose PAQ data were described in Chapter 5. One of these samples was composed of 41 female athletes, the second of 143 male and 18 female Ph.D. holding scientists.

When the WOFO-2 data obtained from each of the male samples were factor analyzed, similar structures were obtained; in each case the analyses yielded a four-factor oblique solution. Four unit-weighted scales were then computed. Since the Ph.D. scientists were tested first, the data from the 143 males in this group were used to form the four scales, although similar scales would have emerged had the responses of the male high school or college students been used instead.

Of the four scales, two are similar in content to the achievement scales developed from WOFO-1—Work Orientation and Mastery. The third, Competitiveness, contains four items and, unlike its forerunner on WOFO-1, is adequately reliable (Cronbach alphas over .50 in both male scientists and female and male students). The fourth scale we have called Personal Unconcern. In content it deals with interpersonal relations influenced by achievement. The item with the highest loading—"I worry because my success may cause others to dislike me"— is reminiscent of Horner's (1968) fear of success concept. The scale was scored such that a high score indicates a *lack* of concern for the opinions of others vis-à-vis achievement. The four scales are all significantly and positively intercorrelated, although the relations are modest in size (average $r = .30$). The instrument, factor pattern matrix, scale composition and reliabilities, and scale intercorrelations for scientists are given in Appendix A, Tables IX through XI.

HIGH SCHOOL STUDENTS

Sex and class differences on WOFO-2 scales. To establish the comparability of the three conceptually similar scales and to investigate relationships with the Personal Unconcern scale, analyses parallel to those made with WOFO-1 were conducted in the high school sample and will be briefly summarized.

Mean scores on each of the four achievement scales were first computed for the four social classes within each sex. No significant main effects or interactions for social class were found with WOFO-2, although a tendency was found for the Lower class to score lower on Work and Mastery but not on Competitiveness. A weak tendency was evident for the Lower class to express *more* personal concern. Overall, class differences are highly similar to those found with WOFO-1.

A main effect for sex was found on Competitiveness, with males again proving more competitive (means of 9.6 and 8.5 for males and females respectively, $p < .01$). A significant main effect was also found for Personal Unconcern, with females showing generally *less* concern about the reactions of others (means of 7.4 and 7.79, $p < .02$). Although this finding seems anomalous at first glance, it probably reflects the fact that women are less likely to operate in competitive, interpersonal situations where success might engender hostility. Further data on this point will be provided in the discussion of female athletes.

Correlates of WOFO-2. Correlations of WOFO-2 scales with the PAQ, Self-esteem, and AWS measures are reported in Table 7-6. As the tabled data indicate, all the PAQ correlations with the four achievement scales are positive in both sexes except for those between Femininity and Competitiveness, which are negative and nonsignificant. The Personal Unconcern scale enters into the fewest significant relationships of the four. Its two strongest correlations are both in females and are parallel in nature, females higher in M and in Self-esteem tending to express fewer concerns about the reactions of others.

Self-esteem is most strongly related to Competitiveness in males and to Work in both sexes. It is significantly and positively related to all scales except Personal Unconcern in males. The magnitude of the relationships, however, is relatively small (average $r = .25$).

Again, the AWS shows rather weak relationships, the strongest being in males, where high Mastery is associated with a profeminist attitude and high Competitiveness with a traditional outlook.

The achievement data were also broken down for each scale by PAQ category. These data, shown in Table 7-7, were then examined by sex by PAQ category analyses of variance on each achievement

Table 7-6. *Correlations of WOFO-2 Achievement Scales with PAQ Scales, Self-esteem, and AWS for High School Students*

	Work	Mast	Comp	Uncon
Masc (M)				
Males	.32	.31	.46	.13
Females	.35	.24	.30	.19
Fem (F)				
Males	.23	.09	−.12	.02
Females	.11	.01	−.02	.05
Masc-Fem (M-F)				
Males	.06	.11	.23	.04
Females	.20	.23	.09	.05
AWS				
Males	.06	.16	−.14	−.04
Females	.05	.10	−.04	.05
Self-esteem				
Males	.30	.19	.35	.11
Females	.35	.26	.22	.23

Note: For $df = 120$, $r_{.05} = .18$; for $df = 230$, $r_{.05} = .14$.

Table 7-7. *Means and Standard Deviations of WOFO-2 Achievement Scales Broken Down by Sex and PAQ Category for High School Students*

PAQ category	Work $\overline{X}$	Work SD	Mastery $\overline{X}$	Mastery SD	Competition $\overline{X}$	Competition SD	Personal Unconcern $\overline{X}$	Personal Unconcern SD
Andro								
Males	7.68	2.49	6.68	2.48	10.06	3.76	7.09	2.21
Females	7.99	2.26	6.58	2.58	9.31	3.80	8.46	1.83
Masc								
Males	7.18	2.49	6.64	2.12	11.24	2.08	7.72	1.92
Females	7.51	2.68	6.77	2.30	9.28	2.82	7.97	2.28
Fem								
Males	6.89	2.31	6.22	2.59	8.33	2.83	7.89	1.97
Females	6.89	2.25	5.84	2.77	7.92	3.28	7.59	2.08
Undiff								
Males	6.10	1.91	5.84	2.60	8.84	2.54	7.00	2.00
Females	5.82	2.43	5.58	2.41	7.68	3.49	7.16	1.99
ANOVA	*p*		*p*		*p*		*p*	
Sex	NS		NS		$<.001$		$<.016$	
PAQ	$<.001$		$<.03$		$<.004$		$<.022$	
Sex $\times$ PAQ	NS		NS		NS		$<.10$	

scale, also shown in Table 7-7. As noted above, significant sex differences on Competitiveness and Personal Unconcern were found, with no interactions reaching significance. The main effect for PAQ category was significant for all scales. With one exception, Masculine and Androgynous individuals of both sexes were higher on each scale than either Feminine or Undifferentiated members of their sex: *Feminine* males expressed the *least* concern with the opinions of others. As individuals manifesting a nontraditional and often derogated personality stereotype, they perhaps tend to react defensively by rejecting concern for the opinions of others.

COMPARISON OF SELECTED SAMPLES ON WOFO-2 ACHIEVEMENT SCALES

WOFO-2 achievement scale scores were also available for several of the selected samples described in Chapter 5. These included the 161 scientists and the 41 female varsity athletes. For comparison purposes, the means of these samples, broken down by PAQ category, as well as the comparable means for the 357 high school students and the 495 college students are shown in Table 7-8. For purposes of statistical comparison, the college students were considered as the baseline group and 2 (college students vs. selected sample) by 4 (PAQ category) analyses of variance on each achievement scale were computed separately for each sex.

Comparing first the overall means of the two student populations, high school males score significantly lower than college students on the Work, Mastery, and Personal Unconcern scales ($p < .01$); they are slightly and nonsignificantly lower in Competitiveness. No inter-

Table 7-8. *Means for High School Students, College Students, Female Varsity Athletes, and Scientists on the WOFO-2 Achievement Scales*

	Males					Females				
	Undiff	Fem	Masc	Andro	Grand mean	Undiff	Fem	Masc	Andro	Grand mean
Work Orientation										
High school students	6.1	6.9	7.2	7.7	7.1	5.8	6.8	7.5	7.9	7.2
College students	5.9	6.6	7.5	8.1	7.4	6.3	6.7	8.4	8.0	7.4
Scientists	7.1	8.1	9.2	9.1	8.7	9.0	8.0	9.7	8.7	8.8
Female athletes						7.0	7.4	8.1	8.8	7.7
Mastery										
High school students	5.8	6.2	6.6	6.7	6.5	5.6	5.8	6.8	6.6	6.2
College students	5.8	6.5	7.2	7.3	6.7	5.7	5.6	7.1	7.0	7.1
Scientists	5.9	7.5	8.1	8.3	7.7	8.0	7.0	8.7	8.7	7.7
Female athletes						6.0	4.2	7.8	8.2	6.8
Competitiveness										
High school students	8.8	8.3	11.2	10.1	10.2	7.7	7.9	9.3	9.3	8.6
College students	8.9	8.9	11.0	11.0	10.4	8.3	8.4	10.0	9.7	9.1
Scientists	8.2	8.4	11.0	11.2	10.4	4.0	8.3	11.7	9.5	9.3
Female athletes						11.1	10.8	11.2	10.4	10.7
Personal Unconcern										
High school students	7.0	7.9	7.7	7.1	7.4	7.2	7.6	8.0	8.5	7.9
College students	6.9	8.5	9.1	9.0	8.6	7.4	8.7	9.6	9.3	8.8
Scientists	9.0	9.1	9.7	9.6	9.5	10.0	11.0	11.0	10.5	10.7
Female athletes						7.9	8.5	7.5	8.1	8.0

Note: N's for males and females respectively are 120 and 237 for high school students, 220 and 275 for college students, 143 and 18 for scientists; the N for female athletes is 41.

actions approach significance. High school females score significantly lower than their college peers on all four scales ($p < .01$), again with no interactions. Although the results are not tabled, an analysis was also performed in which high school students with high educational aspirations (college degree or beyond) were compared with the college sample. In this comparison, there were *no* significant differences on any of the achievement scales in either sex. This pattern of results is reassuring as an indicator of the validity of the instrument. Students from public high schools would be expected to score lower on all measures than a more selective sample of college students and lower than a subgroup of high school students with high educational aspirations.

Comparison of male and female scientists with college students also provides evidence for the validity of the instrument. Both female and male scientists differ significantly ($p < .01$) from same-sex college students on the Work, Mastery, and Personal Unconcern scales, with the scientists exceeding the students on each measure. Scientists and college students of the same sex do not differ significantly in Competitiveness, but females in both groups score lower than their male counterparts.

Male and female scientists do not differ on the Work Orientation and Mastery scales. However, female scientists express significantly *less* concern for the opinions of others than male scientists. As described above, they are also less competitive than their male colleagues.

The comparison of female varsity athletes with their female college peers also produces a psychologically meaningful pattern of results. The athletes score higher, although not significantly, than female college students on the Work factor. Further, they are not only significantly higher in Competitiveness ($p < .01$) than unselected college women but are also higher than male scientists and unselected male students. However, they score significantly *lower* (i.e., they report more concern about others' opinions) on the Personal Unconcern scale ($p < .03$) than female students.

Turning our attention to the differences in Personal Unconcern, we recall that, among both the high school and college students, females expressed less concern than males that others might dislike them because of attainment. We suggested that this sex difference may have come about because many women have achievement goals not likely to result in derogation for successful performance. Therefore, for women whose aspirations and activities are not in traditional male-oriented areas, personal concerns about the effects of success are probably not relevant. In the case of women who participate in competitive varsity athletics, however, success may indeed result in envy or in dislike on the part of others because of the "masculine" nature of these activities. Our sample of female athletes, who tend to be doubly nonstereotypic by virtue of also being Masculine, appears to display considerable awareness of this possibility, showing the greatest expression of personal concern.

Also noteworthy is the fact that, in both sexes in all the other samples tested, the correlation between Personal Unconcern and Competitiveness is significant and positive. In the case of female athletes, the correlation is significantly negative ($r = -.29$). Thus, among these competitive women, a greater degree of competitiveness is accompanied by stronger feelings that others may dislike them for their success. Female scientists, on the other hand, are *less* concerned than female college students. Several possible explanations for this discrepancy suggest themselves. Female athletes may be less able to find an accepting peer group than intellectually oriented women; women who are drawn to lifetime careers may have fewer interpersonal needs; women who fear success may elect not to pursue their interests on a lifetime basis; or adult women may have had their sense of femininity confirmed or may define their femininity in less superficial terms and hence not be plagued by the same fears as young athletes.

Scientific Attainment and Achievement Motivation

Indirect evidence that the self-report achievement scales and the associated M and F scales of the PAQ are related to actual achievement behavior is provided by the demonstration of differences on these instruments between high school and college students and individuals from achieving populations, namely varsity athletes and academic scientists. Direct evidence of the behavioral implications of these self-report variables is provided by analyses of still further data on scientific attainment collected from the sample of scientists described above (Beane 1976; Helmreich, Beane, Lucker, & Spence, in press). Because of the behavioral nature of the findings and the complex relationships they revealed between the various components of achievement motivation and attainment, we will describe them in detail. Before doing so, however, we will discuss briefly the thorny problem of how to measure scientific attainment and the criterion measure that was adopted.

The use of citations to published works as an index of scientific attainment and eminence has gained considerable empirical and theoretical support (Goudsmit 1974; Cole & Cole 1972, 1974; Garfield 1975). That citations are not simply an index of mundane productivity is indicated by the correlation between number of published papers and number of citations received. In a sample of academic psychologists, the correlation was only .27 between the number of first-authored papers and citations received (Helmreich, Beane, Lucker, & Matthews, in preparation).

Citation counts were obtained from the *Science Citation Index* (SCI) for each scientist in the sample. For each respondent the number of publications that received at least one citation and the total number of citations received by the cited publications were recorded for the period 1965–1974. These figures were corrected by eliminating self-citations. A composite criterion called scientific attainment was created by summing the two indices to take into account not only the extent of influence but also the breadth of contributions.[1]

The data to be reported below come from analyses of the scientific attainment of ninety-two Ph.D. holding male scientists and engineers, all on the faculty of the University of Texas at Austin (Beane 1976; Helmreich, Beane, Lucker, & Spence, in press). These men were drawn from the larger sample of male and female scientists described in earlier sections. For purposes of evaluating scientific attainment, the sample was restricted to those who had held the Ph.D. for five or more years and to males, because the number of females meeting this requirement was too small to permit statistical analyses.

Correlations between the PAQ and achievement scales and the composite criterion are given in Table 7-9 for the scientist sample. Two general points can be noted from these data. The first is that the PAQ relates modestly to the criterion. The second is that the achievement scales show very weak relationships.

Looking first at PAQ relationships, we find that M-F shows the strongest relationship, suggesting that the type of aggressiveness and lack of emotional vulnerability associated with M-F may be adaptive for a successful scientific career. M is also positively associated with attainment, supporting the intuitive notion that instrumentality should covary with such a criterion. F scores, on the other hand, show a negative relationship with the criterion.

Initial examination of the correlations between the achievement scales and the criterion was disappointing. Several possible causes for the low correlations were explored. One possibility was truncation of distributions (it will be remembered that the scientists scored significantly higher on three of the four scales than college students).

Table 7-9. *Correlations of PAQ and
WOFO-2 Scales with Journal
Citations for Male Scientists*

	Citation Index
Masculinity	.15
Femininity	−.15
Masculinity-Femininity	.30
Work	.12
Mastery	.10
Competitiveness	.04
Personal Unconcern	.03

Note: For $df = 91$, $r_{.05} = .20$.

1. The two citation indices were subjected to a square root transformation to remove positive skewness. Since years of experience is related significantly and positively to citations, the data were corrected by regressing years since Ph.D. on the total number of citations and on the number of items cited. The residuals from this regression were then summed to form the criterion.

Examination of the variances of scores suggested that this was not the culprit. A second possibility, of course, was a curvilinear relationship between measures and the criterion. Indeed, McClelland et al. (1953) have suggested that very high levels of achievement motivation may impair scientific performance. However, detailed examination of the distributions of the scales with the criterion failed to reveal such relationships.

These alternative explanations for the low relationships with the three major achievement scales having been eliminated, the possibility was explored that the scales combine in an interactive, nonlinear manner in relation to attainment. The four scales were recoded by median splits, and analyses of variance on attainment were computed using the recoded achievement categories as independent variables. The resulting cell N's were too small to permit four-way analyses of variance, so a series of three-way analyses was computed. Personal Unconcern did not show significant effects, so analysis was limited to Work Orientation, Mastery, and Competitiveness. Means and the associated analyses of variance are given in Table 7-10. As predicted from the correlations, no significant main effects were found. However, significant interactions between Work and Competitiveness and Work and Mastery occurred. The Work by Competitiveness interaction is particularly interesting, its nature indicating that attainment is highest when work motivation is high and competitiveness *low*;

Table 7-10. *Means for Scientific Attainment Broken Down by Three Achievement Scales with ANOVA Probabilities*

	Scientific attainment		
	$\overline{X}$	SD	N
Lo Work			
Lo Mastery			
Lo Comp	3.37	1.40	22
Hi Comp	3.83	1.67	13
Hi Mastery			
Lo Comp	2.60	2.31	8
Hi Comp	3.18	1.24	9
Hi Work			
Lo Mastery			
Lo Comp	3.20	1.86	9
Hi Comp	2.51	1.96	7
Hi Mastery			
Lo Comp	4.24	1.16	12
Hi Comp	3.44	1.17	23
	ANOVA		
	F	p	
Work by Mastery	5.15	<.02	
Work by Comp	4.01	<.04	

conversely, high competitiveness and high work motivation are associated with *low* attainment. We can only speculate on the causes of this interaction, but one possible explanation is that those with high competitive as well as work needs channel more of their energy into activities other than scientific pursuits. The highly competitive individual who has high work and mastery needs may also be more influenced by fear of failure. That is, such individuals may be particularly concerned with being better than others and may inhibit the production of innovative work rather than risk being evaluated as less than outstanding.

The Mastery by Work interaction shows a crossover pattern with the highest scientific attainment by those high on both Work and Mastery; it also shows a pattern of lowest scientific attainment by those low on Work and high on Mastery. This result also invites speculation. Certainly the association of high work and mastery needs with scientific attainment is intuitively reasonable. The lower attainment of those with high Work and low Mastery could well result from a concentration on routine research which, although respectable, has little impact on the scientific community. On the other hand, the pattern of high Mastery and low Work may result in a concentration on complex and difficult problems without the necessary motivation to carry them through to completion. The bright but nonpublishing scholars frequently encountered in academia may be among this group.

A second study also investigated the relationship between PAQ variables, achievement motivation, and citations, this time in a sample of 118 male and 18 female Ph.D. holding psychologists (Helmreich, Beane, Lucker, and Matthews, in preparation) belonging to a selective, research-oriented society. This sample was chosen to see if relationships of the various PAQ and achievement variables with citations would hold even within a group whose membership was largely limited to eminent and widely cited scientists. For comparison, the total number of citations was more than six times greater in this sample than in the group studied earlier. PAQ scores and percentage distribution across PAQ categories are highly similar to those reported for scientists in Chapter 5. The only notable difference was that only 11% of the women in this sample were classified as Feminine while 67% were classified as Masculine.

A revision of the Work and Family Orientation Questionnaire (WOFO-3; Helmreich & Spence, in press) was employed in this study. This version was designed to produce more reliable representations of the factors isolated in the earlier forms. The same four factors—Work Orientation, Mastery, Competitiveness, and Personal Unconcern—are found. The unit-weighted scales, however, have average alpha coefficients of .69 in a sample of 965 college students. In both college students and scientists, the relationships of the PAQ scales to the four achievement measures are stronger than those found with WOFO-2. Contrasting this group with college students given the same instrument, the scientists are higher in Work, Mastery, and Personal

Unconcern but markedly lower in Competitiveness. In the earlier comparisons using WOFO-2, scientists and students did not differ in Competitiveness.

The same scientific attainment criterion employed in the previous study was computed, summing the total of items cited and total references and correcting for years since award of Ph.D. Of the PAQ scales, Masculinity was significantly and positively related to scientific attainment.

In this more selective sample, Competitiveness showed a curvilinear relationship with the criterion, those of average attainment (within this group) having the highest degree of Competitiveness. This replication of a negative relationship between high attainment and Competitiveness is perhaps the most exciting finding. Since Competitiveness has implicitly and explicitly been associated with the concept of achievement motivation (e.g., Murray 1938), the finding that it impairs performance, at least in some situations, provides considerable support for a multidimensional formulation of achievement motivation. Of primary concern now is exploring the relationships of masculinity and femininity and achievement indices in other populations with real-life criteria of achievement. One logical area of exploration is the relationship between academic grades and the various scales of the WOFO. Because of guarantees of anonymity to our high school respondents, we were unable to explore this in the core sample. In the case of college students tested, such information is available, as well as information on aptitude, from the Scholastic Aptitude Test. Since most of our respondents were first-semester freshmen, we decided to wait and use overall grade point averages for several semesters as the criterion of attainment. These analyses await only the passage of time.

Summary

1. The educational aspirations and attitudes toward marriage and family of the high school respondents were examined as a function of sex and social class. Overall, males had somewhat higher educational goals than females. Desire for higher education was linearly related to social class, with a higher percentage of Upper- than Lower-class individuals aspiring to a college degree or beyond. Similar but weaker trends for social class were found in evaluation of the importance of marriage and the number of children desired.

2. A factor analysis of the first version of the achievement instrument (WOFO-1) was conducted for each sex. The results for males yielded six factors: Work Orientation, Mastery, Effort, Competitiveness, Job Concerns, and Spouse Career Aspirations. The factor structure for females was much less coherent than that for males. However, when data from those women aspiring to a college degree or beyond were analyzed separately, a factor structure similar to that for males was found. Accordingly, unit-weighted scales were constructed using the

six factors derived from the male factor analysis. These scales were used for all subsequent analyses of the data obtained from high school students on WOFO-1.

3. Scores on the six achievement scales were individually compared by analyses of variance taking sex and social class into account. Significant sex differences were found on four scales—Mastery, Competitiveness, Job, and Spouse—with males scoring higher on all but the latter. Significant class differences were found only for the Mastery and Effort scales, with the Upper classes showing higher scores.

4. Correlations of the PAQ, Self-esteem, and AWS measures with the six WOFO-1 scales were computed for each sex. The strongest PAQ correlations, all positive, were found between M and Work, Mastery, and Competitiveness. Self-esteem related positively to all scales, the largest correlation in both sexes being with Mastery. The AWS related modestly to several scales, with a profeminist attitude being associated with Work, Mastery, and Effort and negatively with Competitiveness in both sexes.

5. Analyses of variance of achievement scales that took both sex and PAQ category into account suggested that most of the sex differences were associated with differences between the sexes in the relative numbers in each PAQ category. In these analyses significant sex differences were found only on the Job and Spouse scales, while significant main effects for PAQ category were found for each scale except Spouse. Overall, Androgynous individuals showed the highest motivation, followed by Masculine, Feminine, and Undifferentiated individuals.

6. Further analyses were conducted separately for each scale to explore differences in achievement motivation as a combined function of sex, PAQ category, social class, and educational aspiration. Significant main effects for educational aspiration were found in both analyses for Work, Mastery, and Effort, with high aspiration individuals scoring higher in each case.

7. An additional analysis was conducted by computing crosstabulations of educational aspirations by PAQ category for each sex in the Upper and Lower middle classes (the two classes with roughly equivalent overall aspirations). In males, a higher percentage of Androgynous and Masculine than Feminine and Undifferentiated individuals had high educational aspirations. In contrast, Masculine females were most likely to have high aspirations, followed by the Androgynous, Feminine, and Undifferentiated.

Correlations of the PAQ, Self-esteem, and AWS measures were also computed separately for low and high educational aspiration groups in each sex. The patterns of correlations were similar in each group, with the exception of elevated correlations of Mastery with M and Self-esteem in the high aspiration groups in each sex.

8. A revision of the achievement instrument (WOFO-2) was administered to a sample of high school students as well as to samples of college undergraduates, female varsity athletes, and female and male Ph.D. holding scientists. Analysis of data from males on the WOFO-2 yielded four oblique factors: Work Orientation, Mastery, Competitiveness, and Personal Unconcern, the latter indicating a lack of concern with the opinions of others vis-à-vis achievement. The same type of sex differences in factor analyses with unselected high school students and the similarity in factor structure between males and females with high educational aspirations found with the WOFO-1 were present. Unit-weighted scales were constructed based on the male factor analysis as with the original instrument.

Class and PAQ category differences in the high school sample were generally similar to those found with the WOFO-1. Significant main effects for sex were found for Competitiveness and Personal Unconcern, with males reporting higher competitiveness and *more* concern with the opinions of others.

9. The WOFO-2 achievement scores of the various samples completing the instrument were compared to provide additional information on the validity of the measures. High school students scored lower on all scales than college students of the same sex and PAQ category. Scientists, on the other hand, scored higher than college students on all scales except Competitiveness. Female varsity athletes, in contrast with unselected female undergraduates, scored significantly higher in Competitiveness and significantly lower in Personal Unconcern (i.e., they reported more concern about others' opinions). It was suggested that this result may have come from the athletes' greater experience with the negative social consequences of achievement-related activities.

10. Additional evaluation of the achievement instrument was undertaken (Beane 1976) by analysis of the relationships between the various scales of the WOFO-2 and the number of citations to their scientific work received by the sample of male scientists. The WOFO-2 scales were reclassified by median splits, and analyses of variance were computed on the criterion of citations. Significant interactions were found between Work and Competitiveness and Work and Mastery. Overall, the highest scientific attainment was found among those high in Work and Mastery and low in Competitiveness. A second study of male and female academic psychologists also confirmed the negative relationship between competitiveness and the criterion of scientific citations. The latter study employed a still further revision of the achievement instrument (WOFO-3), which yields the same four factors found with the WOFO-2 with a cleaner structure and higher reliability.

8. Masculinity, Femininity, and Their Correlates: A Summing Up

THE CASE FOR DUALISM

The current profeminist climate has led behavioral scientists, among others, to question many of the long-standing assumptions underlying previous theoretical and empirical approaches to the study of women and men. Calls by psychologists (Bem 1974; Block 1973; Carlson 1971; Constantinople 1973) for the abandonment of a bipolar model of masculinity-femininity in favor of a dualistic concept (or, as some would have it, the concept of androgyny)[1] were quickly joined by the development of the multiscaled Bem Sex Role Inventory (BSRI; Bem 1974) and the Personal Attributes Questionnaire (PAQ; Spence, Helmreich, & Stapp 1974) and by demonstration that socially

1. Although we recognize the pragmatic value of identifying labels for theoretical concepts, we eschew the word "androgyny" to identify our general conception, preferring to describe it as a "dualistic approach to psychological masculinity and femininity," despite the greater clumsiness of this title and its partial inaccuracy. (As long as our M-F scale continues to behave as it has, ours is only a semidualism.) We have encountered negative reactions to the word "androgyny" among feminists and nonfeminists alike because of its original meaning of biological hermaphroditism. We should note, however, that the psychological usage of the term has a long literary history (see, e.g., Virginia Woolf's discussion of the "androgynous mind" in her 1929 *A Room of One's Own*) and that at least one dictionary, *Webster's New Collegiate* (1974), now includes a psychological definition of androgyny. We therefore have willingly adopted the term as a description of individuals scoring high on both our M and F scales. We are wary, however, of the surplus meaning, both ideological and empirical, that has accrued to "androgyny" as a label for the general model. Our data show that the high masculine, high feminine ("androgynous") combination does not always lead to the most effective behavior; our predictive model is therefore an open, evolving, dualistic one and in this sense is not "androgynous." Further, we are not prepared on the basis of the personality findings alone to draw conclusions about sex roles or to suggest any societal designs for the relationships between the sexes. By the same token, we remain adamant about drawing a clear conceptual line between these clusters of masculine and feminine personality attributes and sex-role attitudes, behaviors, and preferences. In addition to the types of arguments we advanced in favor of this distinction in Chapter 1 and which are carried forward in this chapter, we have already encountered instances in which individuals propose using the PAQ as a "sex-roles" test when superficial inquiry reveals that their questions will be more satisfactorily answered by such instruments as the Attitudes toward Women Scale or role preferences tests. Shakespeare's rose to the contrary, labels for good or ill, do make a difference!

desirable masculine and feminine attributes indeed varied virtually independently of each other within each sex. Quite predictably, these demonstrations, together with those provided by other related instruments (e.g., Berzins et al. 1975; A.B. Heilbrun 1976), have been followed by rapid and widespread acceptance of the dualistic approach.[2] All the published studies, however, reported data from college students who were predominantly late adolescents from white middle-class families. While these results convincingly prove that "masculine," instrumental qualities and "feminine," expressive qualities do not of necessity preclude one another, they do not permit any generalizations about the universality of the independence of these two clusters of attributes in the range of subgroups comprising human societies.

Our fears that the pattern of correlations we have found among the PAQ scales (particularly between M and F) in college students might be restricted largely to the major inheritors of the women's movement—relatively young, middle-class individuals—proved to be groundless. Despite the ethnic, religious, and socioeconomic diversity of our high school sample, the correlations obtained from these individuals were remarkable only because of their invulnerability to these demographic variables. We have found similar correlations among the PAQ scales in a group of fathers and mothers of college students, thus failing to find any evidence that an older generation differs from a younger. (The latter data are presented in some detail in Chapter 10.)

All these samples, however, were almost exclusively white in racial composition. Our attempts to gain access to nonwhite populations have yet to prove successful, but we have obtained highly comparable results from a group of over one hundred male and female U.S. Army enlisted personnel,[3] the majority of whom could be observed to be black. The data from three cross-national samples and from specially selected groups (such as homosexuals) also provided no surprises.

While radically different results may be found in some yet untested cultural or subcultural group, we can nonetheless conclude that the essential orthogonality of the clusters of attributes comprising the Masculinity and Femininity scales holds true across groups that vary widely in demographic characteristics. Similarly stable outcomes have also been found in the relationships between each of these scales and the third, M-F scale, the correlations with the latter being almost without exception moderately positive in the case of M and negative in the case of F. While the M-F scale, both in the criteria used for item selection and in the pattern of its correlations with M and F, seems to be at least quasibipolar in its properties, the magnitudes of

2. See, e.g., the speed with which discussions of "androgyny" have been incorporated into sections on sex typing in such undergraduate texts as Mischel's (1976) *Introduction to Personality* and Raven and Rubin's (1976) *Social Psychology*.

3. We wish to thank Lt. Col. Cecil Harris, now at Fort Ord, California, for his cooperativeness in collecting these data.

the correlations are still sufficiently low to allow the conclusion that there is substantial independence among all three sets of characteristics.

MISCONCEPTIONS ABOUT THE SEXES AND THEIR SOURCES

Despite the note of ambiguity introduced by the M-F scale,[4] the unidimensional, bipolar model of masculinity and femininity that dominated psychological thinking prior to the 1970s is clearly in error. Why, then, has the notion lingered so long? The most immediate answer lies in the psychometric approach that has been used to investigate the topic. Dualistic descriptions of personality phenomena are not new, having been very much a part of early philosophical psychology (Carlson 1971) and of philosophy itself. Dualisms appeared to go out of style with the rise of a more empirically oriented psychology and the development of objective techniques of assessment. Although no psychometric justification (beyond that of parsimony) can be evoked, personality phenomena often considered to be coexisting, dualistic processes (e.g., introversion-extraversion) came to be viewed as unidimensional in character, requiring only single bipolar scales for their measurement. The assumptions on which test construction were based simply precluded consideration of statistical analyses that might have revealed their fallaciousness, particularly in masculinity-femininity tests that limit themselves to the types of characteristics under discussion here rather than omnibus measures that tap a broad range of role and other sex-related phenomena.

While the role of psychometric fashion cannot be dismissed as trivial, belief systems which behavioral scientists have shared with members of society at large may have had a more profound effect in retarding attempts to distinguish among myth, half truth, and reality. The most obviously relevant of these shared beliefs is that masculinity and femininity are in fact psychological antinomies. We have recently gathered evidence suggesting that the implicit personality theory of a substantial majority of both sexes does indeed embrace this bipolar view. In this study (Foushee, Helmreich, & Spence, submitted for publication) male and female students were given a series of descriptions of a group of men or women; the descriptions contained adjectives (drawn from the PAQ) indicative of high or low "masculinity" or high or low "femininity." Students given descriptions suggesting the presence or absence of masculine characteristics were then essentially asked to estimate the probability that each of a number of feminine attributes (F scale items) would be present in these individuals. Conversely, students given descriptions containing information about the

4. Of the items showing consistent stereotyping chosen for the full version of the PAQ, the smallest percentage (30) was assigned to the M-F scale. Since the items were not drawn from any identifiable population, firm conclusions cannot be made from this datum, but it does suggest that characteristics falling into this category may cover a narrower range of personality phenomena than encompassed by Masculinity and Femininity.

presence or absence of femininity were asked to estimate the probability of the occurrence of masculine attributes (M scale items). The data clearly supported the assumption that a bipolar view of masculinity and femininity is normative. That is, the majority were willing to make strong inferences about the presence or absence of attributes belonging to one dimension, given information only about the other dimension—only about 8% consistently chose response alternatives specifying that there was little relationship or no relationship between the two sets of characteristics.[5] While these data show us something about the correlations individuals believe to exist between constellations of characteristics, they do not permit us to assume anything about the stereotypes held about the "typical" woman or man. We have discussed earlier our findings (Spence, Helmreich, & Stapp 1974) that, when these stereotypes are directly assessed, the sexes are usually perceived as differing quantitatively rather than qualitatively; women, for example, are rated not as dependent but as somewhat less *in*dependent than men, and men are rated not as *in*sensitive to others but as somewhat less sensitive than women. These perceptions, coupled with a bipolar view, present something of a paradox. It is this paradox that our present discussion is attempting to resolve.

In trying to account for the persistence of the erroneous bipolar conception, we should point out first that, if regarded as independent statistical statements, many of the commonly accepted beliefs about the differences between women and men cannot simply be dismissed as false. Our PAQ data, for example, indicate that the personality characteristics of males and females do in fact differ, if we can believe their self-reports, in the direction of the accepted stereotype. The self-described differences are doubtless less extreme than the accepted stereotype admits: at least in some quarters, differences between the sexes are perceived on a greater range of characteristics than can be sustained by reality (e.g., Spence, Helmreich, & Stapp 1974) and, even on those characteristics in which the sexes do appear to differ, the stereotype tends to exaggerate the discrepancy between the average woman and man and to underestimate the variability within each sex. But, clearly, the self-images of the sexes are not identical.

We note also that, when the joint occurrence of masculine and feminine characteristics is considered by means of our categorical system, the stereotypically appropriate combination for each sex is frequent and the cross-typed combination rare. Again, the apparently common belief that most males are "masculine" (i.e., relatively higher on M than on F) in temperament and most females "feminine"

5. Our analyses revealed, however, some interesting differences in the strength of the implicit theory as a function of the individual attributes described, the sex of the respondent, and the sex of the described population. Men were particularly prone to attribute high femininity to low masculine women and high masculinity to low feminine men. Women, on the other hand, made the strongest attributions of masculinity to low feminine women and the strongest attributions of femininity to low masculine men.

may be quite grossly exaggerated but is not completely without foundation.

One of the factors contributing to the illusion that strong masculine and feminine characteristics rarely occur together may be the confusion between *role performance* and qualities of *personality*. Traditional sex-role expectations (which, by definition, are dimorphic) specify that men in most of their relationships with women occupy the more dominant, powerful position. In social interactions with those of equal status, women more often than not (whether out of belief in the legitimacy of sex-role expectations or out of self-protection) do defer to men and acknowledge, if not men's greater competence in valued activities, then the priority of their wishes and goals. Although in particular instances this dominant-submissive relationship often demands a good deal of role playing or self-deception in both sexes as to who is more intellectually competent or psychologically stronger, its frequency of occurrence leads easily to the assumption that women are weak and men are strong and that their role relationships are an inevitable consequence of their underlying natures.

Similar statements can be made about other components of traditional sex-role behaviors: differences between the sexes exist but not necessarily to the degree that is ordinarily assumed. The claim that "women's place is in the home," for example, can be regarded not merely as a value judgment but also as an empirical reality, since a smaller percentage of women than men have paid employment outside the home. Yet even here we have been slow to absorb the full reality, to recognize that, while the sexes differ in rate, not merely a few but the majority even of married women with minor children are employed. (As one observer has quipped, the fact that women work has been one of our nation's most carefully guarded secrets.)

Even more mischievous than exaggerated perceptions of the magnitude of differences between the sexes is the tendency (not confined to sex differences or, as a perusal of some of our psychological journals will reveal, to nonprofessionals) to assume that an aggregation of independent statistical facts about a group can be combined to form a composite portrait of the typical member of that group. This inference is legitimate if it can be demonstrated that within individuals the correlations among the various independent components are high. In the absence of strong correlations, special analyses must be undertaken to determine whether any constellation (or series of constellations) of characteristics tends to occur with any frequency, what those frequencies are, and what specific subset of characteristics from the group aggregation appears in these constellations.[6]

The implicit assumption of substantial relationships among "masculine" and "feminine" personality characteristics and the various facets of sex-role behaviors and preferences appears to underlie such

6. For an excellent analysis of the methodological issues in determining modal personality, see the discussion of national character by Inkeles and Levinson (1954).

unidimensional concepts as "sex-role identification" and much of the psychological work on sex-role development. This interdependent model continues to characterize approaches to the study of sex roles and related phenomena, even among those who espouse the dualistic conception of psychological masculinity and femininity. Thus in discussions of this concept (e.g., Bem 1974) it is often strongly implied if not explicitly stated that knowledge of an individual's typological status, as determined by responses to such instruments as the PAQ or the BSRI, permits generalizations about the sex-role behaviors preferred or adopted by that individual: *psychologically* androgynous women or men are expected to be flexible in role performances, while sex-typed individuals are said to be comfortable primarily with the behaviors conventionally defined as appropriate for their sex. While this hypothesis about strong relationships between psychological masculinity and femininity and sex-role behaviors can be entertained, it cannot be logically derived from the data obtained from these measures of instrumental and expressive traits. Conversely, it cannot necessarily be assumed that individuals who are mixed, conventional, or cross-typed in role behaviors (i.e., men whose *sex-role* performances could be classified as Androgynous, Masculine, or Feminine, respectively, or women whose performances could be classified as Androgynous, Feminine, or Masculine)[7] share the same properties, such as degree of self-esteem, as those who fall into parallel categories on psychological measures of masculinity and femininity.

In our introductory discussion in Chapter 1, we proposed a "weak" hypothesis as an alternative to this "strong" one. Personality characteristics, such as those measured by the PAQ, have broad trans-situational significance in both sexes and can be expected to influence the roles (which may or may not be sex-linked) to which an individual is attracted, such as choice of profession in the career-oriented,

7. If individuals were classified on the number or strength of their masculine and their feminine role performances, a fourth category of individuals relatively uncommitted to either would also emerge. In a theory which subsumes psychological masculinity and femininity under the general sex-role rubric, the uncommitted category might be expected to parallel the psychologically Undifferentiated classification. Thus substantial overlap would be predicted between membership in the four categorical groupings produced by the two types of measures, one based on the psychological characteristics found on the PAQ or the BSRI and the other on role commitments. On the other hand, for the purpose of predicting sex-typed interests and the like from psychological measures, Bem's (1974) original balance motion might be more useful. Thus three basic categories would be created—Androgynous, Masculine, and Feminine—with the psychologically Undifferentiated being included in the Androgynous group and expected to exhibit role flexibility. This proposal seems to imply that a three-category model of role commitment, based on the balance between masculine and feminine preferences, might be more useful than one in which classification is based on the strength of each. These multiple possibilities reinforce our conviction that masculine and feminine personality characteristics and role commitments should be measured separately and both the nature and the magnitude of the associations between them empirically determined.

and the manner in which these roles are executed. However, the conjunction between an individual's masculine and feminine attributes and *masculine* or *feminine role behaviors* is likely to be weak. Not only do other types of factors enter in to determine these role preferences and adoptions, but the demands of "feminine" roles for "feminine" characteristics and of "masculine" roles for "masculine" characteristics have been overestimated. Psychologically Masculine women, for example, may marry and stay home to raise children, and psychologically Feminine men work and provide for their families.

Our empirical efforts to date have been focused primarily on the measurement of clusters of socially desirable "masculine" and "feminine" personality attributes and have not included assessment of a range of sex-role behaviors and preferences. The evidence we do have, however, does nothing to refute the theoretical model we have proposed. "Masculine" (high M, low F) girls, for example, do tend to be more egalitarian in their sex-role attitudes than others and to be more likely to have aspirations for a career or higher education, but the associations between these variables are slight. Similarly, in our group of women scientists—who are unlike most women both in their professional attainments and in the relatively high percentage who exhibit "masculine" personalities—most are or have been married, have children, and (from our personal observation) have accepted many other traditional role responsibilities. Others have reported similar observations. In a study of senior women college students, Tangri (1972), for example, found that women who aspired to traditionally male-dominated professions, as opposed to those who had no career aspirations or who planned to enter female-dominated fields, did not reject the role of wife and mother or consider themselves masculine. Still further, various categories of sex-role variables may themselves show substantial independence, as indicated by the relatively low correlations between many masculinity-femininity measures (Lee 1976).

To return to our discussion of modal personalities, the slenderness of the associations among sex roles and personality variables, combined with the relatively small sex differences on several of our measures, suggests that few inferences can be made about the constellation of coexisting qualities that differentially characterize the "typical" woman and man and, indeed, whether any constellation exists with sufficient frequency to make the concept of the typical man as opposed to the typical woman a particularly useful one. We shall be able to find out only after the relevant dimensions are conceptually identified and instruments for their measurement devised.

MASCULINITY AND FEMININITY AS GLOBAL SELF-CONCEPTS

In our investigation of masculine and feminine personality characteristics, we have defined these terms as referring to independent clusters of socially desirable attributes commonly believed to differentiate the sexes. The labels placed on each of these clusters, however, have been supplied by us as investigators rather than by the respondents to our self-report and stereotype questionnaires. Masculinity and femininity can also be regarded as global aspects of the self-concept that men and women directly identify in these or equivalent terms (such as being a "real man" or a "real woman"). Individuals with clear gender identification, in the narrow sense in which we earlier defined this term, have organized belief systems, however poorly articulated, about the psychosocial meaning of being "a man" or "a woman" and can be expected to have incorporated these beliefs into their sense of self. These belief systems, our observations suggest, are compounded of many elements: assumptions about appropriate sex roles, characteristics of the self such as personality attributes and cognitive abilities, physique and physical appearance, styles of speech and body movement, sexual behavior, and so forth.

One can expect that individuals belonging to the same culture or subculture will be reasonably similar in identifying the factors contributing to masculinity and femininity in themselves and others in the sense that they will be drawn from a common pool and will not be completely idiosyncratic. Individuals' definitions of masculinity and femininity, however, are likely to be based on complexly weighted sets of indicators that not only vary from one person to another but also change with age and may even differ when individuals are assessing themselves as opposed to others.

One of the cores of women's and men's self-concept is the degree to which they believe they measure up, or believe it important to measure up, to their abstract conception of what it is to be a proper woman or man. The forging of a self-concept permitting an adequate sense of self-worth may often necessitate efforts to integrate contradictory elements or perceived lacks within a personal belief system. In an attempt (which may or may not succeed) to preserve their own self-concept and feelings of worth, men or women who possess cross-sex characteristics, or who lack a sufficient degree of stereotypically appropriate ones, may variously relabel these characteristics under neutral headings, deny them, or consider them as irrelevant, basing their judgments of their own masculinity or femininity on those conventionally acceptable characteristics they do possess. Psychologically androgynous men, for example, may freely exhibit their expressive characteristics only in limited settings, such as the family in which they are the "protector," or may otherwise integrate their expressive characteristics into their self-concept in such a way that they are in the service of agentic needs and goals. Agency is figure, so to speak, and communion ground. For androgynous women, the emphasis may be reversed, agency being subordinated to communion. Undifferentiated individuals, on the other hand, lacking many of the desirable personality characteristics considered appropriate for their sex, may be forced to organize their self-concepts around conventional role behaviors in order to validate their own sense of maleness or femaleness.

If, as we suspect, there is substantial variability among men and women in the constellations of sex-typed characteristics they possess, differences among individuals in the nature of their self-definitions of masculinity or femininity are the inevitable consequence, even though the majority of men and women may consider themselves as acceptable members of their sex. A more fruitful approach to understanding human behavior than counting the number of ways in which an individual resembles the typical member of her or his own sex to derive a quantitative index of "sex-role identification" or masculinity-femininity is to describe the nature of the individual's self-concept.

Returning to our initial concern—the coexistence of instrumental and expressive characteristics—we should acknowledge the very real dilemma that may arise in any individual, male or female, in trying to balance his or her legitimate needs against the needs and demands of others or trying to reconcile concern with others' feelings and personal well-being with the accomplishment of group goals that may necessarily bring hurt to particular individuals. Reconciliation may be particularly difficult in persons who are high not only in those expressive characteristics contained on our F scale but also have the kind of personal vulnerability, with its associated empathic reactions to the emotions of others, reflected on our M-F scale. Although the overall consequences for the functioning of the individual of the failure to develop or to express both instrumental and expressive characteristics may often be deleterious, the path of least resistance may be to stress the importance of one at the expense of the other and to select for emphasis the constellation of attributes consistent with the demands of the roles that the individual values most highly.

Perhaps it is the attempt to force all these diverse and often contradictory phenomena into the procrustean bed of global self-concepts of masculinity and femininity (which in turn may reflect a need to achieve cognitive consistency) that most fundamentally causes perceptions of the characteristics of men and women, when considered in the whole as opposed to the particular, to become exaggerated and polarized. The existence of these global self-concepts may also partially explain the profound resentments and fears aroused when the legitimacy of traditional social arrangements between the sexes is challenged. Particularly among those whose sense of "personhood" is not secure or well developed and who rely on their correspondence to traditional standards of behavior for their definition of self, attacking these standards may be attacking one of the central aspects of their self-identity.

BLOCK'S THEORY OF EGO AND SEX-ROLE DEVELOPMENT

A self-concept of masculinity or femininity is but one of the elements around which the self is organized and, like other aspects of self, may be expected to change over the life span. In a closely related conceptualization, Block (1973) has presented a theoretical analysis of sex-role development that enriches our discussion.

Block links her analysis to Loevinger's (1966; Loevinger & Wessler

1970) work on the stages of ego development and stresses agentic and communal characteristics as crucial components of masculinity and femininity. A critical period in sex-role development, according to Block, occurs when the child enters what Loevinger labels the conformity stage, in which the child attempts to control impulses by conformity to external rules and is concerned with things, appearances, and reputation. At this period, Block states, "a critical bifurcation in the sex-role development of boys and girls occurs. Socialization patterns impinge differentially on the two sexes: boys are encouraged to control affect, while girls are encouraged to control aggression" (p. 514). At the following, conscientious stage, rules are internalized and inner feelings and motives are differentiated. Here the individual's self-definitions of masculinity and femininity become moderated by inner values and conceptions of responsibility. For those who enter the next, autonomous stage, self-concepts become more clearly articulated and attempts are made to integrate the conflicting aspects of self. It is here, Block theorizes, that the individual becomes aware of values and predispositions that depart from traditional sex-role expectations and must reconcile these contradictory elements. At the highest, integrated stage, men's and women's sex-role identities include an integration of both masculine and feminine—that is, agentic and communal—traits and values; their sex-role definitions are androgynous.

Block's theorizing, for which she has provided some preliminary empirical support, has many obvious implications, among them the expectation that individuals of either sex who fail to develop or to integrate successfully into their sense of self both agentic and communal attributes will not reach the higher stages of ego development, with all that that imports. Ambiguity is introduced into her theorizing, however, by the lack of a more explicit definition of sex-role identity. Is the integrated, androgynous individual one who rejects all sex-role prescriptions and embraces both masculine and feminine life styles? We infer from her discussion that, although using the term "sex-role," she is referring only to clusters of masculine and feminine personality characteristics. Closer to her intent, perhaps, and to our own conceptualization is that integrated, psychologically androgynous individuals are freer than those at lower stages of ego development to develop their own values and goals and to adopt or reject, as suits their own needs and capacities, the sex-role behaviors their society prescribes. Individuals at the higher levels of ego development, having a greater sense of self and individuality, may also define their masculinity and femininity not in terms of their conformity to the behavioral standards for their sex but in terms of inner characteristics. Some individuals may become truly androgynous, in the sense of accepting equally their expressive and instrumental qualities and associating both with "personhood" rather than gender. More frequently, we suspect, these qualities do figure prominently in self-concepts of masculinity and femininity even among those at higher levels of ego maturity, men valuing and giving greater priority to their agentic characteristics and women to their communal ones.

THE NEGATIVE COMPONENTS OF MASCULINITY AND FEMININITY

The main thrust of Block's argument, in agreement with Bakan (1966), is that the fundamental task of all human beings is to balance agency and communion, either unchecked being destructive to the individual or society. For males, the challenge is to temper self-interest with concern for the welfare of others, while for women it is to develop a sense of an effective, actualized self rather than to have an identity reflected only in service to others. Both excessive masculinity and excessive femininity, their discussion implies, are associated with socially undesirable attributes as well as desirable ones.

Recently, with one of our graduate students, Kirk Heilbrun, we have begun to explore the possibility of expanding our Personal Attributes Questionnaire to include not merely the positively valued components of psychological masculinity and femininity but also scales assessing their "dark side." Using the 300-item Adjective Check List as a pool, Heilbrun (unpublished) had groups of college students rate subsets of these adjectives on the degree to which each characterized the typical male or female or the ideal member of each sex. (Adjectives rated both as socially desirable and as differentiating the sexes paralleled in content the PAQ and the BSRI.) Predictably, a number of the attributes judged both as more characteristic of males than females and as undesirable described the *absence* or the *opposite* of socially desirable expressive characteristics (e.g., cruel, hardhearted). Our interest, however, was in the *agentic* adjectives attributed to males and receiving relatively low desirability ratings, items such as boastful, egotistical, greedy, hostile, and (slightly less unfavorable) autocratic, opinionated, and opportunistic. Here we have the "unmitigated agency" of which Bakan (1966) wrote.

No exact parallel of "unmitigated communion" was found among the stereotypically feminine items rated low in desirability, and indeed it is difficult to conceive of many such attributes. Individuals who devote themselves to others and to promoting harmony are seldom faulted for these characteristics per se but, rather, for being indiscriminate in their judgments of others or for lacking balancing agentic characteristics. Aside from adjectives indicating a lack of such instrumental attributes (e.g., weak, shy, submissive), the undesirable qualities attributed to women tended to suggest either a neurotic kind of emotionality—fearful, highstrung, inhibited, moody, whiny—or a stylistically "feminine" type of verbal hostility—complaining, fault finding, nagging.

Data are currently being collected to determine the interrelationships between these socially undesirable masculine and feminine attributes and their desirable counterparts on the PAQ.[8] Information

8. A recent study by Kelly, Caudill, Hathorn, and O'Brien (in press) also investigated the undesirable components of masculinity and femininity and explored their relationships with the socially desirable characteristics on the BSRI. Their negatively toned masculinity scale, however, included a number of items describing the *absence* of socially desirable *feminine* characteristics (e.g., cruel as opposed to kind), and their negatively toned fem-

is also being sought on the possible negative consequences of these characteristics. We anticipate, for example, that males (and perhaps females) who score high on the undesirable masculine items and are relatively lacking in desirable feminine characteristics will be more likely than others to have exhibited sociopathic behavior, while those low in desirable masculine items and high in negative feminine characteristics will be more prone to anxiety, depression, and other similar neurotic problems. Suggestive data have been found by Heilbrun (unpublished) in a post hoc comparison of the items checked by a group of unselected college students and a group of students seeking help at a university counseling center, both groups having been administered the Adjective Check List.[9] Among males, the maladjusted group (whose problems were undoubtedly heterogeneous in nature) checked socially desirable masculine (i.e., instrumental) characteristics only slightly less often than "normal" males, but, on almost all the undesirable masculine items, they more frequently selected the item as characteristic of themselves than did normals. These maladjusted males also selected more often than normals most of the feminine (expressive) items, desirable and undesirable. On the other hand, choice of desirable masculine characteristics clearly distinguished between the normal and the maladjusted females. On most of the adjectives falling into this category, fewer of the latter selected the attribute as characteristic of themselves. Maladjusted females were also somewhat less likely to select desirable feminine items but, like the males, did choose the undesirable feminine items more frequently than their normal peers. Individual profiles were not reported, but it seems reasonable to infer that, while neurotic problems are found in both sexes, those associated with "unmitigated agency" are found more often in males.

SEX DIFFERENCES IN PSYCHOLOGICAL MASCULINITY
AND FEMININITY AND THEIR SOURCES

We return now to our PAQ data and once more call attention to the differences between the sexes. In all the U.S. samples we have tested, with the single exception of homosexuals, significant differences between the sexes in the predicted direction have uniformly occurred on all three scales. Equally impressive are the relatively minor and typically nonsignificant differences in mean scores on the three PAQ scales in each sex when comparisons were made of high school stu-

---

ininity scale included items describing the *absence* of socially desirable *masculine* characteristics (e.g., indecisive). Our interests, however, are in isolating the undesirable aspects of agency (whose possession may well turn out to be facilitated by the relative lack of counterbalancing communal qualities) and, as far as possible, the undesirable aspects of communion (whose possession may be facilitated by the relative lack of agentic qualities).

9. These data were supplied by Prof. A.B. Heilbrun, Jr., of Emory University.

dents from different socioeconomic backgrounds, of high school and college students, and (as will be reported in Chapter 10) of college students and their parents.

More variability was found among the means of the three samples obtained from other countries. Comparisons of the data from males and females within each sample still showed, however, that females scored significantly higher on F and lower on M-F than males. In each instance, the mean of the females on M was slightly lower than that of males, but none of the differences was significant. We hesitate to interpret the meaning of these cross-cultural differences, since it is unclear whether the deviations from American data reflect genuine cross-national differences or such artifacts as sample selectivity or faulty translations of our instruments. Still another possibility is that the particular instrumental or expressive qualities defining masculinity or femininity in one culture may not precisely define them in another. Credence is given to this possibility by data obtained by Block (1973) contrasting students from the United States and five European countries. While male students in all countries chose certain instrumental characteristics more frequently than females as descriptive of their ideal self and females chose certain expressive characteristics more frequently than males, the particular items were not necessarily the same in each country. We remain intrigued by the differences among our samples but, in view of the uncertainties of interpretation, must continue to stress the significance of the similarities across cultures.

We come now to the question of how these temperamental differences between the sexes arise. The evidence that personality development is heavily influenced by environmental factors is incontrovertible, and different cultural expectations for women and men, conveyed to the child by parents and other socializing agents, can be shown to contribute to the appearance of sex-related differences (e.g., Block 1973). A number of serious scholars have further contended that the different personality structures of women and men are to some extent genetically ordained and that the cultural pressures on each sex, while shaped in their particulars by ecological and historical factors, themselves evolve because of the different genetic potential of each sex. A review of the empirical evidence cited in favor of this hypothesis is beyond the scope of this monograph and assessment of its validity beyond our technical competence. Nonetheless, in puzzling over the significance of our M-F scale and its seemingly bipolar properties, we have been struck by the frequency with which the items it contains have been named as being genetically sex-linked. The agentic characteristics on the M-F scale, it will be recalled, refer to aggressiveness and dominance. Examination of the data from such diverse sources as ethological observation, experimental investigation with animals, observation of the social behavior of preschool children, and clinical study of girls androgynized prenatally or early in life has led a number of writers (e.g., Money & Ehrhardt 1972; Wilson 1975; Hutt 1972; E.E. Maccoby 1976) to postulate that hormonal differences between the sexes result in greater aggressiveness in the male than in the female of many species, including humans. In fact, the evidence cited in favor of genetically based sex differences is more compelling for aggression than for other temperamental qualities, and aggression is the sex difference most frequently given a biological explanation.

A close linkage between aggressiveness and the establishment of dominance hierarchies has been suggested (e.g., Montague 1976), and exhibition of more dominance behaviors by males than females in several primate species, again including humans, has been observed. The appearance of these sex differences in dominance has also been attributed to genetically determined hormonal and neurological factors (e.g., Goldberg 1973; Gray & Buffery 1971).

The remaining items on the M-F scale, we have already noted, predominantly reflect (lack of) emotional vulnerability and the need for protection and security. The clustering of these items with aggression and dominance is congruent with hypotheses offered by Gray and Buffery (Gray 1971; Gray & Buffery 1971). Briefly, these investigators propose that in primates males are both more aggressive than females and less fearful, differences that can be traced directly to biological factors. These genetically determined sex differences have adaptive significance and arose during the evolutionary process due to the particular roles played by males and by females in the establishment of dominance hierarchies in primate social organizations. In this connection we will mention suggestive data recently gathered by one of our graduate students, Patricia Kehoe, in the course of her dissertation research. Significant negative correlations were found in a group of over two hundred college women between their scores on the Manifest Anxiety scale (Taylor 1953) and their PAQ M and M-F scores ($-.47$ and $-.37$ for M and M-F respectively). The correlation between anxiety and the F scale, on the other hand, was close to zero.

These and other similar genetic hypotheses, we hasten to add, have not lacked their scientific critics (e.g., Archer 1976), and the case for a biological basis for temperament differences between the sexes has not been unambiguously established. We suggest only that, if biological bases are found for the kinds of sex differences that appear on the Personal Attributes Questionnaire, the current evidence points most directly to the type of items contained on our M-F scale.

Political considerations have too often marred attempts to determine dispassionately what differences among individuals or groups may be influenced by genetic variables: those committed to preserving a social and political system that permits discrimination against members of one sex, socioeconomic class, or racial group may seek to justify their position by appealing to biological factors, while those committed to changing the status quo may deny their significance in creating individual differences. Social policy decisions, however, need not be heavily dependent on the outcome of what should be a purely scientific debate. If differences in innate predispositions between the sexes were large in comparison to the variability within each sex and were relatively resistant to environmental manipulations, societies would obviously be constrained in the kinds of viable cultural designs that could be evolved. None of the evidence at hand, however, suggests that either of these conditions holds. Further, whatever the historical origins or the evolutionary significance of temperamental differences between women and men and rules for division of labor, social arrangements must be functionally adaptive for contemporary conditions. For example, encouraging men to be hostilely aggressive (as opposed to assertive and self-confident) and women to be fearful may have been advantageous for primitive societies but have negative implications for modern societies. It would also seem unnecessary to add that attempts to deny women and men freedom of choice rationalized by pointing to the differences between the sexes are misguided. Even when group differences can be empirically demonstrated, far more valid assessment methods than sexual assignment are available for predicting individuals' behavior or evaluating their intellectual and temperamental capacities for parenting, education, or work.

BEYOND MASCULINITY AND FEMININITY

The above discussion prompts us to address ourselves to a question that has apparently been troublesome to some: why label the PAQ scales with the words "masculinity" and "femininity" and thus, so the reasoning goes, perpetuate erroneous stereotypes and encourage differential treatment of the sexes? Several justifications can be offered. First, the belief that the sexes differ in these clusters of attributes is widespread, these clusters commonly being identified as "masculine" and "feminine" characteristics. Second, the sexes do in fact differ, so that the labels cannot be said to be false. Avoiding the words "masculinity" and "femininity" would do nothing to change either of these empirical facts but, indeed, would invite those interested in sex differences to ignore our findings and their implications.

In another sense, however, the concern is well placed. The terms "masculinity" and "femininity" are not directly descriptive of the content of the three PAQ scales and draw attention away from the fact that they tap personality constellations that have implications for the behavior of both sexes, over and above what they may tell us about sex differences. While the original focus of our research was on the latter, it has been broadened to include the implications for important areas of functioning of instrumental and expressive characteristics per se.

With the exception of our Brazilian sample (particularly the males), for example, we have demonstrated consistent relationships between these characteristics and reports of social competence and self-esteem even in unique samples, including homosexuals, whose distributions of scores differ markedly from those of unselected samples. Androgynous individuals of both sexes reported the highest self-esteem, followed by Masculine, Feminine, and Undifferentiated individuals. Masculinity, as reflected on the M-F scale, was also positively related to self-esteem, those scoring above the overall median within each of the four M and F categories having higher means than those below the median. The behavioral implications of these constellations of personality characteristics, including self-esteem, are shown by the greater frequency of dating and of academic and extracurricular honors reported by Androgynous and Masculine individuals (Beane 1976; Spence, Helmreich, & Stapp 1975) and, in the homosexual sample, by the more frequent participation in psychotherapy by those categorized as Undifferentiated and Feminine.

Further implications for real-life behaviors of instrumental and expressive characteristics, and some of the strongest evidence for the construct validity of the PAQ, are to be found in the demonstration that members of several of our specially selected samples differed predictably in their distributions among the four PAQ categories from unselected groups. For example, when compared to women in general, women varsity athletes were overrepresented in the Masculine and Androgynous categories and underrepresented in the Feminine category. Similar results were obtained in women Ph.D. scientists, particularly in a sample of highly achieving social psychologists.

The striking elevation of instrumental, "masculine" characteristics in these latter groups of women raises an interesting question of interpretation. Were these instrumental qualities, and their accompanying self-esteem, present relatively early in the lives of these individuals, having some causal relationship with their choice of participation in such "masculine" activities as competitive sports or a scientific career? Or were these attributes a consequence of their successful attainments? Longitudinal data that would shed some light on these questions have yet to be collected. A recent study by Wertheim, Widom, and Wortzel (in press) suggests, however, that instrumental and expressive characteristics may be related to career choice. These investigators administered the PAQ, along with several other instruments, to first-year graduate students in two male-dominated disciplines—law and business management—and in two disciplines— social work and education—both more hospitable to women and more oriented to social service. On the F scale, both male and female students in the two male fields scored significantly lower than same sex peers in social work and education. Significant but not clearly sex-typed differences were also found on the M scale, social work students of both sexes scoring lowest and law students next lowest. (Within each field, however, males scored higher on M and lower on F than females.) The students were also given the Attitudes toward Women Scale and an achievement motivation scale taken from Mehrabian (1969). Although males were consistently more traditional in their sex-role attitudes than females, social work students of both sexes were the least traditional and management students the most, differences that probably reflected their general political orientation rather than the influence of masculine and feminine characteristics. No significant differences were found between the sexes or between students from the several fields in their achievement scores, an outcome that may have resulted either from the highly selected nature of these graduate student samples or from the unidimensional nature of the achievement measure. Our evidence concerning the relationships between masculinity, femininity, and the components of achievement will be discussed in the next section.

Achievement Motivation

The expansion of our interests in masculinity and femininity into achievement motivation and the development of instruments for its measurement were prompted by several convictions. First, it appeared to us that, of the many personality variables to which instrumentality, as defined by the M scale on the PAQ, might be related, achievement motivation was one of the most important. Second, achievement motivation is a many-faceted phenomenon that might more profitably be measured by a multifactored instrument than by the unidimensional scales usually employed. Third, we were hopeful that a measuring device could be developed that would be useful in predicting the achievement behaviors of both women and men, at least as far as those behaviors are traditionally defined.

MALE-FEMALE DIFFERENCES IN FACTOR STRUCTURE
AND THEIR IMPLICATIONS

Perhaps the most complex of our findings concerns the structure of achievement motivation in the two sexes. In our high school samples, the factor structure of both preliminary versions of our achievement instrument, the Work and Family Orientation Questionnaire (WOFO-1 and WOFO-2), produced theoretically meaningful and face-valid scales when the data from males were considered, but far less satisfactory results were obtained when the data from females were analyzed. The factor structure for females with aspirations for higher education, however, did parallel that found in males, leading us to develop scales based on the male data to be used with both sexes. This decision proved to be wise but leaves us with several unresolved issues. Our instrument, like most achievement measures, may be tapping motives and thus may be able to predict behaviors relevant only to "achievement" in its traditional, male-oriented sense: vocational aspirations and attainments, educational pursuits (particularly when they are vocationally oriented), competitive games, etc. The desire to achieve, as it pertains to more feminine, family-oriented goals—being an outstanding homemaker or parent or making meaningful contributions as an unpaid volunteer to such service-oriented community activities as the PTA, charitable groups, or neighborhood organizations—may be related to a very different kind of motivational structure.

Even if this were so, our data remind us that an individual's instrumentality and achievement needs may be manifested in a variety of ways and that his or her goals must be understood before accurate predictions of achievement strivings may be made. Lower-class males, for example, produced a factor structure similar to upper- and middle-class males, and class differences in mean scores on the several achievement scales were not strikingly large or uniformly in favor of the latter. Lower-class males, however, had much lower educational aspirations (a class difference that may reflect both subcultural values and students' realistic appraisal of their chances of receiving a higher education) and, one assumes, very different kinds of career aspirations. High achievement needs in many lower-class students may find different modes of expression than in members of higher socioeconomic groups. Similarly, as Raynor (1974) has emphasized, achievement needs may or may not be reflected in excellence of academic performance in high school or college, depending on the degree to which the individual perceives good grades as instrumental to future goals—being admitted to college or postgraduate school, obtaining a job in which intellectual attainments are stressed, and so forth. The adolescent, for example, whose formulation of goals has not progressed beyond striving for fairly immediate success in competitive sports or an interest in hobbies may be an indifferent scholar, even if highly achievement-oriented, as may be the individual who perceives that future job success will be more dependent on personality and the desire to succeed than on academic accomplishment.

An alternate explanation of the different factor structure produced by the high school girls low in educational aspirations is a developmental one. The items on our questionnaire may be interpreted by many girls in terms of intellectual and vocational pursuits in which they presently have little serious interest. The kinds of attitudes and preferences these items describe are not perceived as having any relevance to their future goals, and their phenomenal inner world is not structured in terms of mastery of challenges, hard work, and the like. One does not have to actively strive to *become* a wife or mother (or even a secretary) and it is sufficient simply to *be* one. With maturity and experience a more articulated and realistic motivational system comparable to their peers' may arise even in girls who retain their traditional orientation. However, despite the lack of coherent results produced by these adolescent girls when internal analyses of their responses to our instruments are performed, the externally imposed order produced by our scales may still yield measures that permit some degree of prediction of future behavior, even in domestic spheres.

RELATIONSHIPS WITH THE ACHIEVEMENT SCALES

Factor analyses of our achievement instrument (as it eventually evolved) revealed four factors of particular theoretical interest which we have labeled Work Orientation, Mastery, Competitiveness, and Personal Unconcern. As anticipated, significant positive correlations were found in both sexes between M scores and achievement scores derived from these four factors. Weaker relationships—but more intriguing because they were unexpected—tended to emerge between the F scale and several of the achievement scales, most notably Work Orientation. These correlations were positive except in the case of Competitiveness, which produced a slightly *negative* relationship. Differences that followed from these correlations were found among the groups assigned to the four PAQ categories. Although the sharpest break occurred between those high or low in M, the typical order not only in high school students but also in college students, female athletes, and scientists was Androgynous, Masculine, Feminine, and Undifferentiated. The exception to this order was on the Competitiveness scale, Masculine individuals tending to have the highest means and Feminine individuals the lowest. The presence of expressive, communal characteristics, these data suggest, tends to suppress the desire to best other people and thus to risk hurting them.

By and large, sex differences in achievement motivation were minimal and tended to disappear when PAQ category was taken into account. Differences did occur, however, among the several types of samples, high school students of both sexes scoring lowest on all scales except Competitiveness and scientists scoring highest, with college students in between. Female athletes provided an interesting contrast, being more work-oriented than their female classmates and more competitive than any of the groups, male or female. However, they also expressed more concern about others' reactions to their activities than did their peers (i.e., their mean on the Personal Unconcern scale was lower).

IMPLICATIONS OF THE PERSONAL UNCONCERN SCALE

The similarity between the Personal Unconcern scale and the currently influential fear of success concept (Horner 1968) leads us to examine the results obtained with this scale in more detail. The finding that the scores of the female athletes on this scale were relatively low suggests that, having had more experience with conspicuous attainments than their fellow students, these young women have become sensitized to the negative reactions that successful achievement may elicit, especially when that achievement is in an area particularly valued by their male peers. The mirror image of these findings occurred in the data we have recently collected using a revised version of the achievement instrument (WOFO-3). When college women were classified by educational aspirations, those with the lowest aspirations had high means on the Personal Unconcern scale. This finding suggests that, lacking goals entailing social risk, these young women have little to be concerned about.

The female scientists, however, were also very low in their concern for others' reactions to their achievement, significantly lower, in fact, than their male colleagues. Still further differences were found between the female and male academics in a recent study of scientific attainment and achievement motivation among social psychologists

(Helmreich et al., in preparation). In males, a large number of citations in the scientific literature was associated with *greater* concern
with others' reactions; in females the relationship was reversed. It is
possible that, in males, strong awareness of envy and other negative
reactions to attainment became salient only after they had become
more conspicuously successful than their colleagues. The results of
such awareness may be a greater sensitivity to the responses of others
but not a reduction in achievement-related behaviors. Women scientists, on the other hand, may quite early have become aware of the
potential danger involved in doing well in school and having the kinds
of career aspirations ordinarily associated with males. Highly achievement-oriented women who elect to manifest their achievement needs
in these ways either may be self-selected to be relatively immune to
others' reactions or may have worked through any disturbance they
may once have felt to the point of being relatively indifferent to
others' opinions and thus able to concentrate on scholarly attainments.

ACHIEVEMENT MOTIVATION AND SCIENTIFIC EMINENCE

The behavioral implications of instrumentality and achievement motivation are shown strongly among scientists in the interactions between the achievement factors and eminence, as reflected in the
Science Citation Index. Although even world-famous scientists may
not be immune to the competitive streak that may infect more ordi-
nary mortals (see, e.g., Watson's *The Double Helix*), it makes a certain amount of intuitive sense that influential contributions are more
likely to be made by those devoted to hard work and to mastering
problems, unhampered by trying to best others.

These findings raise important questions about the relationships
among our achievement factors in populations with other goals and
other modes of goal fulfillment. For example, is high competitiveness, when coupled with high work and mastery needs, also deleterious in athletes? Common sense would suggest not, since the point of
most athletic games is to win. We note again that our sample of
female athletes was higher than all other groups on the Competitiveness scale. Even here, however, devotion to some internal standard
of excellence and, in team sports, willingness to subordinate one's
own ambitions to the good of the team may be more important; too
high a level of competitiveness may interfere with effective performance when other components of achievement motivation are
strong.

Still another example that comes immediately to mind is success
in business, often said to be dependent upon an individual's competitiveness. A recent study of businessmen by Michael Maccoby
(1976) provides valuable data, suggesting that competitiveness may
play a highly positive role at some stages of an individual's career
and at some levels of organizations but can prove highly harmful at
others. Maccoby argues that the highly competitive businessman he

describes as the "Gamesman" is not only successful but also widely admired both in society and in the business community. Maccoby describes this type of individual as a collection of paradoxes, co-operative but competitive, detached and playful but compulsively driven to succeed. He sees the main goal of such individuals as being labeled as winners and their main fear as being known as losers.

According to Maccoby's view of individuals and their role in business, the Gamesman is likely to be extremely effective during early years and at lower and middle levels of management. Such individuals, however, are particularly prone to midlife crises and may find themselves frustrated by failures to win new competitions and isolated from others by their long-standing emphasis on the extrinsic rather than the intrinsic aspects of their jobs. As managers, they may lack the broader vision of an organization and its goals necessary for flexible and innovative management. At the least, these observations reinforce the argument that components of achievement motivation such as competitiveness should be assessed separately so that their unique roles at different stages of the life cycle and in different situations can be evaluated in relation to other motives.

The constructs operationalized by the WOFO represent molar aspects of the individual's achievement orientation which should relate more strongly to long-term goal seeking than to performance on a single, isolated task such as routinely employed in laboratory investigations. For this reason, we consider it imperative to explore the manifestations of the various constellations of achievement by comparing groups with different life goals and by relating the measures to objective indices of performance in areas central to the concerns of the individual under investigation.

9. Parental Antecedents of Masculinity and Femininity, Self-esteem, and Achievement Motivation: Background Literature

Theories of socialization differ in the degree to which they emphasize the contribution of internal and external factors in the genesis of response dispositions or patterns of behavior. They differ further in the particular mechanism through which these factors are postulated to have their effects (Looft 1973). Many psychological theories, however, assign a critical and enduring role to the attributes of the parents and to the nature of the parents' behavior in their interactions with their developing child.

The Influence of Child-Rearing Behaviors

Two complementary lines of approach to the impact of parental variables, each with a somewhat different focus, can be discerned. In one, an attempt is made to identify salient aspects of child-rearing behaviors and to relate these behaviors, usually by correlational means, to the characteristics or the behaviors of the child. The paths of influence underlying these observed correlations are seldom spelled out, but they may be assumed to be multiple. Parents affect their children most obviously by direct tuition, encouraging and rewarding some behaviors and discouraging and punishing others. Parents also serve as models whose characteristics and patterns of behavior may be emulated and from whom children may gain information about appropriate modes of behavior. More indirectly, the interactions between parents and the child may be assumed to establish an atmosphere and to create the conditions that facilitate the emergence of certain characteristics and inhibit the development or the expression of others.

As Martin (1975) has observed in a recent review, many of these studies have focused on the relationship between limited patterns of behavior in both the parent and the child (e.g., the relationship between maternal restrictiveness and dependency in the young child or between parental hostility and adolescent aggression). By confining themselves to an examination of a single parental variable rather than the patterning of variables, such studies, although often yielding detailed and richly suggestive data, run the risk that relationships may be overlooked or obscured (Moulton, Liberty, Burnstein, & Altucher 1966). A number of investigators, however, have attempted to get at such patterns by surveying a wide variety of parental child-rearing behaviors and attitudes via parent interviews, self-report instruments, direct behavioral observations, or reports of children about their parents. To bring order into the profusion of data thus generated, factor analyses or other data reduction techniques are often used to identify the major dimensions of child-rearing behaviors and to determine the empirical relationships between various constellations of these parental behaviors and characteristics of the child (e.g., Baumrind 1971). Evidence provided by Schaefer (1959), among others, has suggested that the clusters of behaviors with which most investigators have been concerned may typically be reduced still further to two basic dimensions. These may be labeled acceptance-rejection (or warmth-hostility) and permissiveness-restrictiveness (or autonomy-control).

We will not attempt to survey the results of this literature on patterns of parental behavior. Later in this chapter, however, we will review investigations relating parental child-rearing behaviors to the development of masculinity and femininity, self-esteem, and achievement motivation.

Identification Theories

FREUDIAN THEORY

The second line of investigation of parent-child relations, guided by what have come to be known collectively as identification theories, has emphasized the role of the parent as a model for the child. The earliest identification theory, from which all subsequent theories have been partially derived (Bronfenbrenner 1960), is Freud's. Identification with the mother or father—a process or state whose core elements are the child's emotional attachment to the parent and the desire to be like him or her—leads the child to emulate the parent and to take over as his or her own the parent's values, standards, and behaviors. As Freudian theory eventually evolved, two types of identification were postulated: *anaclitic identification* and *identification with the aggressor* (or *defensive identification*, as Mowrer 1950 has labeled it). Defensive identification, based on fear of punishment from a powerful parent, is said to be more influential in the development of boys, while anaclitic identification, based on fear of loss of the love of a nurturant parent, is said to be more influential in the development of girls. In skeletal outline, psychoanalytic theory states that both sexes typically form a stronger emotional attachment to the mother than the father in very early years because of her nurturing, caretaking role. When the boy is three to five years old, this attachment leads to the emergence of the Oedipal complex, in which he is sexually attracted to his mother and wishes to displace his father. The boy's recognition of his father's greater power, coupled with his fear that his father will retaliate by castrating him (a fear aroused by his belief that females have already suffered this fate), generates an intolerable conflict resolved by renouncing the mother and identifying with the father. This defensive identification leads the boy to adopt masculine characteristics, as exhibited by the father, and to internalize through him the values and the standards set by society for males. Freud postulated that the boy's identification with the father, made strong by his castration fears, has a number of further consequences, the most notable of which is to bring about the assumption of the father's moral values. Identification with the father thus provides the impetus for development of the boy's superego or conscience.

Young girls also undergo Oedipal conflict but in less intense form. Blaming the mother for having castrated her, the girl turns from her and develops a sexual attachment to her father. Failing to supplant her mother and fearing the loss of her mother's love, the girl resolves the conflict by once more identifying with the mother (anaclitic identification). In the absence of castration fears, this identification tends to be less intense than the boy's defensive identification with his father, so the girl is less likely to overcome fully the Oedipal complex or to develop as strong a superego.

IDENTIFICATION BASED ON MODELING

Later identification theories emerging from nonpsychoanalytic traditions share the Freudian view that, through a process of modeling or internalization, children tend to acquire the characteristics of their parents, particularly the parent of the same sex. These theories have minimized or rejected altogether the role of the Oedipal conflict, however, and have sought other mechanisms to explain the socialization process. Most frequently these alternative accounts have drawn heavily on social learning principles, emphasizing the importance of both direct and vicarious reward and punishment in shaping behavior as well as the crucial contribution of observational learning.[1]

Central to identification theories are hypotheses about characteristics of the model that promote imitation. Several theorists (e.g., Kagan 1964; Mowrer 1950; Payne & Mussen 1956; Sears 1957), influenced by Freud's concept of anaclitic identification, stress the importance of nurturance and a positive relationship between parent and child, a parent exhibiting these characteristics being a more ef-

1. In these social learning approaches, identification does not usually have the status of a hypothetical internal state or process, used to explain the appearance of the child's modeling behavior or the similarity between the child and her or his parent. Rather, it is little more than an alternate label for modeling or for parent-child similarity. Although some have therefore advocated eliminating the term as superfluous (e.g., Bandura 1969), it continues to be used as a convenient designation for this group of theories and for such phenomena as parent-child resemblance.

fective model (eliciting more imitation) than a nonaccepting, unaffectionate parent. Other theorists (e.g., Parsons 1955; Whiting 1959) maintain that it is the power of the parent to control all manner of valuable resources—to reward and to punish or withhold reward—that commands identification.

Both hypotheses have received empirical support in investigations in which children's imitation of a model's behavior in a structured situation has been directly observed. Parents who are characteristically nurturant and rewarding in interactions with their children, or an adult confederate of the experimenter who has treated the child warmly before the introduction of the modeling task, tend to elicit more imitation than impersonal, nonnurturant models (e.g., Bandura & Huston 1961; Mussen & Parker 1965; Hetherington & Frankie 1967). Similarly, experimental studies have shown that adult models assigned control over resources or positions of power are imitated more than less powerful models (e.g., Bandura, Ross, & Ross 1963; Mischel & Grusec 1966). This finding is paralleled in studies (Hetherington 1965; Hetherington & Frankie 1967) in which the parents were asked to perform an experimental task. Previously the parents had been observed in a structured discussion of child-rearing problems and the dominant parent identified. The parent classified as dominant was found to stimulate more imitation in the child than did the nondominant parent.

Several theorists (e.g., Kohlberg 1966; Lynn 1969; Tiller 1964) concerned with sex typing have proposed that individuals strive to be similar to those with whom they perceive themselves as having some attribute in common and that this perception of sameness contributes to both the development of sex typing and model effectiveness. Some experimental support has been found for this general contention: subjects led to believe that they have characteristics in common with a person tended to be more influenced by that person than by a dissimilar individual (e.g., Stotland, Zander, & Natsoulas 1961; Rosekrans 1967) or to express greater liking for the more similar individual (Byrne 1969). Congruence between the sex of the model and the sex of the observer also tends to facilitate imitation (e.g., Bandura, Ross, & Ross 1963; Hetherington & Frankie 1967; Maccoby & Wilson 1957).

The sex and other characteristics of the model interact in significant ways, however, with the sex of the child. Hetherington and Frankie (1967), for example, demonstrated that girls tended to imitate most a warm mother and boys a dominant father, as would be expected from psychoanalytic theory. In an investigation in which children observed an adult model dispensing desirable resources (in the form of toys and snacks) to an adult of the opposite sex, Bandura, Ross, and Ross (1963) reported that girls preferred to imitate the powerful controlling model more than the adult recipient, whether the model was female or male. Boys were more likely to imitate the male even when faced with a controlling female adult model and a recipient male. This may be because they refused to accept that the male actually had less power. Bandura, Ross, and Ross (1961) have also reported that girls showed greater imitation of an adult female when she modeled nonaggressive rather than aggressive behavior.

Freud's theory of identification with the aggressor has frequently been interpreted as suggesting that a child will attempt to be like a parent who is not only powerful but also actively threatening and punitive. In one of the few formal studies providing confirmatory evidence for this hypothesis, Hetherington and Frankie (1967) suggested that this type of identification might take place under the limited conditions proposed by Sarnoff (1951): the individual both is dependent on the aggressor and is in a situation that prevents escape from the hostile behavior of the aggressor. In support of this contention, Hetherington and Frankie found that, in homes in which conflict had been observed between the parents and both were low in warmth, young children modeled the behavior of the dominant parent on an imitation task regardless of the sex of the parent or the sex of the child. In homes in which conflict was low or the nondominant parent was warm, the greater imitation of the hostile dominant parent was reduced, except in the case of boys with a dominant father. When either of these conditions obtained, boys continued to imitate the dominant father markedly more than they imitated the nondominant mother.

Parental variables and the development of sex typing. Identification hypotheses are also assessed in studies examining the relationship between parental behaviors and the degree to which children's characteristics resemble their parents or to which children exhibit appropriate sex-typed interests. Bronson (1959) has shown that elementary school children tend to resemble the same-sex parent in sex-typed interests when the parent-child relationship is warm and supportive but not when the relationship is stressful and unrewarding. In an investigation of preschool and elementary school children, Hetherington (1965) obtained ratings on a series of non-sex-typed personality traits for both the children and their parents. Also obtained was a measure of mother vs. father dominance, based on observation of the parents in a discussion of child-rearing problems. Both girls and boys showed greater similarity in their personality characteristics to the dominant parent, a result attributed to children's greater identification with (modeling after) this parent. In boys, sex-typed interests, as measured by the It scale (Brown 1956), were also related to parental dominance. Those with dominant mothers had less masculine scores than those with dominant fathers, a finding also interpreted as reflecting greater identification with the dominant parent. In all age groups girls from father dominant homes showed somewhat more masculine interests than those from mother dominant homes, but the differences were not significant.

Results reported by Moulton et al. (1966) suggest that parental affection and warmth must be taken into account in addition to dominance. Male college students were classified into masculine and feminine groups on the basis of their sex-typed interests and attitudes revealed on Gough's (1952) Femininity scale; they were also classified as perceiving either their father or their mother as having been the primary disciplinarian. Ratings of the affection and support given by each parent were also obtained. Students with a dominant father (i.e., a father who was the primary disciplinarian) were more likely to be masculine if their father was high in affection, while those with a dominant mother were more likely to be feminine if she was high in affection. (Affection in the nondominant parent, however, had no influence on sex typing.)

In a related series of studies, Mussen and his colleagues have investigated the influence of the parent as a source of reward and of punishment on the child's identification. Payne and Mussen (1956) administered three California Personality Inventory (CPI) scales, one of them the Masculinity-Femininity scale, to male high school students and their parents; they also obtained from the students an assessment of their fathers' (as opposed to their mothers') rewardingness. The extent to which the sons were more similar to their fathers than to their mothers on the two non-sex-typed CPI personality scales was significantly correlated with father rewardingness. Father identification (i.e., father-son similarity) was also highly related to the students' scores on the Masculinity-Femininity scale, the more masculine males being more highly identified. Still further studies (Mussen & Distler 1959, 1960; Mussen & Rutherford 1963) conducted with five- and six-year-old boys also implicate the role in sex typing of the same-sex parent as a source of nurturance and, to a lesser extent, as a source of punishment. Thus high masculine boys— that is, boys high in sex-typed interests as assessed by the It scale— tend to perceive their fathers (but not their mothers) as a more powerful source of reward and punishment than do low masculine boys. Mussen and Rutherford also demonstrated that girls high in feminine interests perceived their mothers and, to a lesser extent, their fathers as being more nurturant that did girls low in femininity. The mothers of high feminine girls also scored higher on the CPI Self-acceptance scale, a scale measuring feelings of self-worth, self-acceptance, and a capacity for independent thinking and action. (Despite the association of high Self-acceptance scores in mothers with feminine *interests* in their daughters, one suspects that their Self-acceptance scores would be positively correlated with the *masculinity* scale of the Personal Attributes Questionnaire [PAQ].)

The results of these and other similar studies have been cited in favor of the argument that children's personality characteristics tend to resemble those of a powerful or nurturant parent more than those of a parent lacking these properties because they have modeled themselves after that parent. The finding that the sons of nurturant and/ or dominant fathers and the daughters of dominant mothers show more sex-appropriate interests has also been interpreted as demonstrating the influence of identification or modeling. This latter interpretation seems to rest on the undemonstrated assumption that, regardless of personal characteristics, fathers are almost uniformly masculine and mothers almost uniformly feminine in their interests, so that variations in the child's sex-typed interests are a reflection of the parents' effectiveness as a model. This assumption is not necessarily valid, however, and it is quite possible that the relationship between parental characteristics and children's sex-typed interests is brought about by more complex factors than simple modeling.

This possibility is given credence by evidence suggesting that the development of appropriate sex typing is not heavily dependent on parental variables. In the Mussen and Rutherford (1963) study, for example, no relationship was found between the mother's or the father's CPI Femininity score and the child's score on the It scale in either males or females. Also unrelated to the child's masculinity or femininity was the mother's encouragement of sex-typed interests in girls and both parents' encouragement of these activities in boys. The children, it will be noted, were old enough to have entered kindergarten or elementary school, where they were exposed both to adult models other than their parents and to peers. Sex-role stereotypes were also available to the children in books and television. Mussen and Rutherford suggest that, quite early in the life of the child, such extraparental sources begin to make important contributions to the development of sex-typed interests and attitudes, thus minimizing the parents' roles as teachers and models of society's sex-role expectations. A similar hypothesis, which emphasizes the critical contribution of children's knowledge of societal expectations to sex-role development, has been advanced by Kohlberg (1966).

These contentions raise questions about the influence of parental vs. extraparental variables on the acquisition of masculine and feminine personality characteristics. If, as we have suggested, the linkage between these clusters of attributes and many role-related phenomena is not strong, one could argue that, for both parents and children, these attributes tend not to be as salient in defining "maleness" and "femaleness" as more obvious characteristics such as physical appearance and recreational and vocational interests. The factors that influence the development of masculine and feminine personality characteristics may thus be more similar to those influencing non-sex-typed characteristics than to those contributing to the acquisition of sex-typed interests.

The theories of socialization we have discussed above were devised as general theories rather than as accounts of sex-role development per se although, by their nature, they have inevitably paid a good deal of attention to this topic. A brief description of one additional theory specifically designed to explain sex-role development will be useful.

Johnson's reciprocal role theory. Johnson (1963), in an extension of Parsons' (1958) reciprocal role theory, proposed that identification with the father is critical for producing appropriate sex-role orientation in both males and females. Following Parsons, Johnson defines identification as the internalization of role relationships rather than as the assumption of the totality of the parents' characteristics. These change with age so that, during the course of development, the child successively identifies with a series of increasingly differentiated roles. Johnson also adopts Parsons' position that women's personality and roles are expressive, their orientation being to please others and to give them warmth and understanding, while male roles are instrumental and demand instrumental personality characteristics for their execution. Within the family, the mother's responsibility is thus to care for the family members; the father's responsibility is to provide for his family and be its representative in the outside world.

Crucial to Johnson's formulation is the claim that fathers tend to treat their daughters and sons differently while mothers are more prone to treat them similarly. Her reading of the empirical literature suggested that fathers are more nurturing, less demanding, and less punitive with their daughters than with their sons and, in general, are attentive to appropriate sex-typed behavior in both sexes. Mothers, on the other hand, are less likely than fathers to make differentiations in their treatment of female and male children and less likely to be concerned with sex-typed behavior.

Early in life both boys and girls identify with the warm, nurturing mother in an asexual way and from her learn her expressive characteristics. The boy as he matures is expected by his father to develop instrumental skills and personality traits, these paternal demands being fostered not by love but, congruent with the father's instrumental orientation, by punishment or the threat of withholding rewards. The task of the boy is to shift from an expressive orientation to an instrumental one and from attachment to his mother to identification with his father and the masculine role. Development of the instrumental male role is facilitated by the pressure placed upon the boy by his father and by the clear distinction the father makes between female and male roles. The task of the girl is simpler because she "need only be expressive" (Johnson 1963, p. 323) and thus does not have to develop instrumental qualities. Like the boy, however, the girl does have to overcome her infantile dependency relationship with her mother. The father, by rewarding her and being appreciative of her femininity, encourages her to identify with him and, by their reciprocal role relationship, facilitates her acquisition of and identification with the adult female role.

Parsons' (1958) and Johnson's (1963) assumption that women are quite uniformly characterized by the relative absence of instrumental attributes is contradicted by the data we have presented, as is their assumption that role preferences and behaviors and the possession of expressive or instrumental personality characteristics are strongly related. These disagreements do not necessarily invalidate, however, the essential details of sex-role learning that Johnson proposed or the claim that fathers typically make a more influential contribution to the development of girls than mothers make to the development of boys. Relatively few empirical studies have included fathers as well as mothers but, in support of Johnson, the existing evidence tends to suggest that fathers are more demanding of their sons than of their daughters and more likely to be concerned about sex-typed interests and activities in their sons, a pattern of differentiation not paralleled in degree or in kind by mothers. (See Maccoby & Jacklin 1974 for a recent review.)

Data particularly relevant to our concerns with instrumentality and expressiveness are provided by Block (1973) in a report of the results of four studies in which the parents of males and females ranging from nursery school to college age were questioned about their child-rearing practices. For males, there was a consistent emphasis on achievement and competition and on the control of feelings. For females, greater emphasis was placed on warm, affectionate interactions, particularly by the fathers. The differences in socialization practices used with boys and girls were also greater for fathers than for mothers. Similar results were reported by Heilbrun (1973) in college students' perceptions of their fathers' nurturance. The students also rated their fathers on a bipolar masculinity-femininity scale composed of a series of instrumental and expressive psychological characteristics. Feminine fathers were perceived by males as more nurturant than masculine fathers, but both types of fathers received lower ratings than were given by females. Further, females with masculine and feminine fathers did not perceive them as being differentially nurturant.

In opposition to Johnson, however, we might expect that a girl who has a nurturant, accepting father high in instrumental characteristics (e.g., high on the PAQ M scale) will develop some of these same instrumental traits, either because she models herself after him or because his support sets up the conditions that permit these characteristics to develop, even if she is simultaneously feminine in *role* behaviors. Boys might similarly acquire expressive characteristics from their fathers, as well as from their mothers, particularly if the father is also high in instrumental characteristics and thus perceived as both a powerful and an appropriate model.

Parental Variables and Psychological Masculinity and Femininity

Although considerable attention has been paid to the parental variables that contribute to sex-role development, as they affect both modal differences between the sexes and individual variations within females and males, the literature on the development of masculine and feminine personality attributes is scanty. The reasons are not hard to find. First, as we have indicated earlier, masculine and feminine "sex roles" have been used as umbrella terms, referring to all the internal characteristics and overt patterns of behavior that may be presumed to distinguish between men and women. This practice has in turn encouraged the search for single theoretical or empirical models to account for all gender-related phenomena and the use of measures that tap only a limited behavioral domain to define the multifaceted concept of masculinity-femininity. Most frequently these measures have been heavily, if not exclusively, concerned with sex-typed interests and activities (e.g., children's toy preferences) and have an uncertain relationship with masculine and feminine personality characteristics. Second, until recently even masculinity-femininity measures that contain only personality trait names or dimensions have been set up as bipolar scales. In addition, social desirability of the attributes has not been one of the criteria for item selection (e.g., Heilbrun 1973). These differences between the PAQ and other masculinity-femininity measures make it difficult, if not impossible, to determine the implications of the results of studies employing such measures for our conceptual model. For this reason, we will not attempt to summarize the findings of these prior investigations but will focus on studies having some bearing on the acquisition of instrumental and expressive attributes.

EMPIRICAL STUDIES

To date only one study directly relevant to the parental variables associated with the development of psychological masculinity and femininity, as we have defined these terms, has appeared in the literature. Kelly and Worell (1976), working with female and male college students, obtained students' masculinity and femininity scores on the PRF ANDRO scale (Berzins, Welling, & Wetter 1975), derived from Jackson's Personality Research Form (Jackson 1967). The item content of this scale, as was discussed in Chapter 2, is more heavily loaded with descriptions of role behavior, as opposed to personality traits, than either our Personal Attributes Questionnaire or such other similar measures as the Bem Sex Role Inventory, but the scale yields masculinity and femininity scores moderately correlated with the latter instruments. Also administered to the students was the Parent Behavior Form (Worell & Worell 1974), a questionnaire divided into thirteen scales describing parental behaviors. On each item respondents were asked to indicate how much each parent resembled the description when the student was sixteen years old. Factor analyses of the data indicated three dimensions underlying the thirteen scales that could be labeled acceptance, cognitive encouragement, and control.

The students were categorized on their joint masculinity and femininity scores using the median split method, and the mean scores of those in each category on each of the parent behavior scales were determined. Androgynous men, in comparison to Masculine men, reported receiving significantly greater warmth from both their mother and father and were more involved with their father and more conforming in their dealings with him. Feminine men, in comparison to Masculine, also reported greated conformity with their father, greater warmth from both parents, and more active involvement on the part of their mother. Like the Masculine males, the Undifferentiated men also perceived their mother and father as lacking in warmth and active involvement and themselves as low in conformity to the father.

In sum, the appearance of expressive (feminine) characteristics in males was associated with parental scales related to the acceptance factor, the major difference between Androgynous and Feminine men being in their active involvement with the father vs. the mother. No scale was uniformly related to the appearance of instrumental (masculine) characteristics. There was a striking difference, however, between the Undifferentiated men and all other groups on scales related to cognitive encouragement. These Undifferentiated students, in contrast to the other groups, saw both parents, but particularly the father, as placing relatively little stress on cognitive independence, curiosity, and competence.

In women, scores on the cognitive encouragement scales also distinguished between groups. Parental warmth was not particularly implicated in the appearance of masculine characteristics (as they occurred in both Androgynous and Masculine groups), but laxity of disciplinary control and the setting of achievement goals appeared to be. Thus Masculine women, relative to Feminine, reported that they received more encouragement from their father of cognitive curiosity and competence, that their mother was less actively involved, and that both parents were relatively lax in discipline. Androgynous women reported greater maternal involvement and encouragement of curiosity than the Masculine group and less disciplinary laxity on the part of their father. Like the men, the Undifferentiated women received less cognitive encouragement from their parents than other groups. Relative to the Androgynous women, the Undifferentiated also had mothers who set lower achievement goals and who were less actively involved with their daughters but were stricter in their disciplinary control. In both sexes, then, different constellations of parental behaviors were associated with the masculinity-femininity category into which the student fell.

Suggestive data on the influence of parental behaviors on the development of masculine, instrumental attributes can also be found in studies by Baumrind (1967, 1971) involving nursery school children and their parents. Baumrind identified three major patterns of parental behaviors that she labeled authoritarian, authoritative, and permissive. In terms of a two-dimensional conceptualization of parental behaviors, the prototypic *authoritarian* parent is highly restrictive (as opposed to permissive) but relatively low in acceptance of the child, although not necessarily lacking in nurturance. That is, the parent imposes demands with little explanation or allowance for the child's needs and opinions and is generally nondemocratic in disciplinary procedures, but the parent may or may not be affectionate and emotionally responsive to the child. The *authoritative* parent tends to be high on the restrictiveness dimension but also tends to be accepting. Thus, the authoritative parent exercises firm control but, at the same time, recognizes the child's needs and shares with the child the reasons underlying disciplinary decisions. The parent "values both expressive and instrumental attributes, both autonomous self-will and disciplined conformity" (Baumrind 1968, p. 261). The *permissive* parent is high on acceptance of the child but low on restrictiveness. Thus this parent attempts "to behave in a nonpunitive, accepting, and affirmative manner toward the child's impulses, desires and action" but is not "an active agent responsible for shaping or altering his ongoing or future behavior" (Baumrind 1968, p. 256). Baumrind (1971) has also described a pattern in which the parent is relatively nonauthoritarian (not highly restrictive) but is rejecting and neglectful.

In her 1971 study, Baumrind first identified clusters of parent behaviors by statistical means. The patterning of these clusters was then examined for each couple and, where possible, the couple was assigned to one of the four basic groups described above. Extensive observation of the nursery school behavior of the children suggested that those from authoritative homes were more likely to exhibit social and instrumental competence than those from other types of homes. The daughters of authoritative parents were thus more dominant, independent, purposive, and achievement-oriented than the daughters of authoritarian, permissive, or rejecting parents. The sons were more friendly and achievement-oriented and, if their parents (particularly their fathers) actively promoted nonconformity and individuality, they also tended to be more independent and dominant than boys from other types of homes.

Similar results were obtained in an earlier study (Baumrind 1967) in which the children had initially been separated into three groups according to their social and emotional behaviors; the parental behaviors associated with memberships in these groups were then determined. Parents of a group of children observed to be high in self-reliance, self-control, and friendly relationships with peers tended to exhibit the authoritative pattern, being warm and nurturant with their children but also high in control. Parents of a group of children who were relatively discontented, moody, and unsuccessful in peer relationships were also controlling but tended to be more detached and less nurturant than the parents of the first group. These parents tended to exhibit the authoritarian pattern. Children in the third group were relatively more cheerful and less irritable than those in the second but had the least self-reliance and self-control. The parents of these children tended to be permissive. Baumrind's data thus suggest that the development of instrumental characteristics related to self-esteem and social competence is facilitated when the parents combine warmth, reasoning, and acceptance of the child with the imposition of standards of behavior that they expect the child to meet. These results, based on the direct observation of nursery school children and their parents, parallel quite nicely the self-report data collected from college students by Kelly and Worell (1976).

Sex differences uncovered by Baumrind (1971) are also worthy of note. Boys were rated as significantly more hostile and domineering than girls and more resistive to adult control but were not significantly more dominant, purposive, independent, or achievement-oriented than girls, despite the fact that, in older groups, these characteristics tend to differentiate the sexes and indeed form the core of stereotypic "masculinity." A clear association was found in girls between dominance, purposiveness, and independence and authoritative parental behaviors, suggesting that the development of counterstereotypic, instrumental attributes in females is fostered by high demands coupled with warmth and acceptance. In boys, however, weaker relationships emerged between these characteristics and parental behaviors. Such data suggest, Baumrind observed, that socialization practices within the family may have greater influence on independence and related characteristics in girls than in boys, a hypothesis also suggested by Lynn (1969), among others. Baumrind also suggested that what she labeled social responsibility (reflected in such characteristics as friendly, cooperative, tractable, and achievement-oriented as opposed to hostile, resistive, domineering, and less achievement-oriented) is more heavily influenced by parental practices in boys than in girls. In boys, for example, achievement motivation was facilitated by the authoritative pattern, in which achievement was encouraged and expected, but was inhibited by the permissive pattern, in which no emphasis was placed on achievement. In girls, however, not only authoritativeness but also permissiveness led to greater achievement motivation. The latter result is reminiscent of the association reported by Kelly and Worell (1976) between masculinity in girls and laxity of discipline.

THE INTERACTION OF PARENTAL CHARACTERISTICS AND BEHAVIORS

Although the possibility cannot be ruled out that the behavior of the child elicits these differential reactions on the part of the parents, the usual interpretation given to correlational studies of parent-child relationships is that the causal flow is primarily in the reverse direction, variations in parental practices bringing about differences in the child. Granting the validity of this assumption, the data in the studies reviewed above still yield little insight about how parental behaviors influence the development of instrumental and expressive characteristics in the child. In particular, the role of the parents' own masculinity and femininity (or instrumentality and expressiveness) cannot be discerned. It seems quite conceivable that these parental characteristics are themselves correlated with the socialization techniques the parent employs. One would not be surprised to find, for example, that Androgynous individuals are more likely than others to be the kind of parent Baumrind (1968) described as authoritative. That is, they are warmer and more accepting of the child than those who are relatively lacking in feminine, expressive attributes. At the same time they impose relatively high demands on their children, expecting them both to develop the same level of instrumental competence that they exhibit and to defer to the parent as an autonomous, powerful adult. A doctoral dissertation by Stapp (1975) that employed the PAQ and an abbreviated form of the Life History Questionnaire (Radloff & Helmreich 1972) in a sample of college students supplies evidence supporting several aspects of these hypotheses.

If a conjunction occurs between parental behaviors and the parent's level of masculinity and femininity, and both are similarly related to the appearance of masculine and feminine characteristics in the child, modeling or identification could be evoked as an explanatory concept of the parent-child resemblances, with parental child-rearing techniques being of secondary significance. The Androgynous father, for example, may be an attractive individual for his son to emulate, both because his personal characteristics are themselves attractive and because his behaviors toward the child further enhance the probability that the child will attempt to model himself after the father.

It would also not be too surprising to find that an Undifferentiated individual not only has a parent relatively low in supportiveness and nurturance, as Stapp's (1975) and Kelly and Worell's (1976) data suggest, but also that the parent tends to be Undifferentiated. In this instance the argument that parent-child similarity comes about because the individual identifies with the Undifferentiated parent or has modeled himself after this parent is counterintuitive. If these empirical relationships were found, a more reasonable assumption is that, in the absence both of an individual who can serve as a model of instrumental and expressive characteristics and of the kinds of parental support and encouragement that permit the child to develop his potential, the child may fail by default to acquire these socially desirable characteristics.

Commonsense considerations suggest that parents' masculinity and femininity and their child-rearing behaviors are not only correlated but also interact with each other in complex ways to exert both direct and indirect influence on the appearance of the masculine and feminine characteristics in their children. Children may model themselves after their parents, but parental socialization techniques have effects on children over and above those that determine the attractiveness of the parent as a model, effects that may themselves be enhanced by parental masculinity and femininity. The evidence we have reviewed also suggests that the sex of the parent who exhibits these characteristics and patterns of behavior interacts with the sex of the child to determine the child's characteristics. Given socially desirable characteristics in the parents (high masculinity, high femininity) and effective child-rearing techniques (e.g., a high degree of acceptance of the child), we anticipate that males will be more influenced by the father and females more equally by both parents.

THE JOINT CONTRIBUTIONS OF MOTHERS AND FATHERS

With rare exception, prior studies attempting to investigate the differential influence of mothers and fathers have approached the problem by comparing the data obtained from fathers as a group with those from mothers as a group. Children in intact homes, however, have two parents whose characteristics affect the relationships they have worked out between themselves and with their children. For example, the dynamics of a home in which the father is Masculine (high instrumental, low expressive) may be quite different when the mother is Feminine than when she herself is Masculine or is Undifferentiated or Androgynous.

In searching for the parental variables associated with masculinity and femininity, we therefore sought information not only about students' perceptions of their fathers' and mothers' child-rearing behaviors but also about their perceptions of their parents' masculine and feminine characteristics. In analyses of the data, each parent was assigned to one of the four categorical groups reflecting her or his joint M and F score, and each couple was then assigned to one of the sixteen possible father-mother combinations (e.g., both Androgynous, father Masculine and mother Feminine, etc.). The relationship between couple type and the students' masculinity-femininity classification was then determined, as well as the relationship between couple type and patterns of parental behaviors.

The relationships between these parental measures and other student variables, most notably self-esteem and achievement motivation, were also explored. Prior research relevant to these factors will be reviewed in the sections that follow.

Development of Achievement Motivation

Given the consistent, positive correlations between our measures of masculinity, femininity, and achievement motivation, a reasonable expectation is that similar constellations of parental behavior should be associated with the development of these attributes.

Despite contradictions and conceptual problems surrounding research in the area, some progress has been made in isolating the antecedents of achievement orientation, with results that suggest that this may indeed be the case. We have previously mentioned Baumrind's (1971) research, in which young children whose parents exhibited an authoritative pattern of behavior showed stronger achievement motivation. Her findings stress that, even with a positive affective environment, competence and achievement come not from permissiveness but from guidance and encouragement of achievement behaviors.

The specific concept of childhood independence training as a precursor of achievement motivation has been suggested by several investigators (e.g., Winterbottom 1958; Rosen & D'Andrade 1959; Baumrind & Black 1967). Callard (1964), using an adaptation of Winterbottom's measure of child-rearing practices, asked mothers of four-year-old females and males to indicate the appropriate age to permit or encourage such specific behaviors as using potentially dangerous utensils or staying away from home without prior permission. Two indices were derived from the scale items: *independence granting* and *achievement induction*. Mothers of girls considered the appropriate ages to be later than mothers of boys, although the difference was only significant for independence granting.

Similarly, Hoffman (1975) suggests that parents' unambivalent pleasure in independent and achieving behaviors may foster such motivation in their children and that greater ambivalence may be found among mothers of daughters than mothers of sons. Hoffman also suggests that establishing a separate self is a critical component of independence training and that this is more readily accomplished in boys because they have more conflict with the mother. She reasons that girls may experience too much maternal support and protection during early years and that this may result in inadequate motivation for autonomy. (Johnson 1963, however, assigns an even more critical role to the father, who tends to demand independence in his son but not in his daughter.) Conversely, Hoffman argues that boys' achievement is more likely to be impaired by too much conflict. Her position is that some conflict may facilitate the development of independence, with females more likely to experience too little and males more apt to experience too much.

The research just described suggests that differences in the treatment of girls and boys may lead to differences in achievement motivation but does not address the question of whether differences are qualitative. As we have noted in Chapter 7, one postulated theoretical position is that socialization produces different kinds of motivations underlying achievement-related behaviors in the two sexes—achievement per se in males and affiliation in females. Such hypotheses have been proposed by Crandall (1967) and Veroff (1969), each of whom has suggested that achievement in very young children may be similar in both sexes but that males then usually progress to a more internalized motivation while females frequently do not.

VEROFF'S STAGE THEORY

Veroff's (1969) theory will be described in some detail because it illustrates several important points regarding the development of achievement motivation. His theory defines three developmental stages for achievement motivation: autonomous achievement orientation, social comparison, and integrated achievement motivation. Like other stage theorists, Veroff believes that complete mastery of earlier stages is necessary before later stages can be achieved and integrated. His theory stresses a shift from the importance of parental behaviors to a primary concern with the peer group during elementary school years. Another important element of his theory is the specification of differential, motivational outcomes as a result of incomplete mastery and integration of autonomy and social comparison. The contellations of motives defined bear a strong conceptual resemblance to the factor structure obtained from our work with the Work and Family Orientation Questionnaire (WOFO) and can provide a framework for examining parental influences.

The first stage—autonomous achievement—is seen as beginning between the ages of one and one-half and two and one-half and continuing through early elementary school. In autonomous achievement, the child is aware of a sense of personal agency in his accomplishments and develops and employs internalized standards of perform-ance. This early sense of competence in autonomous achievement does not involve comparison of the self with relevant others.

Veroff's second stage, beginning roughly at the onset of school is based on social comparison. In the school setting, children receive continuous, relative evaluation vis-à-vis their peers. Such comparisons are functional in allowing children to accommodate to their own fail-ures and to note the accuracy of their aspirations. Social comparison serves both an informative and a normative function, providing feed-back on performance and presenting norms for acceptable levels of attainment. When social comparisons are favorable, the concomitant is often widespread social approval, which may increase not only so-cial comparison needs but also the individual's self-esteem. Finally, Veroff proposes that, if both autonomous and social comparison mo-tivations are successfully achieved, a third stage—integrated achieve-ment motivation—may develop. Individuals who achieve the integra-tion of autonomous and social comparison needs are defined as those who have a strong internal sense of competence, the ability to utilize others as referents, and the further capacity to weigh both sources of information as a function of situations and to employ the resultant data to evaluate and guide achievement-related behavior.

Parents' behavior, through provision of appropriate independence training, is regarded as essential to the development of autonomous achievement motivation. Parents must encourage free exploration of the environment and foster the acquisition of a broad range of verbal and manipulative skills. Their primary responsibility is to pace these opportunities so the child acquires a sense of effectance. Where par-ents are totally permissive and provide no pacing, the child may ac-quire no sense of autonomous achievement. Too early or ineffective pacing may lead to partial mastery and anxiety about autonomous achievement.

Veroff contends that parental rewards are not critical for the devel-opment of the sense of mastery associated with autonomous achieve-ment, while White (1959) argues similarly in his discussion of com-petence. Veroff, however, suggests further that parental criticisms of a child's performance adequacy can be strong deterrents to the de-velopment of autonomous achievement. In a similar vein, Sarason, Davidson, Lighthall, Waite, and Ruebush (1960) contend that early criticism of a child's performance may underlie a sense of dependency, which in turn may be the major determinant of debilitating anxiety in such evaluative situations as examinations.

The role of parents is seen by Veroff as less central to the develop-ment of social comparison motivation. He suggests that only very considerable reinforcement for relative performance evaluation can cause the development of social comparison as a general disposition in the young preschool child. For mastery of social comparison, the child must compare favorably with a reasonably large majority of others of the same age and sex with respect to valued attributes of the reference group. Veroff reasons that, by eight or nine years, chil-dren typically have sufficient awareness of steps of difficulty in performance to recognize relative improvement in their achievement vis-à-vis others. Too early emphasis on social comparison may blind the child to *relative improvement* and lead to an overemphasis on incompetence relative to peers and to general anxiety about performance. On the other hand, if demands for social comparison come too late, they may have little relevance for the child. That is, if demands are not applied to the child until later elementary school years, they may present little challenge and may fail to generalize to other situations. Veroff concludes that for essential, favorable comparisons to occur the child must be in a group where he or she can excel at something but also be challenged.

Typological outcomes. Finally, Veroff defines a typology of five major outcomes of the socialization of achievement motivation. The first type is called *integrated achievement motivation.* An individual in this category has mastered both autonomous and social comparison orientations. Such a person is motivationally engaged not only when her or his internalized goals are clear but also when goals are ambiguous and means of evaluations are unclear. In the latter case the individual uses social comparison informatively. Relating this condition to the factors we derived from the second version of the WOFO, such a person should be high in Work and Mastery needs but not particularly high in interpersonal Competitiveness and not overly concerned with the reactions of others to personal attainment (i.e., should be relatively high in Personal Unconcern). Individuals falling in this category have had successful experiences both in parental guidance for independence and in social comparison with peers.

The second type is defined as *competitive orientation.* Such individuals are assumed to have failed to integrate mastered autonomy with imperfectly mastered social comparison. As Veroff describes it, "this type includes people who overly evaluate the competitive situation. Even when a situation in fact demands autonomous strivings and standards of excellence are clear without resort to social comparison, such people tend to interpret the situation as one where competition is required" (1969, p. 57). In such individuals, competitive needs seem strongly to interfere with the expression of other strong aspects of achievement motivation. Here parental independence training is assumed to have been as successful as in the first type; the deficit resulting in overcompetitiveness is assumed to come from unsuccessful social comparison experiences. A case in point may be the relatively low attainment of scientists high in Work, Mastery, *and* Competitiveness noted in Chapter 7.

The third typology is defined by those *high in fear of failure orientation.* In contrast to the use of this term by Atkinson and his colleagues to include those fearful of failure in competition with standards of excellence as well as in competition with others, Veroff defines this group as those overly concerned with failure in interpersonal competition. He suggests that two patterns of experience may cause this outcome—such individuals may have achieved considerable success in the autonomy stage but have experienced difficulty in comparing themselves favorably with others; alternatively, they may have experienced intermittent failure and success in both the autonomy and social comparison stages. In either case, Veroff argues that the major concern of such individuals is to avoid disapproval from others and to do what is socially desirable. One antecedent may have been unsuccessful independence training by parents. The individual, due to improper pacing of parental demands, may have had both successful and unsuccessful autonomy experiences. Such incomplete autonomy then adds to difficulties in making appropriate comparisons.

In terms of the constellation of factors isolated by the WOFO, such individuals might be expected to inhibit the expression of Mastery and Competitiveness needs while retaining a strong Work orientation. The role of Personal Unconcern is less clear because, as we have noted in Chapter 7, success in competitive achievement appears to be a necessary precursor of the manifestation of concern with the reactions of others.

In his fourth typology, defined as *fear of success orientation*, Veroff makes a similar point. He considers such individuals to be those who have had some difficulty with autonomous achievement but have had success in competition with others and have hence learned the price one must pay for achievement. Such a person by our typology should be one high in Competitiveness and low in Personal Unconcern and probably high in Work and moderate or low in Mastery. Veroff suggests that one familial precursor of such a syndrome may be inconsistent parental reinforcement. That is, achievement in a particular area may be praised by one parent and derogated by the other, or the same parent may criticize some aspects of achievement while praising others. Although he argues, along with Horner, that this condition is more frequent in females, the dynamics are likely to be similar in each sex.

The fifth and final type is defined as *low achievement orientation*. Individuals in this group have found little emphasis on or satisfaction from autonomy striving. Here the initial problem seems to stem from unsuccessful independence training by the parent in preschool years. The failure could lie in total permissiveness without guidance or encouragement or in inappropriately high demands for achievement and autonomy. Having failed to achieve an autonomy orientation, the individual subsequently fails to confront demands for social comparison.

The weight of the evidence suggests that early but appropriate independence training of the type most often associated with Baumrind's (1968) "authoritative family" is an essential antecedent of an integrated achievement motivation. In looking at the outcomes of socialization for achievement motivation, it appears essential to consider combinations of the components comprising achievement motivation, such as are found on the WOFO, instead of speaking of the relative strength or weakness of a unitary construct.

While parental actions and examples may be necessary, they may not be sufficient for the development of high achievement motivation; as Veroff suggests, the role of social comparison with age and sex peers may be crucial. If these speculations are valid, the relationships between achievement motivation and parental variables may be less clear-cut than those between masculinity and femininity and self-esteem.

Antecedents of Self-esteem

The preponderance of evidence from diverse samples suggests that there are no reliable sex differences in self-esteem (see, e.g., Maccoby and Jacklin's 1974 review of thirty comparative studies and Helmreich, Stapp, & Ervin 1974).[2] One of us (Helmreich 1977) has recently argued that the failure to find racial and class as well as sex differences in self-esteem stems from social comparison processes. That is, individuals tend to employ peers of the same sex and social milieu to evaluate their own social competence.

Our evidence indicates, however, that in each sex the agentic characteristics measured by the masculinity scale of the PAQ are strongly correlated with a measure of self-esteem. The communal characteristics tapped by the femininity scale of the PAQ are also significantly though less strongly related to self-esteem. We should expect therefore to find the antecedents of self-esteem to be similar to those of masculinity and femininity in each sex. As noted above, however, it seems likely that much of the individual definition of personal worth takes place through social comparisons with peers in school and play settings. While parental attitudes may have some influence on their children's self-esteem, parents' primary role may be to foster the kind of instrumental and expressive skills valued by their children's primary reference groups.

Perhaps the classic study of the parental antecedents of self-esteem is that of Coopersmith (1967), who studied ten- to twelve-year-old white males from middle-class families. Although his sample is highly restricted, Coopersmith's findings are congruent with those of Baumrind (1971), cited above, and other investigators such as Wessman and Ricks (1966) and Rosenberg (1965), who have looked at both sexes and a broader social and ethnic spectrum. Coopersmith found that three parental characteristics (as reported in interviews with mothers) were most strongly associated with the development of a positive self-concept: acceptance of the child by the parents, establishment of clearly defined and enforced limits for child behavior, and respect and latitude for the child's individual actions within the defined limits. Families that establish and define clear limits on behavior permit more deviation from conventional behavior and freer individ-

2. This is not to ignore those researchers and theoreticians who have suggested that many women, especially homemakers, may experience a drop in self-esteem during midlife, often at the same time that men are experiencing feelings of self-worth (e.g., Gurin, Veroff, & Feld 1960; Rossi 1968; Birnbaum 1975). Much of this speculation centers around midlife transitions in women's roles when children are grown or when widowhood or divorce change social status.

ual expression. These authoritative (in Baumrind's sense) parents also utilize less drastic forms of punishment while exerting stronger demands for academic achievement and excellence in performance.

Coopersmith reports further that the parents of children with higher self-esteem also tend to be on relatively good terms with one another and to have established clear lines of authority and responsibility. He further notes that in such families both parents tend to lead active lives outside the family and do not necessarily rely upon the family setting as their primary source of gratification. He also suggests that the provision of limits by such families provides the child with settings to facilitate social comparison by delineating conditions under which evaluation of personal performance is reasonable.

Coopersmith also provides an important qualification of his data by emphasizing that "first and foremost there are virtually no parental patterns of behavior or parental attitudes that are common to all parents of children with high self-esteem" (1967, p. 239). This statement serves to underline the complexity of the parent-child environment, the likelihood that child characteristics and behaviors interact with those of parents to determine the climate of the home, and the fact that the peer group also plays a major role in determining stable attributes measured during adolescence or later.

Recently, the significance of such characteristics as ability, physique, and physical attractiveness in influencing the treatment of the individual has come to be recognized (e.g., Smith 1969; Berscheid & Walster 1974). Clearly a child who is stigmatized or markedly deviant on one of these dimensions can be expected to elicit differential treatment from peers and teachers. Berscheid and Walster, in their review of the attractiveness literature, point out that even very young children differentiate between the more and less attractive. It is hardly daring to postulate that parental behaviors may be similarly influenced by such factors as well as by the child's behaviors. Unfortunately, most studies of socialization and resultant child characteristics, including the present one, have not been designed to investigate the reciprocal influences of child characteristics and behaviors and parental behaviors.

Despite these limitations, the theories and data we have considered in this chapter suggest that the attributes and behaviors of parents do play a role in the development of masculinity and femininity, achievement motivation, and self-esteem. We therefore anticipated that perceptions of parent characteristics and behaviors should show modest but significant relationships with children's characteristics.

10. Relationships with Parental Masculinity and Femininity

Two types of information were gathered about the parents of high school students: the students' perceptions of their mothers' and their fathers' masculine and feminine attributes and their perceptions of their parents' child-rearing attitudes and behaviors. Data on perceived parental attitudes were also obtained from college students. These college data were supplemented by self-reports by the parents themselves so that the congruence between student perceptions and the parents' view of themselves could be determined.

In this chapter, the relationships between parental attributes and the several student variables will be examined. The relationships with parental behaviors will be presented in Chapter 11.

High School Samples

In order to obtain as uncontaminated a picture as possible of the interrelationships between parent and parent-child variables, the decision was made to analyze data only from white students from intact homes, that is, students who had from birth or shortly thereafter been brought up by their natural or adoptive parents. This restriction decreased the size of the sample only slightly, since over 90% came from such homes. Considerably more shrinkage was brought about by two additional factors. First, the parental scales were placed at the end of the test battery, and some students were unable to complete the full battery in the time available. Second, in analyses involving social class comparisons, data from a number of students were lost because the information they supplied about father's occupation was not sufficient to permit assignment to class. Complete data were available from 374 males and 589 females, and these were used in making social class comparisons. Since complex interactions with social class were not observed, a number of analyses were performed that did not include this variable as a factor. In order to increase the stability of the findings, these latter analyses were based on all students for whom relevant data were available, without regard to the availability of data on measures not entering into the comparison, such as social class.

PARENTAL MASCULINITY AND FEMININITY

The students rated their parents, it will be recalled, on the items going to make up the M and F (but not the M-F) scales of the Per-

sonal Attributes Questionnaire (PAQ). Each parent was first classified jointly on her or his M and F scores by the four-way median split
method. In making this assignment, we were forced to decide whether
to use the same median values as had been used in classifying students on their own self-ratings or to establish new norms, based on
their ratings of their parents. We could find no compelling substan-
tive reason in favor of one procedure over the other and opted to use
the previously established student norms so that direct comparisons,
based on a common metric, could be made between the two sets of
data. We should note, however, that the mean of the medians for this
sample of fathers turned out to be somewhat higher than the males'
self-ratings on M (22 for fathers vs. 20 for males).

The first data to be reported involve social class comparisons.
Before presenting the percentages of mothers and fathers falling into
each of the four Masculinity and Femininity categories within the
four socioeconomic classes, data on their children's PAQ scores will
be reported so that direct comparisons with parent ratings may be
made. The percentages of students, male and female, falling into
each category at each of the four socioeconomic levels are shown in
Table 10-1. Significant ($p < .01$) differences were found in the distributions of the class groups in each sex, the nature of these differences in general confirming what was reported earlier for the larger
sample from which these students were drawn. Thus, in males, the
percentage of Undifferentiated students increases as one goes from
Upper- to Lower-class status, and the percentage classified as Androgynous decreases. Similar but less striking results are found in
females, the major discrepancies being between the Lower-class individuals and those in the other groups. Greater percentages of these
Lower-class girls fall in the Undifferentiated and Feminine categories
than in the other class groups and, correspondingly, lesser percentages fall in the Masculine and Androgynous categories.

Parallel data for the mothers and fathers of these students, reported separately for female and male students, are shown in Table 10-2.
The distribution of mothers of males across categories was similar to
the distribution produced by the female students' self-ratings, but the
females' rating of their mothers led to an elevation in all socioeconomic groups in the percentage in the Androgynous category and a
depression in the percentage in the Feminine category. In like fashion, the distribution of the fathers of females was fairly similar to
the self-ratings of the male students, but the males' ratings of their
fathers resulted in a greater percentage of the fathers being classified
as Masculine in all socioeconomic groups than was found in their
self-ratings; this elevation in Masculinity came about at the expense
of the Androgynous and Feminine categories. In short, the females
perceived their mothers as Androgynous more frequently than they
so perceived themselves and the males perceived their fathers as
Masculine more frequently than they so perceived themselves. The
discrepancy between the perceptions of the two sexes of their fathers
could reflect a tendency of adolescent boys to exaggerate the tradi-

Table 10-1. *Percentage of Students in Each Masculinity and Femininity Category within Each Socioeconomic Class for High School Students from Intact Families*

Class	Males				Females			
	Undiff	Fem	Masc	Andro	Undiff	Fem	Masc	Andro
Upper	15	8	44	33	17	35	11	37
Upper middle	17	5	49	29	16	30	19	35
Lower middle	23	8	39	29	14	32	12	42
Lower	36	7	43	14	23	42	4	30
Total	20	7	44	28	16	33	14	37

PAQ category

Note: Sample is restricted to students for whom parental data were obtained.

tional masculine attributes of their fathers (which includes a denial of their more feminine characteristics), thus distorting their perceptions of the father in the direction that they define as normatively appropriate. It is even more likely that the discrepancy arises because, in the father-son interaction, the masculine aspects of the father's personality are emphasized to a greater degree than their feminine attributes. Mothers, on the other hand, may more freely express their agentic characteristics with their daughters than with their sons or be perceived by their daughters but not by their adolescent sons as relatively more powerful than themselves.

Comparison of the socioeconomic groups shows, for the ratings of fathers, a pattern of differences among the classes similar to but less pronounced than the males' self-ratings. Thus, more Upper-class fathers were perceived by both male and female students as Androgynous and fewer were perceived as Undifferentiated than in the other classes. A chi square showed that these differences were significant ($p < .01$). Slight and nonsignificant trends in a similar direction were observed in the data for mothers.

Having classified each parent into one of the four masculinity and femininity groups, we proceeded to determine how the parents looked as *couples* vis-à-vis these categories. We thus set up a 4 by 4 table to reflect the sixteen possible couple types. The percentages in each of these couple types are shown in Table 10-3 for 506 males and 745 females. Inspection of the table shows that what might be considered the "traditional" couple—Masculine husband and Feminine wife—occurs frequently, being found in 16% of the males and 15% of the females. (Within each sex, however, one of the types including an Androgynous parent occurs most frequently, in part because of the relatively high percentage of mothers and fathers falling into this category, compared to the students themselves.) Three other couple types, in which the father is high in masculinity (M) and may or may not be high in femininity (F) and the mother is high in femininity (F) and may or may not be high in masculinity (M), could be classified as "near-traditional": Androgynous-Androgynous, Masculine-

Table 10-2. *Percentage of Parents in Each Masculinity and Femininity Category (Student Perceptions) for High School Students within Each Socioeconomic Class*

Class	Males				Females			
	Undiff	Fem	Masc	Andro	Undiff	Fem	Masc	Andro
Upper	17	32	16	35	18	18	15	49
Upper middle	24	25	14	37	14	32	11	43
Lower middle	23	23	17	37	20	27	16	37
Lower	22	25	16	37	24	24	12	40
Total	22	25	16	37	18	27	14	41

Note: Presented are the data from parents of the students reported in Table 10-1.

Androgynous, and Androgynous-Feminine (in these and subsequent descriptions, father's category appears first and mother's second). When traditional (i.e., Masculine-Feminine) and near-traditional couples are considered, the majority of homes are accounted for: 58% in females and 54% in males. Four nontraditional types occurred with sufficient frequency to permit further study: Undifferentiated-Undifferentiated (5% of the females, 12% of the males), Masculine-Undifferentiated (9% of both sexes), Masculine-Masculine (5% of the females, 10% of the males), and Undifferentiated-Feminine (4% of the females, 3% of the males). These four nontraditional types accounted for an additional 34% of the homes of males and 23% of the homes of females. Completely cross-sex couples (Feminine-Masculine combination) were rare, accounting for less than 1% of the cases, both because of the small percentage of fathers classified as Feminine and because Feminine men may be found with wives in all four categories.

Within the smaller sample for whom socioeconomic data were available, the numbers of cases were too few to permit meaningful inspection of the frequency of all sixteen parent types within each class level or separation of the students by sex. Inspection of the data showed, however, that the eight couple types observed to occur most frequently in the group as a whole also occur most frequently in both females and males in this small sample and in a similar rank order. The data from males and females whose parents fell in one of the eight types were therefore combined, and the percentages within each socioeconomic group across these types were determined. These results are reported in Table 10-4. Only minor differences can be observed across socioeconomic groups. The one discrepancy to which attention will be called is the descending frequency of the Masculine-Undifferentiated combination, this couple type occurring twice as often in Lower-class as in Upper-class families. Overall, however, the modest class differences in the classification of the individual parents, seen in Table 10-2, are still further diluted when the parents are jointly considered as couples.

	Males			Fathers	Females		
Undiff	Fem	Masc	Andro	Undiff	Fem	Masc	Andro
15	0	53	32	7	6	38	49
19	0	56	25	14	3	49	34
20	4	57	19	20	2	42	36
19	0	66	15	15	6	39	40
19	1	57	23	15	4	44	37

156   *Parental Masculinity and Femininity*

Table 10-3. *Percentage of Couples in Each of the Sixteen Masculinity and Femininity Couple Types (Student Perception) for High School Students*

		Mother category							
		Males				Females			
		Undiff	Fem	Masc	Andro	Undiff	Fem	Masc	Andro
Father category	Undiff	12	3	3	2	5	4	3	5
	Fem	<1	<1	<1	<1	<1	<1	<1	<1
	Masc	9	16	10	19	9	15	5	15
	Andro	1	6	2	13	4	7	5	21

PARENT-CHILD RESEMBLANCES IN MASCULINE AND
FEMININE ATTRIBUTES

In attempting to uncover the relationships between the students' masculinity and femininity and their perceptions of their parents, we first determined the correlations between the students' self-ratings on the M and F scales and their ratings of their father and mother on these measures. These correlations are shown in Table 10-5. All the correlations are positive and significant, the highest relationships occurring between the student and the same-sex parent on the same sex-appropriate scale (M for males, F for females). Even these r's are quite low in magnitude, however, the largest value being only .29.

Our next approach was to determine the pattern of the relationships between the masculinity and femininity category to which each parent had been assigned and, for each, the distributions of their sons or daughters with respect to these categories. As the low correlations suggested, the results were not particularly enlightening, and we will

Table 10-4. *Percentage of Occurrence within the Eight Most Frequent Couple Types for Each Socioeconomic Level (Male and Female High School Students Combined)*

Couple type (Father-Mother)	Upper	Socioeconomic class		Lower	Total %
		Upper middle	Lower middle	Lower	Total %
Andro-Andro	28	21	20	24	22
Masc-Andro	22	18	21	18	20
Andro-Fem	8	9	6	6	7
Masc-Fem	18	19	18	16	18
Masc-Masc	7	10	9	6	9
Masc-Undiff	8	11	10	17	11
Undiff-Fem	2	4	5	6	4
Undiff-Undiff	8	7	11	6	9

Note: Only the data from the eight couple types enter into the analysis so that, except for rounding errors, each column totals 100%.

Table 10-5. *Correlations between High School Students' Self-ratings and Ratings of Their Parents on M and F Scales*

Ratings of parents	Self-ratings			
	Males		Females	
	M	F	M	F
Mothers				
M	.24	.09	.22	.13
F	.17	.23	.08	.24
Fathers				
M	.29	.14	.19	.10
F	.10	.20	.12	.17

Note: For $df = 500$, $r_{.05} = .08$.

not report them here. More instructive patterns of parent-child relationships emerged, as we had anticipated, when the distribution of the students among the four PAQ categories within each parental *couple type* was examined.

Couple type and student PAQ category. The percentage of students in each of the four PAQ categories within each of the eight most frequent couple types is shown for males and females in Table 10-6. (The numbers and percentages for all sixteen couple types are shown in Table I, Appendix D.) For expository purposes, we will frequently describe the systematic trends noted in these data as though parent-child resemblances reflect modeling phenomena. We will seriously examine this hypothesis and alternatives to it after presenting data on the students' perceptions of their parents' child-rearing behaviors in Chapter 11.

Inspection of Table 10-6 indicates that, in traditional and near-traditional homes, there is a marked congruence of father-son category, moderated to some degree by mother category. Thus, in Androgynous-Androgynous couples, the majority (51%) of the sons are Androgynous; an additional 33% are Masculine. The percentage of Androgynous boys systematically decreases and the percentage of

Table 10-6. *Percentage of Students in Each Masculinity and Femininity Category in Each of the Eight Frequent Couple Types for High School Students*

Couple type (Father-Mother)	PAQ category							
	Males				Females			
	Undiff	Fem	Masc	Andro	Undiff	Fem	Masc	Andro
Andro-Andro	10	6	33	51	7	27	11	55
Andro-Fem	17	7	35	41	6	42	12	40
Masc-Andro	17	8	46	29	12	32	15	41
Masc-Fem	18	10	48	24	22	33	18	27
Masc-Masc	19	2	58	21	20	40	23	17
Masc-Undiff	33	2	44	21	22	39	14	25
Undiff-Fem	31	19	31	19	38	28	10	24
Undiff-Undiff	38	7	39	16	38	26	18	18

Masculine boys increases as one goes from this parental combination to Androgynous-Feminine, Masculine-Androgynous, and Masculine-Feminine. It appears that, in these traditional and near-traditional homes, boys are highly likely to exhibit the masculine characteristics they perceive in their fathers but are likely to be high in feminine characteristics as well only if one or both parents, but most particularly the father, is perceived as *Androgynous*. Parental modeling of expressive, feminine characteristics thus seems to have an influence on the appearance of these characteristics in males only when the parent is simultaneously perceived as exhibiting masculine characteristics.

The Masculine-Masculine combination continues this trend of decreased Androgyny and increased Masculinity in males, this couple type producing the greatest percentage of Masculine sons (58%), primarily at the expense of the Androgynous category. In going from Androgynous-Androgynous to Masculine-Masculine couples, in the order listed in Table 10-6, there is also a suggestion of a simultaneous trend toward an increase in Undifferentiated boys; Masculinity in the father, particularly when untempered in the mother by Androgyny or at the very least by Femininity, appears to increase the likelihood of males falling into the Undifferentiated category.

The negative impact of a Masculine father is particularly marked in the couple in which the father is perceived as Masculine and the mother as Undifferentiated; here one-third of the boys are Undifferentiated. "Raw" masculinity in the father, balanced by neither masculinity nor femininity in the mother, seems to have a particularly inhibiting influence on the development of both masculine and feminine characteristics in many males.

Undifferentiated boys are also frequent in the two couple types in which the father is perceived as Undifferentiated (Undifferentiated-Feminine, Undifferentiated-Undifferentiated). These couple types also produced the lowest proportion of boys in the two high M categories (Masculine and Androgynous), the number of Androgynous individuals being particularly depressed. The absolute percentage of Masculine males, however, remains quite high (31% and 39% in Undifferentiated-Feminine and Undifferentiated-Undifferentiated couples, respectively).

In girls, examination of the PAQ distributions for traditional and near-traditional couples reveals a more complex pattern and a more equal influence of both parents. Androgyny is most likely to occur when both parents are reported to be Androgynous, next more likely when either the father or the mother is Androgynous, and least likely in the traditional Masculine-Feminine couple. In the Masculine-Feminine combination (and to a lesser extent in the Masculine-Androgynous couple), the decrease in the frequency of Androgynous daughters is accompanied by an increase in the Masculine and Undifferentiated categories. These latter findings suggest the important influence of the father, whose masculinity, in the absence of feminine characteristics, can often have the effect either of suppressing the girl's personality development or of encouraging the appearance of her father's agentic characteristics at the expense of communal ones.

In the two nontraditional couples in which the father is seen as Undifferentiated, the greatest percentage of girls also falls into the Undifferentiated category. Perhaps the most confusing outcome among females is found in the couples in which the father is Masculine and the mother Masculine or Undifferentiated. In both of these couple types, the most frequent classification of the daughter is Feminine; in fact, the percentages of Feminine girls are among the highest of all the couple types. Rather than speculating on this outcome, it will merely be pointed out that the number of cases is small and, as will be seen shortly, that the results were not replicated in college students. In the latter, these two combinations most frequently produced Undifferentiated girls. Clearly, however, these two nontraditional types—in which the father is Masculine and the mother low in femininity—do not encourage the appearance of agentic characteristics in girls.

Finally, a word might be said about the characteristics of the students whose fathers were Feminine. Reference to Table I in Appendix D indicates that only eight (out of a total of almost five hundred) males come from such homes. None of these boys is Feminine and half are Undifferentiated. Of the four remaining boys, three are Androgynous (and have Androgynous mothers) and one is Masculine (and has a Masculine mother). Of the twenty-eight girls (out of a total of over seven hundred) with Feminine fathers, fifteen (54%) are Feminine, thirteen of them having an Androgynous or Feminine mother. Four girls are Undifferentiated, two are Masculine, and seven are Androgynous, five of the latter having Androgynous or Masculine mothers. Feminine fathers as well as Feminine mothers, one infers, are unacceptable models for their sons. Boys with Feminine fathers thus fail to resemble their fathers in this pattern of characteristics but tend to become Masculine or Androgynous (rather than Undifferentiated) if their mother exhibits these qualities. Females are more flexible, tending to be responsive to the instrumental or the expressive attributes or to both in whichever parent they perceive as exhibiting them.

COUPLE TYPE AND M-F

The sample was not sufficiently large to permit an eight-way breakdown of students' scores on all three PAQ scales within the eight most frequent types of families. The mean M-F scores for males and females within each type were instead computed. For males, minimally significant ($p < .05$) differences occurred, those with Undifferentiated fathers tending to score slightly lower on M-F than those with Masculine or Androgynous fathers. For females, the differences among couple types were not significant ($p > .05$). In stark contrast to M-F, highly significant ($p < .0001$) differences among couple types were found in both sexes in their mean scores on the M and F scales. The ordering of the students' means on the individual M and F scales was predictable from the analyses reported in Table 10-6 of the differential distribution among the four M and F categories within couple types. For this reason, the means have not been tabled.

COUPLE TYPE AND IDENTIFICATION

A series of items aimed at measuring more directly and more globally students' perception of similarity or closeness to their father or mother concluded the Parental Attitudes Questionnaire. These parent-identification items inquired into which parent the students perceived themselves as resembling in ideals and in personality and the parent in whom the students confided or to whom they felt closer. Results obtained from the several items were highly correlated. Chosen for presentation here are the data obtained from the item that asked about the similarity between the students' and parents' ideals. The item contained five alternatives, ranging from "Much more similar to my father's [ideals] than my mother's" through "Equally similar to both my parents (or not similar to either)" to "Much more similar to my mother's than my father's." Combining in the middle category equally similar to both and equally dissimilar to both, rather than putting them into separate alternatives, was dictated by the constraints of the machine-scorable answer sheet, which contained only five response alternatives per item. As will be seen, failure to isolate the two components—equally similar and equally dissimilar—turned out to be unfortunate and to complicate interpretation of the results.

In scoring the item, the five alternatives were collapsed into three, yielding a three-point scale: More similar to Father, Equally similar (or dissimilar) to both, and More similar to Mother. In Table 10-7, the percentage of males and females choosing each of the three alternatives is shown separately for each of the eight most frequent couple types.

In the two types of homes in which the mothers were perceived as

Table 10-7. *Percentage of High School Students Perceiving Themselves as Similar in Ideals to Father or Mother or Equal to Both*

| Couple type (Father-Mother) | Similarity in ideals | | | | | |
| | Males | | | Females | | |
	Father	Equal	Mother	Father	Equal	Mother
Andro-Andro	42	55	3	22	59	19
Andro-Fem	56	44	0	36	48	16
Masc-Andro	30	51	19	16	46	38
Masc-Fem	47	37	15	22	52	26
Masc-Masc	36	51	13	21	55	24
Masc-Undiff	54	39	7	34	51	15
Undiff-Fem	7	47	47	18	36	46
Undiff-Undiff	30	54	16	22	61	17
Total	39	48	13	23	52	25

Androgynous (Androgynous-Androgynous and Masculine-Androgynous), over half of the males chose the Equal alternative. Father similarity was the next most frequent choice in these two types of homes but, when the fathers were Masculine rather than Androgynous, fewer of the males not selecting the Equal alternative chose the Father alternative (61% in Masculine-Androgynous vs. 93% in Androgynous-Androgynous). In the Androgynous-Feminine combination, 56% of the males identified with the Father and the remaining 44% with both. These data, as did the analyses reported above, suggest that for males Androgynous fathers and, secondarily, Androgynous mothers are more attractive individuals with whom to identify than are parents seen as exhibiting only the stereotypic characteristics of their sex. As might be expected from these results, males whose parents were the traditional Masculine-Feminine couple most frequently chose the Father alternative, but the percentage was somewhat less than half of the group (47%), and the split among the three alternatives was more even than in the homes in which one or both parents were Androgynous.

In the females from traditional and near-traditional homes, the contribution of fathers and mothers was more balanced, just as in the analyses in which parent-child resemblances on M and F were examined. Thus, in all four of these homes, the Equal alternative was the most frequently chosen (although highest in the Androgynous-Androgynous combination). Of the girls who did not choose Equal, about the same number chose Mother and Father in the Androgynous-Androgynous and Masculine-Feminine combinations, while the girls who had one Androgynous parent were more likely to choose that parent, regardless of sex.

In nontraditional homes, boys with a Masculine father and an Undifferentiated mother were most likely to perceive themselves as similar to their fathers, 54% falling into this category and only 7% in the Mother category. In the Masculine-Masculine combination about half of the boys chose the Equal alternative, and about a third chose Father. In the two combinations in which the father was Undifferentiated, the Equal alternative was also the most frequent choice. It seems reasonable to infer, especially in light of the results obtained from the Parental Attitudes Questionnaire, to be reported in Chapter 11, that the significance of the choice of the Equal alternative by male students with nontraditional parents was not the same as this choice by students in the traditional and near-traditional couple categories. Many of the former students, particularly those with Undifferentiated fathers, probably selected this alternative because they felt identified with neither parent and thus perceived themselves as equally *dissimilar* to both.

It is also interesting to note that boys with Undifferentiated fathers and Feminine mothers were not only the least likely of all the male groups to see themselves as more similar to their fathers, only 7% choosing this alternative, but also the most likely to see themselves as similar to their mothers, 47% choosing the Mother alternative. Although interpretation is clouded by the ambiguity of the Equal alternative, it seems safe to assume that males tend not to identify with either parent when they do not exhibit masculine characteristics but, when they do not reject both parents, find a Feminine mother a more worthy person with whom to identify than an Undifferentiated father.

In girls from nontraditional homes, almost half (46%) of those with an Undifferentiated father and a Feminine mother identified with the mother, just as had the boys. A more substantial proportion, however, identified with the father (18%) than did the boys (7%). In each of the remaining nontraditional combinations, over half selected the Equal alternative, a choice that can also be assumed primarily to reflect their lack of identification with either parent. In the Masculine-Undifferentiated home, almost 70% of the girls who did not select Equal chose the Father alternative while, in the other two (Masculine-Masculine and Undifferentiated-Undifferentiated), choice between the Father and the Mother category for those not selecting Equal was about the same.

Still further clarification of these relationships was sought by examining, within each of the eight couple types, the Masculinity and Femininity classification of students giving each category of response to the question about ideals, with the results shown in Table II, Appendix D. In each of the five types of homes in which neither parent was Undifferentiated, males who chose the Father similar response fell proportionately more often in the same category as their fathers (Masculine or Androgynous) than males choosing the Equal or Mother similar response. In the homes in which one or both parents were Undifferentiated, the major discrepancy in the PAQ distributions was found between those selecting the Mother response and those selecting the Father or Equal response: those perceiving themselves as similar to their mother were more likely to be Undifferentiated than those in the other response groups.

In females, those who had at least one Androgynous parent and were themselves Androgynous were more likely to perceive themselves as similar to both parents. Other than the tendency in Masculine-Feminine homes for the girls who choose the similar to Mother response to be Feminine more frequently than the other groups, no other systematic trends were discernible in the other types of homes.

In summary, when asked to assess their similarity to their mother or father on a global dimension such as "ideals" or "personality," these adolescents did not in overwhelming numbers identify themselves with (perceive themselves as similar to) the same-sex parent. While males identified less frequently with their mothers than females identified with their fathers, a very frequent choice in both sexes was equally similar (or dissimilar) to both. The data also indicated that the two measures of parent-child resemblance (similarity of masculinity and femininity category vs. direct report of similarity) did not fully track each other. The masculine and feminine attributes of the parents and of the students were jointly related to the items inquiring directly about similarity but in a complex fashion.

COUPLE TYPE, SELF-ESTEEM, AND ATTITUDES TOWARD WOMEN

The mean Self-esteem and AWS scores for female and male students coming from the eight frequent types of families are presented in Table 10-8. In both sexes, an analysis of variance revealed significant (p's < .05) differences in mean AWS scores among the eight groups. In females, no theoretically coherent pattern could be discerned to explain these differences. In males, a slight pattern could be detected, the two couple types in which the father was Androgynous producing sons with more liberal attitudes than all but one of the other groups and the Undifferentiated couple producing sons with the most traditional attitudes. Without replication, however, it seems unwise to make much of these observed differences.

Highly significant differences in mean Self-esteem scores were also found in both the males and females from the eight parent combinations. Except for the unexpected depression in the mean of the males with Androgynous-Feminine parents, the ordering of the means follows quite directly from the different distributions in student PAQ category across couple types that have already been reported. For example, the greatest percentage of Androgynous students of both sexes and the smallest percentage of Undifferentiated students are found in the families of Androgynous couples. In view of the relationship between Self-esteem and PAQ category, the finding that students with Androgynous parents have the highest Self-esteem was to be anticipated. Similarly, students who came from homes in which the father was Undifferentiated predictably tend to have the lowest means.

The Self-esteem data were examined in greater detail by computing, for each sex and couple type, the mean score for members of each of the four PAQ groups. These data are presented in Table 10-9. (A number of cells contain only a small number of cases; means based on an N of five or less are marked by an asterisk.) In males, there is a tendency for the differences in Self-esteem associated with couple type to remain, even when students' PAQ category is held constant.

Table 10-8. *Mean Self-esteem and Attitudes toward Women Scores for High School Students within Each Couple Type*

Couple type (Father-Mother)	Males Self-Esteem	AWS	Females Self-esteem	AWS
Andro-Andro	44.13	24.07	41.57	30.18
Andro-Fem	36.07	28.31	42.28	27.31
Masc-Andro	41.31	22.94	40.12	29.99
Masc-Fem	38.90	22.68	37.38	31.31
Masc-Masc	40.45	23.47	38.97	31.68
Masc-Undiff	37.48	20.69	35.69	33.00
Undiff-Fem	34.00	25.13	36.50	30.83
Undiff-Undiff	36.11	19.75	34.92	32.50
p	<.0001	<.001	<.0001	<.04

Table 10-9. *Mean Self-esteem Score for Each PAQ Category within Each Couple Type for High School Students*

Couple type (Father-Mother)	Males				Females			
	Undiff	Fem	Masc	Andro	Undiff	Fem	Masc	Andro
Andro-Andro	37.33	36.00*	43.43	46.88	30.36	36.94	44.06	44.75
Andro-Fem	26.40*	21.50*	39.10	40.00	41.33*	38.47	42.00	46.83
Masc-Andro	35.06	36.29	42.05	45.19	31.69	34.83	44.88	45.21
Masc-Fem	32.07	31.38	40.38	44.05	31.46	36.53	38.80	42.20
Masc-Masc	36.56	29.00*	42.78	38.80	39.60*	33.36	44.71	44.83
Masc-Undiff	31.71	37.00*	40.42	40.78	30.15	32.17	41.00	42.50
Undiff-Fem	33.20*	33.33*	34.00*	37.00*	29.73	38.14	48.67*	40.29
Undiff-Undiff	32.86	36.50*	36.38	42.89	29.15	31.11	43.33	45.00*

PAQ category

*N ≤ 5.

Sons of Androgynous parents, for example, have the highest mean Self-esteem in all categories, while those with Undifferentiated fathers tend to have the lowest. Weaker and less consistent trends in the same direction were noted in females in the Undifferentiated and Feminine categories. Discussion of the implications of these data will be postponed until the findings on parental behaviors have been presented.

College Students

In order to determine the replicability of the results obtained with high school students, a sample of 586 male and 724 female college students in introductory psychology courses, all from intact homes,[1] was administered the Parental Attributes Questionnaire as well as the self-report version of the PAQ. Self-report data on the PAQ (and on the AWS) were also obtained from the mothers and fathers of many of these students. Both PAQ instruments included all three scales.

Before describing in detail the relationship between student self-reports and each of the two types of parental data, mention should be made of the intercorrelations among the three PAQ scales within each of the three sets of data, that is, student self-report, parent self-report, and student report of parents. (See Table III, Appendix D.) In each instance, the expected relationships occurred, M and F showing a low but positive relationship with each other, M-F showing a moderately high, positive relationship with M and a somewhat lower, negative relationship with F. These data are of interest in two respects. First, the results obtained from parent self-reports demonstrate that the dualistic conception of psychological masculinity and femininity continues to have validity in individuals a generation removed from the student samples. Second, they provide comforting reassurance that students do not perceive their mothers and fathers in a radically different manner from the ways in which their parents perceive themselves.

Also shown in Table III, Appendix D, are the correlations between each of the three PAQ scales and the AWS. As usual, most of the correlations were low, and many were nonsignificant. However, one interesting relationship did emerge. In all three types of data—student self-report, parent self-report, and student perception of parents—the highest correlations with the AWS (all in the .20s) were found in females with the M-F scale, women scoring higher (more masculine) on this scale tending to be more egalitarian than their lower scoring, more feminine contemporaries.

---

1. Comparisons of the data of students from intact homes with those reared by only one parent would undoubtedly yield valuable information. However, as in the high school sample, the number of single parent homes was too small to permit meaningful analyses to be conducted.

RELATIONSHIPS BETWEEN STUDENT AND PERCEIVED PARENTAL
ATTRIBUTES

Significant correlations were found between students' M and F scores
and their perceptions of their same-sex parent on the same scales, but
their magnitudes were low. The correlations between parents and students on M-F were even lower and consistently nonsignificant. (These
results, along with the parallel results for the parental self-report
data, are presented in Table 10-11.) Thus, as in the high school sample, perceived parent-child resemblance on the PAQ scales was
minimal.

Next, the students' ratings of their parents were used to classify
each parent into one of the four masculinity and femininity groups,
based on the college student norms. A comparison of the percentages
in each category with the percentages determined from students' self-
reports indicated that, by and large, the distribution for fathers and
mothers was very similar to the distribution of the male and female
students themselves. (See Table IV, Appendix D.) The major discrepancies concerned the elevated percentages of Fathers classified as
Masculine, as compared to male students' self-reports, and of Mothers
classified as Androgynous, as compared to female students' self-
reports. As might be suspected from these differences, the mean M
score for Fathers was noticeably as well as significantly ($p < .001$)
higher than the mean for male students (24.13 vs. 22.46), a difference paralleling that found in the high school data. The Fathers' mean
on M-F was also significantly ($p < .001$) higher than the mean for
males: 18.57 vs. 16.61. For Mothers, the mean F score was significantly ($p < .001$) higher than the mean for female students (25.74
vs. 24.13), thus accounting for the somewhat greater percentage of
Androgynous mothers. (The complete set of means is presented in
Table V, Appendix D.)

Each of the parents having been classified into one of the four PAQ
categories, the percentage falling into each of the sixteen couple types
was then determined. These data are reported at the top of Table
10-12. A comparison of the data shown in Table 10-3 for high school
students with the college sample reveals only minor differences between them. As in the high school sample, the four traditional and
near-traditional types were the most frequent, together accounting
for 60% of the parents of males and 64% of the parents of females.

The percentage of female and male students in each PAQ category
within each of the sixteen parental couple types was next determined.
The data for college students obtained for the eight types which occurred most frequently in high school students[2] are shown in Table

2. The four most frequent nontraditional types for college students
were Masculine-Masculine, Masculine-Undifferentiated, Undifferentiated-
Feminine, and Undifferentiated-Androgynous. The first three of these were
also among the four most frequent for the high school students, Undifferentiated-Undifferentiated substituting for Undifferentiated-Androgynous.
Since the percentages in the latter categories were small for both groups,
this discrepancy between samples has little significance. Because of the

10-10. (The distributions for all sixteen types may be found in Table VI, Appendix D.) As can be seen by comparing these data with those presented in Table 10-6, the overall trends in the college sample are similar to those observed in the high school students. Thus, when the father or both parents are perceived as Androgynous, males are more likely to be Androgynous and less likely to be Undifferentiated than males whose parents are not perceived as exhibiting these characteristics. Conversely, males whose fathers are perceived as Undifferentiated are least likely to be Androgynous. Similarly, Androgynous parents of either sex are more likely to produce Androgynous girls and are less likely to produce Undifferentiated girls than the other couple types, while couples in which both parents are perceived as Undifferentiated produce the opposite pattern.

Several major discrepancies between the high school and the college samples may be observed, however. For example, in the high school sample, substantial percentages of males with parents perceived as Undifferentiated-Undifferentiated fell not only into the Undifferentiated category but also into the Masculine category; in the college sample, the lowest percentage of Masculine males was found in this couple type, with over 60% being Undifferentiated. However, the number of college students whose parents exhibited this combination was low (N = 26). Inspection of the distributions in the other couple combinations in which the father was Undifferentiated suggests that sampling error may have led to this extreme elevation in the Undifferentiated category and the corresponding depression in the Masculine category. Still another discrepancy may be found in the distribution of females in the Masculine-Masculine and Masculine-Undifferentiated combinations. In the high school sample, it will be recalled, the percentage of Feminine girls from such homes was strikingly high. In the college sample, the females were more evenly distributed between the Undifferentiated and Feminine categories, a more intuitively reasonable finding. Again, attention will be called to the relatively small number of cases in these nontraditional combinations in both high school and college students; such discrepancies are thus to be expected. Overall, the similarities in the patterns of relationships found in the high school and the college samples far outweigh their differences.

RELATIONSHIPS WITH PARENTS' SELF-RATINGS ON THE PAQ AND THE AWS

The analyses of parental data reported above were all based on the high school and college students' ratings of their parents rather than their parents' self-reports. The use of children's perceptions of their parents' characteristics in determining parent-child resemblances has

---

theoretical interest of the Undifferentiated-Undifferentiated couple, this combination was selected for special study rather than Undifferentiated-Androgynous.

Table 10-10. *Percentage of College Students in Each Masculinity and Femininity Category in Each of the Eight Most Frequent Couple Types*

Couple type (Father-Mother)	PAQ category							
	Males				Females			
	Undiff	Fem	Masc	Andro	Undiff	Fem	Masc	Andro
Andro-Andro	9	7	25	59	11	33	10	46
Andro-Fem	13	15	37	35	17	44	4	36
Masc-Andro	14	9	44	33	10	34	14	42
Masc-Fem	29	8	39	24	20	34	23	23
Masc-Masc	33	4	42	21	32	23	23	23
Masc-Undiff	32	2	36	30	31	33	13	22
Undiff-Fem	19	24	38	19	39	30	12	18
Undiff-Undiff	61	8	12	19	42	32	10	16

Note: Parent classification is based on student's ratings of parents. The eight couple types are those occurring most frequently in the high school sample. See Footnote 2.

been both criticized and defended. Reflecting the critics' suspicions that only pseudorelationships are being revealed, Child (1954), for example, has contended that resemblances between individuals' perceptions of themselves and their parents may simply reflect their projections. The minimal correlations reported above between the students' ratings of themselves and their parents on the PAQ scales suggest that the pattern of relationships found between the students' and parents' masculinity and femininity category cannot be dismissed on these particular grounds. Others (e.g., Heilbrun 1973) have argued, to the contrary, that children are more appropriate sources of information about their parents than are outside observers or the parents themselves. Children's *perceptions* of their parents, it is claimed, most critically influence their development; stronger parent-child relationships are therefore likely to be found when the children supply information about their parents than when the information comes from other sources. In the present instance, for example, it seems quite possible that parents' overt expression of instrumental and expressive behaviors may not be the same in their interactions with their children as with others and may even vary according to the child's age, sex, or other characteristics. Not only are children more likely to be affected by the nature of their personal experience with their parents, but they may also be better reporters of their parents' behaviors toward themselves than objective observers who have access only to temporally limited behavioral samples or even than the parents themselves, particularly when the latter are asked to assess themselves on general instrumental and expressive traits that contain no reference to situation.

Even if one accepts the validity of these contentions, it is nonetheless important to the interpretation of the results reported above to determine whether similar relationships would emerge if parental self-reports on the PAQ were used rather than student perceptions.

Political considerations discouraged us from approaching the parents of high school students, but no such barriers existed in the case of the college population. After filling out a test battery that included the AWS, the PAQ, and the Parental Attributes Questionnaire, members of the introductory psychology classes from which the sample of students described above was drawn were asked to supply their mothers' and fathers' names and addresses if they were willing to have us send the PAQ and the AWS to their parents. The parent or parents were each sent a test booklet containing the AWS and the twenty-four-item PAQ, along with a cover letter explaining in general terms the purpose of the study and, for each parent, a stamped return envelope. Parents were asked to specify their sex but not their names on the test booklet although, as the cover letter explained, each booklet contained the code number assigned to their son or daughter so that parent-child correlations could be calculated. Approximately 66% of the students (N = 946) complied with the request for their parents' names and addresses, and usable forms were returned by 685 mothers and 641 fathers. The number of couples in this pool of data was

586, 258 of them the parents of a male student and 328 of them parents of a female.

The first analyses that will be reported are the correlations between the students' self-ratings on the three PAQ scales and the two types of parent ratings, shown in Table 10-11. The correlations between the students' and the parents' self-ratings, it will be observed, are even lower than those between the students' self-ratings and their perceptions of their parents, and most are nonsignificant. Thus, whether student perceptions or parent self-reports are used to measure parental attributes, parent-child resemblances are minimal.

At the bottom of Table 10-11 are shown the correlations between the students' ratings of their mothers and fathers on the three PAQ scales and the parents' ratings of themselves. The correlations, which range in value from .20 to .51, are all highly significant. Although the magnitudes of the relationships are modest, they do provide evidence that there is some veridicality between students' perceptions of their parents and their parents' self-image. Inspection of the pattern of correlations suggests that females were somewhat better predictors of parental self-report than males and that, in both sexes, predictions were better for M and M-F than for F. Whether the former result reflects the greater social sensitivity of females or the tendency of parents to behave differently with their sons and daughters cannot be determined. Also unclear is the reason for the lower relationships with F, even in mothers.

The next series of analyses were aimed at determining whether the two sets of parent ratings yielded similar results. First, a comparison was made of the means on each scale produced by students' ratings of themselves and of their parents and the parents' self-reports.[3] These data may be found in Table V, Appendix D. What is most remarkable about these means is the similarity across the three types of ratings, almost all the differences between pairs of means being less than one scale point. (Because of the large N's, even small mean differences were often statistically significant but, practically, they seem to have little meaning.) The only notable discrepancies, as was discussed earlier, were the students' perceptions of their fathers as being higher on M and M-F than the males reported themselves and of their mothers being higher on F and lower on M-F than the females reported themselves. With the possible exception of fathers on M, these parent-child differences are not borne out in the parents' self-ratings.

Minor differences between the three types of ratings were also found when the parents or the students were classified into the four PAQ categories. (See Table IV, Appendix D.) Only two differences, which seem to follow from the just reported discrepancies, are worth noting. First, when student ratings were used to classify the parents,

---

3. In these analyses, parental self-data were used even if only one member of the couple returned usable data. Analyses were also run using data from only the subset of students for whom both father and mother self-reports were available. Since no evidence of systematic differences between the total sample and the subsample was found, the latter analyses will not routinely be reported.

Table 10-11. *Correlations between College Student Self-ratings on the PAQ, Perceived Parental Ratings, and Parent Self-report Ratings for 586 Students and Their Parents*

	Male students						Female students					
	Fathers			Mothers			Fathers			Mothers		
	M	F	M-F	M	F	M-F	M	F	M-F	M	F	M-F
Student ratings of parents vs. student self-ratings												
M	.21	.11	.06	.17	.11	.03	.20	.02	.13	.10	.17	.01
F	.15	.20	-.00	.21	.25	-.04	.18	.16	-.03	.09	.27	-.06
M-F	-.04	-.04	.23	-.07	-.07	.10	.04	-.04	-.16	-.00	-.09	.10
Parents' self-ratings vs. student self-ratings												
M	.11	.08	.00	.07	.09	-.03	.10	.01	.08	.07	.08	.04
F	-.01	.06	.02	.07	.16	-.09	.11	.10	-.05	-.03	.07	-.06
M-F	.06	.09	.02	.01	.02	.02	.03	.00	.17	.08	-.04	.10

	Fathers	Mothers	Fathers	Mothers
Parent self-ratings vs. student ratings of parents				
M	.33	.41	.37	.51
F	.21	.27	.26	.20
M-F	.26	.38	.30	.45

Note: For $df = 256$, $r_{.05} = .11$.

a greater percentage of mothers was found to be Androgynous and a lesser percentage to be Undifferentiated than was found in mothers' or female students' self-ratings. Second, when both sets of father ratings were compared with males' self-ratings, a smaller percentage of the male students than fathers was classified as Masculine.

These discrepancies appear to be at least partially responsible for differences in the percentages falling into each of the sixteen couple types, shown in Table 10-12. In both sexes a somewhat greater percentage of the couples is categorized as Masculine-Feminine when student perceptions, as opposed to parent self-reports, are used to classify the parents and, in females, a somewhat greater percentage of Androgynous-Androgynous couples occurs. Overall, however, the distributions are highly comparable.

In sum, the group relationships produced by the several sets of PAQ ratings (e.g., patterns of intercorrelations among the scales, distributions among masculinity and femininity categories) are quite comparable. Further, there was a modest correspondence between the individual student's ratings of his or her father and mother and the parents' ratings of themselves.

A question of critical significance is whether the patterns of relationships between perceived couple type and the students' PAQ category reported earlier are replicated when parent self-reports are used to classify the couples. The distributions for all sixteen couple types, based on parents' self-report, may be found in Table VII, Appendix D. Data from the eight combinations we have been selecting for special scrutiny are reproduced at the bottom of Table 10-13. At the top of the table are shown the equivalent distributions, based on student perceptions, obtained from the daughters and sons of these specific couples.

Table 10-12. *Percentage of Couples in Each of the Sixteen Masculinity and Femininity Couple Types for College Students*

		Mother category							
		Males				Females			
		Undiff	Fem	Masc	Andro	Undiff	Fem	Masc	Andro
Student ratings of parents									
	Undiff	4	7	2	6	4	5	2	4
Father	Fem	<1	2	<1	2	1	1	1	1
category	Masc	8	21	4	15	6	20	3	14
	Andro	2	9	2	15	3	12	4	18
Parent self-ratings									
	Undiff	5	7	2	5	5	6	2	5
Father	Fem	<1	2	2	2	1	2	<1	2
category	Masc	8	16	4	13	12	17	6	12
	Andro	8	9	3	15	5	9	6	10

Table 10-13. *Comparison of Percentage of College Students in Each Masculinity and Femininity Category within Selected Couple Types for Student Ratings of Parents and Parent Self-ratings*

Couple type (Father-Mother)	PAQ category							
	Males				Females			
	Undiff	Fem	Masc	Andro	Undiff	Fem	Masc	Andro
Student ratings of parents								
Andro-Andro	8	11	22	59	20	30	7	44
Andro-Fem	4	19	38	38	16	42	3	40
Masc-Andro	16	3	50	31	16	34	14	36
Masc-Fem	23	12	36	29	17	35	17	32
Masc-Undiff	37	0	42	21	33	40	13	13
Undiff-Fem	20	27	40	13	50	22	11	17
Undiff-Undiff	63	12	12	12	20	50	20	10
Parent self-ratings								
Andro-Andro	3	18	44	36	19	45	13	23
Andro-Fem	9	9	44	39	21	35	14	31
Masc-Andro	30	12	33	24	21	26	13	40
Masc-Fem	20	5	30	45	19	41	9	31
Masc-Undiff	24	5	43	29	13	41	10	36
Undiff-Fem	22	6	44	8	10	38	14	38
Undiff-Undiff	33	0	42	25	33	20	20	27

Note: Student ratings were obtained for the subsample of students for whom parental data were available.

For males, the results obtained from student perceptions are both more orderly and more dramatic than those obtained from parents' self-ratings. Nonetheless, the overall trends are similar, homes in which the father is Androgynous and the mother Androgynous or Feminine tending to produce Androgynous sons more frequently and/ or Undifferentiated sons less frequently than the other couple types. Conversely, homes in which the father is Undifferentiated and the mother is Feminine or Undifferentiated tend to produce sons who are less frequently Androgynous and/or more frequently Undifferentiated.

In females, the patterns observed when student perceptions were used to classify couples are even more diluted when parent self-reports are substituted. When the full table is inspected, the mildest of trends can be detected, homes in which one parent is Androgynous, according to self-report, and the other not Undifferentiated tending to have a higher percentage of Androgynous daughters and a lower percentage of Undifferentiated daughters than homes in which the father is Masculine or Undifferentiated and the mother not Androgynous.

The difference between the sexes in the reproducibility of the patterns of perceived parent-child resemblance when parental self-reports are used may be real, mediated through the differential treatment by parents of boys and girls (see Chapter 11). Or it may be a psychometric artifact, occurring as a by-product of the greater influence of the father than the mother on males' self-perceptions, as opposed to the more equal influence of both parents in females. Lack of concordance between the two methods of classifying parents has consequences for the pattern of parent-daughter relationships when either mother or father is categorized differently but has consequences for patterns of parent-son relationships primarily when there is a discrepancy in father classification. Whatever the explanation, students' masculinity and femininity are clearly more highly related to their perceptions of their parents' attributes than to the parents' perceptions.

THE RELATIONSHIPS BETWEEN PARENTS' AND STUDENTS' ATTITUDES TOWARD WOMEN

Parents were asked to respond to the AWS as well as to the PAQ. Shown in Table 10-14 are the data both for the couples who returned the questionnaire and for their sons or daughters. Inspection of the means shows that parents are more traditional in their attitudes than students and, within each generation, males are more traditional than females, all of the mean differences being significant ($p < .001$). The greatest difference occurred between the female students and the other groups. Thus the means for fathers and sons were closer than for mothers and daughters and the means for husbands and wives closer than those for male and female students.

Also reported in Table 10-14 are parent-child and husband-wife correlations. Substantial correlations were found between husbands and wives and between daughters and each of their parents, but par-

Table 10-14. *Means and Correlations on the AWS for*
College Students and Their Parents

	$\overline{X}$	SD	Fathers	Mothers	Sons	Daughters
				Correlations		
Fathers	24.2	8.14	1.00	.40	.03	.36
Mothers	26.9	8.97		1.00	.12	.51
Sons	25.9	9.00			1.00	
Daughters	31.6	7.82				1.00

Note: For $df = 110$, $r_{.05} = .18$.

ticularly the mother. These findings essentially replicate an earlier study (Spence & Helmreich 1972b) of the resemblance between college students and their parents that employed the full version of the AWS. In that study, significant father-son correlations were also found. In the present sample, the scores of the sons were significantly related to neither parent.

Relationships between Parental Attributes and Achievement Motivation in High School Students

Examination of relationships between the attributes of parents and their children's achievement motivation is made more complicated because two different forms of the Work and Family Orientation Questionnaire were administered in the high school population. Because of these noncomparable forms, sample sizes are much smaller than in the preceding comparisons.

In the initial examination of parent-child relationships, correlations between students' perceptions of parent masculinity and femininity and the five scales of the WOFO-1 were computed for the 420 males and 562 females for whom these data were available. The magnitude of these correlations was small, the largest r in males being .09 and, in females, .13. These data are not of sufficient interest to warrant tabulation or further exploration, and the remainder of the discussion will deal with the data from the sample given the revised scale, WOFO-2.

Correlations were also computed between parental M and F and the four conceptually cleaner and more reliable scales of the WOFO-2 for the 104 males and 200 females for whom these data were available. Although still modest, several of the correlations obtained with these scales were higher than those with the earlier form and are therefore presented in Table 10-15.

CORRELATIONS WITH PARENTAL MASCULINITY AND FEMININITY

In the case of males, the strongest correlations with the fathers' characteristics are between masculinity (M) and the Competitiveness

Table 10-15. *Correlations between Parental Masculinity and Femininity and the WOFO-2 Scales for 104 Male and 200 Female High School Students*

| | Males | | | | Females | | | |
| | Fathers | | Mothers | | Fathers | | Mothers | |
	M	F	M	F	M	F	M	F
Work	.16	−.08	−.05	.16	.10	.20	.03	.12
Mastery	.07	−.14	−.07	.10	.04	.18	.09	.03
Competitiveness	.21	−.01	.04	.17	.16	.08	.05	.00
Personal Unconcern	.05	−.13	−.03	.10	.15	.24	.07	.07

Note: For $df = 102$, $r_{.05} = .19$; for $df = 198$, $r_{.05} = .14$.

and Work scales. Mothers' F (rather than M) also relates at about the same level to these same two scales. What is intriguing about the correlations is the pattern of their signs. Fathers' M relates positively to all four scales, while Fathers' F relates negatively to each. In contrast, Mothers' F is positively related to all four scales, while M shows a negative relationship with three of the four.

The pattern of results for females is quite different. All correlations with parental attributes are positive, but those with maternal M and F are lower than those with the father's attributes, and none of the maternal correlations is significant. These data imply that the father tends to play a more important role in the development of his daughter's achievement motivation than the mother. The three strongest correlations are between fathers' femininity and Work, Mastery, and Personal Unconcern. Fathers' masculinity is significantly related to Competitiveness (as it was in males) and to Personal Unconcern.

Couple type and achievement motivation. The small sample makes extensive analyses by couple type a precarious undertaking; however, several explorations were conducted. Two indices were formed for the analyses. The first—Work-Mastery—was computed by summing scores on the Work and Mastery scales and making a split at the median of the total sample and assigning respondents to a high or low category. Work and Mastery were combined because of their high intercorrelation and conceptual similarity in order to keep the number of cases per group as high as possible. The second—Competitiveness —was formed by making a similar median split and assignment to category. In the resultant classifications, 53% of the males and 49% of the females were classified as high Work-Mastery, while 53% of the males and 31% of the females were classified as high Competitive, the latter discrepancy reflecting the strong sex difference on this scale. The percentage of students falling in each category of Work-Mastery and Competitiveness for seven of the eight most frequent family types is shown in Table 10-16. (The Undifferentiated-Feminine type had fewer than five cases in each sex and was therefore not considered.)

The results for Work-Mastery bear out the implications found in

Table 10-16. *Percentage of High School Students Given the WOFO-2 Classified as to High or Low Work-Mastery and Competition in the Seven Most Frequent Couple Types*

Couple type (Father-Mother)	Males					Females				
	Work-Mastery Low	High	Competitiveness Low	High	N	Work-Mastery Low	High	Competitiveness Low	High	N
Andro-Andro	42	58	42	58	12	37	63	68	32	38
Andro-Fem	50	50	62	38	8	43	57	43	57	14
Masc-Andro	56	44	39	61	18	54	46	54	46	13
Masc-Fem	24	76	52	48	21	49	51	71	29	35
Masc-Masc	55	45	64	36	11	56	44	81	19	16
Masc-Undiff	70	30	30	70	10	70	30	78	22	23
Undiff-Undiff	60	40	29	71	7	67	33	78	22	9

the pattern of correlations. The largest percentage of highly motivated males (76%) is found in traditional (Masculine-Feminine)
families. The lowest percentage of motivated males is found in
the Masculine-Undifferentiated and Undifferentiated-Undifferentiated
families (30% and 40%, respectively), with the other groups distributed between these extremes. On the other hand, the *largest* percentages of high Competitive males were found in the Undifferentiated-Undifferentiated and Masculine-Undifferentiated families (71%
and 70% respectively), with the percentage of those from traditional
families so classified being among the lowest.

In contrast, the greatest concentration of females high on Work-
Mastery is in the couple types with an Androgynous father (Androgynous-Androgynous and Androgynous-Feminine), rather than in the
traditional Masculine-Feminine couple. This finding parallels the
stronger correlations of both paternal M and F with the achievement
scales. As in males, however, the smallest percentage of those above
the median on Work-Mastery was found in the Masculine-Undifferentiated and Undifferentiated-Undifferentiated couples. These couple
types also produced a low percentage of girls high in Competitiveness,
only the Masculine-Masculine couple being lower.

Given the limited number of students per couple type, it is risky to
speculate on dynamics within family constellations which may determine different expressions of achievement needs. In particular, to
understand more completely parental influence, both the constellation
of achievement needs (i.e., the distribution of scores on all scales)
and the masculinity and femininity of each individual should be considered. Obviously, this could not be attempted in the present, restricted sample.

The data do provide additional evidence for the usefulness of a
multidimensional conception of achievement motivation by suggesting that high Work-Mastery and Competitiveness may occur with differential frequencies in the various couple types.

Summary

1. Using the high school students' ratings of their mothers and
fathers on the M and F scales and the student norms, each parent in
an intact home was classified into one of the four masculinity and
femininity categories. A comparison of these data with students' self-
reports indicated that by and large the two sets of distributions were
similar. Females, however, tended to perceive their mothers as Androgynous more frequently than they so perceived themselves, and
males tended to perceive their fathers as Masculine more frequently
than they so perceived themselves. Reflecting the trends found in students' self-reports, more Upper-class fathers were perceived as Androgynous and fewer as Undifferentiated than in the other socioeconomic groups. Slight and nonsignificant trends in the same
direction were noted in the distribution of mothers.

2. The parents of high school students from intact homes were classified as couples vis-à-vis the masculinity and femininity categories to which each was assigned, an analysis that yielded sixteen possible couple types. The majority of parents fell into traditional or near-traditional categories (i.e., the father-mother types of Androgynous-Androgynous, Androgynous-Feminine, Masculine-Androgynous, and Masculine-Feminine, all combinations in which the father was above the median on M and the mother on F). Four nontraditional father-mother types occurred in 3% or more of the homes of both males and females: Undifferentiated-Undifferentiated, Undifferentiated-Feminine, Masculine-Undifferentiated, and Masculine-Masculine. Only minor differences occurred across the socioeconomic groups in the distribution of the sixteen types.

3. Significant but low correlations were obtained between the high school students' M and F scores and their ratings of each of their parents on the parallel scales. The congruence between the category to which the student and each parent was assigned was also minimal.

4. More revealing relationships occurred when the distributions of the students were related to their parents' couple type in the eight most frequently occurring combinations. In males from the four traditional or near-traditional homes, father-son congruence was high but was moderated to some degree by the mother's classification. In these homes, boys are highly likely to exhibit the masculine characteristics they perceive in their father but are likely to be above the median in feminine characteristics only if one or both of their parents, but particularly the father, is Androgynous. In the two nontraditional types in which the father was perceived as Masculine and the mother as low in F (Masculine or Undifferentiated), there were proportionately fewer Androgynous and proportionately more Undifferentiated males than in the traditional and near-traditional types. This trend continues in the two types in which the father was Undifferentiated, these homes producing the largest percentage of Undifferentiated boys and the smallest percentage of Androgynous. A substantial number of these boys were Masculine, however, suggesting the role of extraparental influences.

The two parents appeared to exert a more equal influence on females. In the traditional and near-traditional homes, Androgyny was most likely to occur when both parents were Androgynous, next most likely when one or the other parent was Androgynous, and least likely in the Masculine-Feminine couple. This decrease was accompanied by a corresponding increase in Undifferentiated and Masculine girls, these results suggesting the importance of the Masculine father in either suppressing the girl's personality development or encouraging the appearance of her father's agentic characteristics at the expense of communal ones. The couple perceived as Undifferentiated-Undifferentiated produced the highest percentage of Undifferentiated girls, followed by the Undifferentiated-Feminine.

5. In an attempt to assess both globally and directly the association between students' perceptions of similarity to their father or mother (parent identification) and to parental characteristics, the results of an item inquiring into their similarity to their parents' ideals were related to couple type. Males from traditional and near-traditional homes were least likely to identify with the mother, the percentages being particularly low in the couple types in which the father was Androgynous. Males from these homes were most likely to identify equally with both parents when the mother was Androgynous. Females from traditional and near-traditional homes were most likely to identify equally with both parents, those not choosing this response selecting the Father and the Mother alternative more equally than males.

More complex relationships occurred in nontraditional homes. Overall, students of both sexes tended to choose the Equal alternative, an outcome that may be inferred to indicate that they did not identify closely with either parent. Identification with the opposite-sex parent was most likely when that parent was perceived as being high in either feminine or masculine characteristics and when the same-sex parent was perceived as low in both.

6. Highly significant differences in mean Self-esteem scores were found in both female and male high school students from the eight most frequent parent combinations. The order of the means followed quite directly from the differences in PAQ distributions associated with couple types. For example, the highest means occurred in students from Androgynous-Androgynous homes and the lowest in students from Undifferentiated homes. There was a tendency for these differences in self-esteem associated with couple type to remain even when students' PAQ category was held constant.

7. In order to determine the replicability of the results with high school students, college students were asked to supply their perceptions of their parents on all three scales of the PAQ as well as their ratings of themselves. Fathers were rated higher (particularly by males) on M and M-F than the male students reported themselves, and mothers were rated (particularly by females) higher on F and lower on M-F than the female students. When the individual parents were classified into the four PAQ categories, the resulting distribution of sixteen couple types was highly similar to that found with high school students. Although several discrepancies were noted in non-traditional homes (probably attributable to small N's), by and large the PAQ distributions of the students within each of the eight most frequent couple types also paralleled the high school data.

8. Self-ratings on the PAQ scales were obtained from the parents of a number of the college students given the questionnaire. Except for the discrepancies noted immediately above, the means produced by the three sets of ratings (student ratings of self and parents, parent self-ratings) were highly comparable, as were correlations between

the PAQ scales. In all cases, M-F was moderately correlated in a positive direction with M and more modestly correlated in a negative direction with F, while M and F showed a very low relationship. For both males and females significant correlations (ranging from .20 to .51) were found between their ratings of their fathers and mothers and their parents' self-ratings, with females tending to be superior predictors of their parents' responses.

9. Distribution of the parents among the sixteen couple types, based on PAQ self-ratings, was quite comparable to that found when assignment was based on student perceptions of their parents. A comparison of the patterns of student PAQ distributions across the most frequent couple types produced by the two types of parent ratings showed that, in males, similar but less clear-cut differences among couple types occurred when parent self-ratings were used to classify couple types. Less satisfactory results were obtained from the females, the patterns observed when parent classification was based on student perceptions all but disappearing when parent self-ratings were substituted. Whether this difference between the sexes is genuine or a psychometric artifact cannot be determined. Whatever the reason, the relationships between students' and parents' PAQ (couple type) are clearly more dramatic when student perceptions are employed.

10. The scales of the WOFO-1 achievement instrument failed to correlate significantly with parental masculinity and femininity. Low but more consistent correlations were found with the more reliable scales—Work, Mastery, Competitiveness, and Personal Unconcern—derived from the WOFO-2. For males, fathers' M correlated positively and fathers' F negatively with all scales, while the mothers' correlations tended to exhibit the opposite pattern of signs. All correlations of parental attributes with the achievement scales were positive for females, but correlations with fathers' attributes were generally stronger than with mothers'.

11. Examination of the distributions of binary classifications of students on Work and Mastery combined and on Competitiveness across the seven most frequent couple types indicated that, in males, high Work-Mastery was found most frequently in traditional (Masculine-Feminine) families and least frequently in Undifferentiated-Undifferentiated and Masculine-Undifferentiated families. High Competitiveness, however, was *most* frequent in these latter couple types. Females with high Work-Mastery were found most often in the families with an Androgynous father and least often in the families with an Undifferentiated mother. Unlike males, females from these latter homes also tended to be low in Competitiveness.

11. Relationships with Parental Behavior and Attitudes

In this chapter we will present the results obtained from the Parental Attitudes Questionnaire given to the sample of high school students. The items on the questionnaire, it will be recalled from Chapter 3, were subjected to a separate factor analysis for each sex. Seven factors emerged from these analyses that were highly similar in both males and females. Scales containing items on which the loadings were high in both sexes were developed to reflect each of these factors. These scales were labeled Father Positivity, Mother Positivity, Father Democracy, Mother Democracy, Rule Enforcement, Family Protectiveness, and Sex-Role Enforcement. (In all instances labels were chosen to describe the high end of the scale.) Two additional factors emerged from each sex that were similar but did not contain a sufficient number of items in common to permit the building of unisexual scales. Four additional scales were therefore developed, two based on the data from males and two on the data from females. The first set of these scales was labeled Male Family Harmony, and Female Family Harmony and Mother Supportiveness, respectively. As the names imply, the primary difference between this pair of scales was the inclusion of a number of items on the female scale relating to the mother's affection, encouragement, and support. Both scales in the second set had to do with setting of standards but had different emphases. The female scale (labeled Female Standards) contained items referring to mother strictness and criticalness and to the setting of "high standards" by both mother and father. The male scale (labeled Male Achievement Standards) included both high standards and achievement-oriented items (e.g., "My mother encouraged me to do my best on everything I did," "If I go on after I finish my education and have a very successful career, my parents will be very pleased"), set within a context of parental encouragement and support (e.g., "I feel that my father has almost always approved of me and the things I do"). In order to determine whether scales based on a factor analysis of data from one sex would reveal meaningful relationships when applied to data from the other sex, scores were obtained for all students on all eleven parent behavior scales. It will also be recalled from Chapter 3 that a second-order factor analysis revealed three similar factors for each sex. These may be labeled Mother and Family Acceptance, Father Acceptance, and Strictness of Family Rules and Standards.

Correlations with the PAQ, Self-esteem, and Attitudes toward Women Measures

The correlation matrix between scores on the eleven parent behavior scales and the students' scores on the three PAQ scales, the Self-esteem measure, and the Attitudes toward Women Scale (AWS) may be seen in Table 11-1.

Table 11-1. *Intercorrelations of PAQ Scales, Self-esteem, and AWS with Parent Behavior Scales for High School Students*

Parent Behavior scales	PAQ categories				
	M	F	M-F	Self-esteem	AWS
Fa Posit					
Males	.22	.13	.04	.27	.03
Females	.16	.15	.04	.25	−.06
Mo Posit					
Males	.19	.12	.04	.20	.11
Females	.12	.17	−.02	.21	.00
Fa Democ					
Males	.18	−.01	.06	.18	.07
Females	.02	.09	.01	.09	−.05
Mo Democ					
Males	.12	.09	−.05	.16	.08
Females	.12	.15	.00	.24	−.08
Rule Enforce					
Males	−.02	.10	−.05	.04	.02
Females	.10	.09	−.02	.07	−.02
Fam Protect					
Males	−.10	.06	−.19	−.11	.04
Females	−.04	.07	−.03	.00	−.14
Sex-Role					
Males	.04	.05	.04	.01	−.27
Females	−.12	.02	−.10	−.13	−.36
Male Fam Harm					
Males	.07	.06	−.04	.10	−.02
Females	.11	.14	−.01	.21	−.12
Fem Fam Harm					
Males	.27	.20	.02	.33	.04
Females	.19	.21	−.03	.30	−.04
Male Ach					
Males	.28	.21	.01	.34	.05
Females	.21	.17	.00	.30	.01
Fem Stand					
Males	.00	.06	−.03	.06	−.11
Females	.08	−.07	.05	.06	.00

Note: For $df = 530$, $r_{.05} = .08$.

In both sexes, but to a somewhat greater degree in males, relatively small but usually significant correlations were found between the M scale and the scales related to the second-order factors of Mother and Family Acceptance and Father Acceptance: Father and Mother Positivity, Father and Mother Democracy, Female Family Harmony and Mother Supportiveness (hereafter referred to as Female Family Harmony), and Male Achievement Standards. Essentially orthogonal relationships were found between M and the remaining parent scales.

The pattern of correlations of the students' F scores with the parent scales was similar to that obtained with M scores, although the values tended to be even lower and less often significant. Few significant correlations were found with the M-F scale.

As anticipated, the parent scales significantly correlated with M and F were also related to the TSBI Self-esteem measure, with correlations being somewhat higher in most instances than the values obtained with the M and F scales alone. The relationships of the parent behavior measures with the Attitudes toward Women Scale were essentially orthogonal except for the Sex-Role Enforcement scale. Students of both sexes who were more traditional in their attitudes toward women's roles tended to have fathers and mothers more traditional in their attitudes and more concerned about sex-role training.

In a later section, comparisons will be made of the scores on the parent behavior scales obtained from the students assigned to the four PAQ masculinity and femininity groups.

Sex and Class Differences in Parent Behavior

To determine whether reports of parent behaviors differed among the socioeconomic groups, the mean z scores on each of the scales were determined separately for males and females and compared across the four classes. These values, along with the p values obtained from simple analyses of variance comparing the means of the four classes for each sex, are shown in Table 11-2.

For females, differences that are significant ($p < .05$) or of borderline significance ($p < .20$) occurred on all scales except Male Family Harmony and Rule Enforcement. Lower-class or Lower- and Lower-middle-class females reported that their fathers and mothers were less positive and less democratic and that the family was less harmonious (Female scale) than females from the other socioeconomic groups. Lower- and Lower-middle-class parents were also perceived as having lower achievement standards and as being more traditional about sex roles and more protective.

Similar class differences were noted in males on the scales related to achievement standards, sex roles, and protectiveness. With the exception of Rule Enforcement, on which Upper-class parents were the most strict and Lower-class parents the least, nonsignificant differences occurred among the socioeconomic groups on the remaining scales, although the trend of the means paralleled the differences found in females.

Table 11-2. *Mean z Scores on Parent Behavior Scales by Social Class for High School Students and p Values from Analyses of Variance*

Parent scale	Males					Females				
	p	Upper	Upper mid	Lower mid	Lower	p	Upper	Upper mid	Lower mid	Lower
Fa Posit		.14	.02	−.02	−.15	<.09	.22	.07	−.04	−.08
Fa Democ		.09	.00	.02	−.21	<.04	.13	.09	−.08	−.19
Mo Posit		−.09	.09	.04	−.20	<.004	−.01	.19	−.05	−.19
Mo Democ		.03	.00	−.08	−.03	<.16	.01	.09	−.03	−.14
Rule Enforce	<.03	.26	.06	−.14	−.20		.12	−.03	−.04	−.01
Fam Protect	<.10	−.04	−.10	−.01	.28	<.0001	−.22	−.17	.10	.26
Sex-Role	<.008	−.29	.04	.13	.33	<.0001	−.28	−.13	.19	.23
Male Fam Harm		.02	−.02	−.11	.17		.10	.01	−.06	−.09
Fem Fam Harm		.16	.06	.05	−.09	<.001	.12	.20	−.05	−.25
Male Ach	<.11	.27	.07	.03	−.20	<.0001	.28	.21	−.04	−.30
Fem Stand		.17	.02	−.07	.10	<.02	.29	.02	−.05	−.11

In summary, class differences were not large, particularly in males, but they were generally congruent with the results of prior studies relating child-rearing to socioeconomic variables (e.g., Minton, Kagan, & Levine 1971; Radin 1972; Sears, Maccoby, & Levin 1957). The stronger child acceptance exhibited by the upper socioeconomic groups in comparison to the lower groups is similar (though less marked) to that reported earlier for the Androgynous couples vs. the nontraditional couples and may be associated with the tendency of Androgynous parents of both sexes to appear more frequently in the upper socioeconomic groups.

Comparisons were also made of the data provided by female and male students in each PAQ category. Since the numbers of each sex and the distribution of the sexes across PAQ categories were not equal, means of the raw scores on each scale were found for the males and females in each of the four categories, and these data were subjected to 2 (male vs. female) by 4 (PAQ category) analyses of variance. (The means and results of these analyses are presented in Table I of Appendix E.)

We will consider at this point the differences between the sexes in their perceptions of their parents' behavior and the interactions between sex and PAQ category. Discussion of the relationships for each sex between the parent behavior scales and the students' PAQ category will be postponed until a later section.

The absence of a significant main effect for sex or of a significant interaction of sex with PAQ category was noted for only two scales: Rule Enforcement and Male Achievement Standards. In a third scale —Male Family Harmony—no main effect for sex was observed, but sex did interact with PAQ category. The data for the two sexes were parallel, however, in the sense that in both there was less family harmony in the homes of Undifferentiated and cross-typed students (Masculine girls, Feminine boys) than in the homes of Androgynous and conventionally sex-typed students. On the remaining scales, significant or near-significant sex differences were found, males, in comparison to females, reporting that their parents were more concerned about sex-role training, had stricter standards (Female Standards scale), and were less positive, democratic, and protective. In the absence of direct behavioral observation, it is unclear whether parents are actually less accepting and more demanding of males than of females or whether males more actively resist and resent parental control, particularly in adolescence, and therefore perceive their parents differently or elicit more negative behavior from their parents. A survey of the parent-child literature (see, e.g., Martin 1975) lends credence to each of these possibilities.

Parent Behavior and Identification

The relationship between the Parental Attitudes scales and students' identification with their father or mother was examined by determining the mean z score on each scale for the males and females choosing each of the three alternatives on the question about similarity to the father's or mother's ideals. These data, along with the results of simple analyses of variance, are shown in Table 11-3.

For males, significant (p's $< .05$) differences were found for the Father Positivity and Father Democracy scales, and a difference of borderline significance ($p = .09$) was found for the Male Family Harmony scale. In all instances, the means of the males who chose the Father alternative were highest and the means of those who chose the Mother alternative lowest.

In females, the Positivity and Democracy scales for both the father and the mother were significant. On the two Father scales, those selecting the Father alternative rated their fathers highest in positivity and democracy, while those selecting the Mother alternative rated their fathers lowest. The reverse pattern of identification was found for the Mother scales, those selecting the Mother alternative having the highest means on Mother Positivity and Democracy and those selecting the Father alternative having the lowest means. Three additional scales were also significant for females. On the Female Family Harmony scale, those identifying with the mother have the highest mean (a mirror image of the results for males on the Male Family Harmony scale) and those choosing the Equal alternative have the lowest mean, a result probably reflecting rejection of both parents. On the Female Standards scale, mother-identified girls have the lowest means and father-identified girls the highest, suggesting that strong pressure on the females in the ways specified by this scale was more likely to lead to alienation from the mother and to father identification. On the Rule Enforcement scale, those who chose the Equal alternative had the highest mean, a result that is not easy to interpret since it is probable that the individuals in this category were a mixture of those who perceive themselves as equally similar and as equally dissimilar to their parents.

Parent Behavior and Student Masculinity and Femininity Classification

We will examine here the relationships for each sex between parent behaviors and the masculinity and femininity category to which the students were assigned. The mean z scores on each parent scale for each of the four PAQ categories for male and female students are shown in Table 11-4.

In males, the means of all four categories are close to the overall mean of the Sex-Role and Female Standards scales, and analyses of variance indicated that they do not differ significantly. On all the remaining scales, significant ($p < .05$) differences were found. Inspection of Table 11-4 shows that the Androgynous group falls near the overall mean on the Protectiveness scales but is above average on the rest of the scales, particularly on Female Family Harmony and Male

Table 11-3. *Mean z Scores on Parent Behavior Scales in Each Category of Similarity in Ideals (Father, Mother, or Equal to Both) for High School Students and Results of Analyses of Variance*

Scale	p	Males Fa	Equal	Mo	p	Females Fa	Equal	Mo
Fa Posit	<.0001	.26	−.07	−.39	<.0001	.35	.06	−.40
Mo Posit		.00	.04	.08	<.0001	−.31	.04	.27
Fa Democ	<.0001	.30	−.04	−.43	<.0001	.34	.04	−.06
Mo Democ		−.27	−.32	−.22	<.0001	−.36	−.20	−.01
Rule Enforce		.02	.00	.02	<.03	−.11	.11	−.09
Fam Protect	<.18	−.36	−.34	−.17	<.12	−.15	−.28	−.29
Sex-Role	<.24	.02	−.07	.13		−.02	.00	.00
Male Fam Harm	<.09	−.20	−.33	−.40		−.16	−.19	−.25
Fem Fam Harm		.03	−.02	.13	<.0001	−.19	−.34	.24
Male Ach		.06	−.04	.02		.03	.01	−.01
Fem Stand	<.28	−.04	−.11	.08	<.006	.16	−.03	−.16

Table 11-4. *Mean z Scores on Parent Behavior Scales for High School Students in Each PAQ Category and Results of Analyses of Variance*

	PAQ category									
	Males					Females				
Scale	p	Undiff	Fem	Masc	Andro	p	Undiff	Fem	Masc	Andro
Fa Posit	<.001	−.21	−.22	.02	.24	<.001	−.30	−.02	−.08	.22
Mo Posit	<.001	−.29	−.08	.07	.20	<.0001	−.20	.00	−.18	.18
Fa Democ	<.007	−.18	−.29	.12	.08	<.0001	−.09	.07	−.20	.08
Mo Democ	<.01	−.22	.14	.01	.09	<.0001	−.18	−.02	−.13	.17
Rule Enforce	<.15	−.01	.22	−.08	.10	<.01	−.25	.00	−.06	.12
Fam Protect	<.035	.08	.26	−.10	−.03	<.22	.03	.02	−.17	.01
Sex-Role		−.07	−.03	.03	.02	<.06	.02	.12	−.07	−.09
Male Fam Harm		−.06	−.07	.00	.05	<.0001	−.15	−.03	−.15	.18
Fem Fam Harm	<.0001	−.31	−.11	.03	.31	<.0001	−.32	−.02	−.21	.27
Male Ach	<.0001	−.27	−.06	.01	.29	<.0001	−.34	−.05	−.01	.24
Fem Stand		.02	−.02	−.09	.06	<.01	−.06	−.08	.26	−.01

Achievement Standards. The Masculine males are lower than the Androgynous group on all but one of these scales (Father Democracy), and their means cluster around the overall mean. The lowest means tend to be found in the Undifferentiated group.

Particularly instructive data in Table 11-4 are those obtained with the Feminine group, since the low frequency of cross-typed males and their wide distribution across parent couple types permit them to be studied only *en masse*. The means for these males are negative but still close to the average on Mother Positivity, Male and Female Family Harmony, and Male Achievement Standards. However, they are discernibly below average on Father Positivity and Democracy and above average on Mother Democracy, Rule Enforcement, and Protectiveness. (In fact, on these latter scales their means are higher than those of any other group.) Feminine boys, then, tend to come from protective, nonpermissive homes in which the mother is relatively warm and accepting but the father is less emotionally supportive and more authoritarian. The profile of parent behaviors (particularly father behaviors) for these Feminine boys is less favorable than reported by Kelly and Worell (1976) in their study of college students using the PRF Androgyny scale. Their results, as we described in Chapter 9, did suggest, however, that the mothers of Feminine males were more actively involved with their sons than were the fathers. Examination of the responses of these high school boys to the question about the parent whom they resembled in ideals revealed that, despite their more benign treatment by their mother, they were not particularly different from the other groups in the percentage who identified with her. Only 18% of the Feminine boys indicated that they were more similar to their mothers, a figure somewhat greater than found in Masculine boys (12%) but somewhat less than in Undifferentiated boys (20%).

In girls, nonsignificant differences were found among the PAQ groups for Protectiveness, and differences of borderline significance were found ($p = .06$) for Sex-Role. On the latter, the Feminine group deviated from the others in the direction of more traditional sex-role emphasis. On the remaining scales (on all of which the groups differed significantly), the Androgynous girls were markedly above average on all but the Female Standards scale, and the Feminine girls were about average. In contrast, the Masculine girls were below average, and the Undifferentiated girls tended to have the lowest means of all. This ordering of means—Androgynous highest followed by sex-traditional, cross-sex, and, finally, Undifferentiated—is parallel to what was found in males.

Again, the individuals in the cross-sex category are of particular interest. As was described above, on the scales relating to Father and Mother Positivity, Father and Mother Democracy, and Family Harmony, the means for these Masculine girls were below average, although generally not as low as those for the Undifferentiated groups. They differed most strikingly from those in the other PAQ categories in their high score on the Female Standards scale. They were only average, however, on the Male Achievement scale, suggesting that, while Masculine girls were treated strictly and expected to meet high standards of behavior, these behaviors did not necessarily involve conventional achievement-oriented activities. To throw further light on this finding, one particular item that appeared on the Male Achievement scale—"If I go on after I finish my education and have a very successful career, my parents will be very pleased"—was selected for specific analysis. The means for this item did differ significantly among the female PAQ groups, but this result was primarily attributable to the very high scores obtained by the Androgynous girls in comparison to other categories. The mean of the Masculine girls was similar to those for girls classified as Feminine or Undifferentiated. These results also differ in critical respects from those reported by Kelly and Worell (1976) for Masculine college women, particularly with respect to encouragement of achievement behaviors. The inclusion of items on the PRF Androgyny scale that go beyond instrumental and expressive attributes may be responsible for these discrepancies.

Parent Behaviors and Couple Type

It seemed quite likely that the various PAQ couple types, as defined by their children's perceptions, would also be reported to differ in their behaviors. The mean scores on each of the parent behavior scales were therefore determined for each of the eight most frequent couple categories. (Data from the parents of females and males were analyzed separately.)

Since the scales have different numbers of items, the means were converted to z scores (based on means and standard deviations of the total group of males or the total group of females) to facilitate comparisons across scales. These converted means, together with the results of simple analyses of variance, are reported in Table 11-5. Differences between the reported parent behaviors for the various couple types may be observed that are even more striking than those found with students' masculinity and femininity category.

Significant differences were found among the couple types in all comparisons except Rule Enforcement and Female Standards in males and Family Protectiveness in females. (Even in these comparisons, however, the F values were of borderline significance.)

The first group of scales to which attention will be called in discussing these differences includes Father Positivity and Democracy, Mother Positivity and Democracy, Male Family Harmony, and Female Family Harmony and Mother Supportiveness (hereafter referred to only as Female Family Harmony). The couples perceived as Androgynous-Androgynous and Androgynous-Feminine are reported to be high in all these factors by both males and females. In the homes with parents perceived as Masculine-Androgynous, the means on this cluster of scales were quite consistently lower, particularly in females, than in homes with an Androgynous father. In the Masculine-Feminine homes, this downward trend continues, even the Feminine mother being reported as less positive and less democratic than her Feminine or Androgynous counterparts who are married to Androgynous men.

In all four nontraditional types, both parents tend to be low on all the scales under discussion (z scores for the means are, with a single exception, negative in sign in both sexes). The Undifferentiated fathers tend to be lowest in Positivity and Democracy, as are the Undifferentiated mothers. Thus, overall, the homes in which both parents are Undifferentiated are reported as being the least supportive, democratic, and harmonious.

A similar pattern is noted in both sexes for the Male Achievement scale, the means for the homes with Androgynous fathers tending to have the highest values of the eight types, those for the Masculine-Feminine couples being close to the overall mean, and, finally, those for the Undifferentiated-Undifferentiated couples having the lowest values. For the Female Standards scale, however, the couples perceived as Masculine-Masculine and Masculine-Undifferentiated are strictest with their daughters, and the Masculine-Masculine couples are strictest with their sons; no discernible trends differentiate the other groups.

The Family Protectiveness scale yielded less than enlightening data for females. Masculine-Masculine and Undifferentiated-Undifferenti-

Table 11-5. *Mean z Scores for Parent Behavior Scales for the Eight Most Frequent Couple Types and Results of Analysis of Variance for High School Students from Intact Families*

Couple type (Father-Mother)	Fa Posit	Mo Posit	Fa Democ	Mo Democ	Rule Enforce
			Males		
Andro-Andro	.92	.62	.69	.33	.10
Andro-Fem	.84	.51	.99	.05	.00
Masc-Andro	.18	.44	.02	−.07	.11
Masc-Fem	.00	.14	−.20	−.19	.17
Masc-Masc	−.22	−.42	.04	−.64	−.01
Masc-Undiff	−.33	−.22	−.22	−.75	−.19
Undiff-Fem	−.77	−.10	−.34	−.40	−.22
Undiff-Undiff	−.52	−.55	−.34	−.74	−.27
p	<.0001	<.0001	<.0001	<.0001	<.09
			Females		
Andro-Andro	.70	.46	.53	.27	.10
Andro-Fem	.81	.55	.51	.32	.04
Masc-Andro	−.13	.32	−.19	.12	.10
Masc-Fem	−.17	.25	−.24	−.12	−.15
Masc-Masc	−.45	−.52	−.32	−.78	.16
Masc-Undiff	−.62	−1.10	−.74	−1.12	.32
Undiff-Fem	−.78	−.11	−.55	−.47	−.30
Undiff-Undiff	−.77	−.62	−.17	−.90	−.30
p	<.0001	<.0001	<.0001	<.0001	<.04

ated parents were least protective of girls, but the differences among the parent groups as a whole did not reach significance. Minimally significant differences did occur in males, couples in which the father was Masculine tending to be less protective than the others.

Special attention will be called to the Rule Enforcement scale. In both males and females, the couple types with the lowest means were those in which the fathers were perceived as Undifferentiated. Although the parents in these homes are reported as being relatively nonsupportive and authoritarian, they also appear to be perceived as ineffectual enforcers of discipline and family rules. These results are reminiscent of the Kelly and Worell (1976) findings that students classified as Undifferentiated on the PRF ANDRO scale (many of whom, one suspects, perceived their fathers as Undifferentiated) reported their parents to be relatively powerless in control of resources and in disciplinary matters.

Finally, differences were found in both sexes on the Sex-Role scale, a scale that contains items referring to each parent's attitudes toward "women's lib" and their concern about their children playing with opposite-sex toys when they were young. In males, the couples in which the father was perceived as Masculine were rated highest in this factor (i.e., were most traditional). A different pattern was exhibited in the females' data. Most permissive about sex roles were

ct	Sex-Role	Male Fam Harm	Fem Fam Harm	Male Ach	Fem Stand
			Males		
7	−.07	.51	.92	.78	−.09
7	−.34	.09	.39	.32	−.50
1	.10	−.14	.51	.46	−.12
4	.12	−.34	.15	.14	−.06
6	.18	−.62	−.39	−.16	.20
5	.24	−.60	−.58	−.60	−.20
4	−.33	−.97	−.41	−.37	−.34
0	−.29	−.53	−.75	−.85	−.10
5	<.01	<.0001	<.0001	<.0001	<.09
			Females		
7	−.24	.36	.55	.49	−.18
9	−.15	.53	.67	.52	−.18
3	.10	.04	.50	.35	.02
0	.02	−.32	.16	.12	−.19
2	−.06	−.65	−.62	−.51	.28
5	.29	−.87	−.99	−.62	.60
6	.16	−.75	−.20	−.28	−.27
3	.44	−1.02	−.97	−1.10	−.17
1	<.001	<.0001	<.0001	<.0001	<.0001

the couples in which the father was Androgynous, and most traditional were the couples in which one or both parents were Undifferentiated.

Constellations of Parent Behaviors

We have shown that the distributions of students among the four PAQ categories based on M and F scores are related both to the patterns of parent behaviors they report and to the parents' joint classification with respect to these PAQ categories (perceived couple type). Couple type and parent behaviors are, in turn, related to each other. Either of these perceived parental variables could be primarily responsible for the association with the students' masculinity and femininity category, the other being a correlated variable with no direct causal significance. It seems more likely, however, that both variables make a contribution, both independently and in interaction with each other.

In part to assess these possibilities and in part to clarify further the relationships between perceived parent behaviors and attributes, we sought to identify a series of constellations of parent behaviors that could be specified independently of parent classification on the PAQ scales. The methodological problem was to find combinations of the expression of parent behaviors that occur with considerable frequency and that are systematically related to other criterion attributes in the child.

For this purpose, we used Self-esteem as the criterion because of its psychometric property of being a continuous, normally distributed variable in both sexes, while at the same time being related to PAQ category. Initial analyses using stepwise multiple regression suggested that complex interactions were probably occurring in the equation as striking changes in the magnitude and even signs of beta weights resulted as scales were added to the equation. Therefore, to isolate the interactions between scales, we employed as the analytic tool the Automatic Interaction Detection (AID) technique of Sonquist, Baker, and Morgan (1973).[1] In this technique, the subject population is first split on the best predictor; then the resultant subject groups are *independently* split on the best predictor for each group, and so forth. Thus, the technique can detect complex interactions that would not be seen in stepwise linear regression.

1. These AID analyses were conducted using the computer program developed by L. L. Gooch (1972). The program permits isolation of the maximum amount of criterion variance through a splitting process on independent variables based on maximizing the between groups' sum of squares while minimizing the within sum of squares. The technique is designed for large N studies and is somewhat unreliable when applied to samples of less than one thousand. Although aware of a violation of this rule of thumb, we used the technique as a heuristic to isolate constellations of parental behaviors with a strong relationship to self-esteem.

The AID program was run using nine of the eleven parent behavior scales as predictors (Male and Female Family Harmony scales were dropped because of collinearity with several other scales). Separate analyses were conducted for males and females and resulted in nine discrete patterns for males and eleven for females. Not all predictors entered into the solution, and varying numbers entered into the determination of each group of parents. The groups defined by the AID program thus consist of students with parents showing the program-defined clusters of attributes.

This procedure can be illustrated by giving an example of a constellation defined by the program. One group of males with high Self-esteem was defined by splits on the Male Achievement, Democratic Mother, and Father Positivity scales. High Self-esteem was associated with higher values for the Achievement and Mother factors, with the splits occurring at z values of $-.17$ and $.49$, respectively. High Self-esteem was, however, associated with *less* than extreme paternal positivity, the program selecting respondents with z scores of *less* than $.97$ on this variable.

Having identified the males who fell into each of the nine parent behavior constellations and the females who fell into each of the eleven constellations, we computed for each sex the mean z score on each of the eleven parent behavior scales (including the two dropped from the AID run). These values, along with the mean Self-esteem scores, for each constellation are shown in Table II, Appendix E. For each sex, the family constellations are ordered according to mean Self-esteem score, Constellation 1 having the highest score, Constellation 2 the next highest score, etc.

In both sexes, Constellation 1 is highest in the cluster of scales having to do with Father and Mother Positivity and Democracy, Male Family Harmony and Female Family Harmony, and is high, if not highest, on Male Achievement. Conversely, the constellation that produces the lowest Self-esteem in both sexes is low on all these scales. (In females, Constellation 1 families were also least traditional on the Sex-Role scale and Constellation 11 most traditional.) The constellations between the two extremes show other patterns. For example, Constellations 3 and 4 in males, whose Self-esteem means are almost identical, have generally similar values on the scales except for Father and Mother Positivity and Democracy. In Constellation 3, the father is only average on these scales and the mother is above average while, in Constellation 4, the father is somewhat above average and the mother is below average. Since our primary interest is not in the constellations per se, we will not attempt to describe them further.

The association between these constellations of parent behaviors and the eight most frequent couple types (based on PAQ classification) was next determined for each sex. In Table 11-6, the families of males belonging to each constellation are broken down by couple type. Inspection of the table shows, for example, that 44% of the couples exhibiting Behavior Constellation 1 are Androgynous-Androgynous, even though only 14% of the eight types of couples fall into this category. Similarly, 7% of the couples are Androgynous-Feminine but go to make up 12% of the couples in the first constellation; the parallel figures for Undifferentiated-Undifferentiated couples are 14% vs. 0%. Inspection of Table 11-6 indicates that, in general, couples in which one or both parents are Androgynous are over-represented in the constellations producing the highest Self-esteem. As one moves down the couple types in the order listed, overrepresentation shifts to the middle constellations and then, in the types in which the father is Undifferentiated, to the lower constellations, that is, those associated with the lowest Self-esteem.

Considerable variability in patterns of behavior exists within each couple type, however. The intratype variability in males is most clearly shown in Table 11-7. This table reports the percentage *within each couple type* exhibiting each behavioral constellation. In the Androgynous-Androgynous couples, for example, the largest proportion, 31%, fell into Behavior Constellation 1, but some Androgynous-Androgynous parents of males can be found in every constellation but the lowest. At the other extreme, 49% of the Undifferentiated-Undifferentiated couples are in the lowest constellation, but some couples of this type are found in all constellations but the first.

Parallel data for females are found in Tables 11-8 and 11-9. The data for the sexes are similar in that the higher ranked constellations tend to be predominantly composed of couples in which one or both parents are Androgynous and the lower ranked constellations tend to be predominantly composed of couples in which the father is Undifferentiated (see Table 11-8). The most notable difference between the sexes is observed in Tables 11-7 vs. 11-9. In males, Constellation 1 was the modal pattern in Androgynous-Androgynous couples. In females, the mode for these couples was Constellation 5, 43% falling into this classification. Other female groups were similarly displaced downward; the mode in Androgynous-Feminine couples, for example, was also Constellation 5. Although the "best" couple types made up

Table 11-6. *Distribution (in Percent) of PAQ Couple Types within Each Behavioral Constellation for High School Males*

Couple type	Behavioral Constellation									
(Father-Mother)	1	2	3	4	5	6	7	8	9	Total %*
Andro-Andro	44	36	28	10	6	15	4	9	0	14
Andro-Fem	12	13	0	9	6	7	0	11	1	7
Masc-Andro	23	30	24	39	18	21	15	14	4	22
Masc-Fem	12	7	28	25	21	18	4	20	15	18
Masc-Masc	7	7	10	8	18	10	35	6	14	11
Masc-Undiff	2	7	3	5	27	8	23	13	15	10
Undiff-Fem	0	0	3	2	0	7	4	4	8	4
Undiff-Undiff	0	0	3	2	3	15	15	24	42	14

*These figures represent the percentage of each couple type within the total group of eight types.

most of the families falling into the first four constellations for females, the frequencies of these constellations were relatively small.

The percentage of females and males falling into each of the four PAQ categories within each behavioral constellation is shown in Table 11-10. In general, constellations producing the highest Self-esteem have the highest percentage of Androgynous individuals of both sexes and the lowest percentage of Undifferentiated individuals. As one goes down the constellations, the percentage of Androgynous individuals decreases, and elevations occur in the sex-traditional (Masculine for males, Feminine for females) and Undifferentiated categories. In the lowest constellations, the percentage of Undifferentiated students is elevated further, primarily at the expense of the traditional and Androgynous categories. Since Self-esteem and PAQ category are highly related, these results were to be anticipated.

To a large extent, the pattern of PAQ distributions across behavioral constellations parallels those found when the breakdown is by couple types (see Table 11-6). The analysis is instructive primarily in showing more refined groupings of parent behaviors and their relationship to masculinity and femininity and does nothing to disentangle the influence of perceived parent behaviors and attributes on the attributes of their children. An analysis that would throw light on the independent contribution of these two parental variables is one in which the kind of constellation by PAQ category breakdown shown in Table 11-10 is conducted separately for each couple type. Such a breakdown, however, would require a considerably larger sample than was available. Approximations of these analyses were carried out, however. In these analyses, three representative couple types with sufficient N were selected for further study: Androgynous-Androgynous, Masculine-Feminine, and Undifferentiated-Undifferentiated. The numbers assigned to the behavioral constellations, it will be recalled, reflected their rank based on the mean Self-esteem scores of students belonging to each correlation. Within each couple type, the cumulative frequency of the students assigned to the ranked constellations was determined, and the constellations were divided into an Upper (high Self-esteem) and a Lower (low Self-esteem) group. The distribution of the students assigned to the Upper and Lower groups across PAQ category was then determined.

In males, the split into Upper and Lower Groups for each couple type was based on the closest possible approximation to a median split. It may be seen in Table 11-11 that, in Androgynous-Androgynous couples, the Upper group of behavioral constellations primarily results in more Androgynous and fewer Masculine sons than the Lower group. In the Masculine-Feminine couples, the Upper group yielded more Androgynous and Masculine and fewer Feminine and Undifferentiated sons than the Lower group. Both of these analyses suggest that perceived parent behaviors contribute to sons' masculinity and femininity, even when couple type is held constant. It will also be noticed, however, that differences still remain between the Androgynous-Androgynous and Masculine-Feminine couples. This difference is in part a function of a different constellation split for the two types,

Constellations 1 to 3 constituting the Upper group for Androgynous-Androgynous and Constellations 1 to 4 for Masculine-Feminine couples. However, when the data were reanalyzed for the latter group, so that Constellations 1 to 3 vs. 4 to 9 were compared in both couple types, differences still remained. For example, of the males with Masculine-Feminine parents, 33% in Constellations 1 to 3 and 19% in Constellations 4 to 9 were classified as Androgynous. The comparable figures for those with Androgynous parents are 55% and 41%. Such data suggest that both parent attributes and behaviors may independently contribute to sons' characteristics.

The data produced by the analysis of the Undifferentiated-Undifferentiated couples are interesting in two respects. First, the Upper group contains more Androgynous and fewer Undifferentiated and Feminine boys than the Lower, again suggesting the importance of parent behaviors. But the Lower group contained the same substantial proportion of Masculine boys (41%) despite the low degree of masculine attributes perceived in either parent and the unfavorable pattern of parent behaviors. Both here and in previous analyses, we have been unsuccessful in pinpointing the factors that determine whether the sons of Undifferentiated-Undifferentiated couples will be Undifferentiated or Masculine (the modal categories). One strong possibility is that the Masculine boys have adopted extraparental models to emulate or have received emotional support from others that has made the development of masculine attributes possible.

A similar analysis was performed for females. Because of the high proportion of females with Androgynous-Androgynous parents within a middle-ranked constellation (5), a median split was not possible. Instead, the females in the modal category and above (Constellations 1–5) were assigned to the Upper group and those below to the Lower group. Females from Masculine-Feminine homes tended to cluster in Constellations 4 to 6. Those in Constellation 6 and above were therefore assigned to the Upper group. In like fashion, the modal categories for those with Undifferentiated parents were Constellations 9 and 11. Constellations 1 to 8 were therefore designated as the Upper

Table 11-7. *Distribution (in Percent) of Constellations of Parent Behaviors within Each PAQ Couple Type for Male High School Students*

Constellation	Andro-Andro	Andro-Fem	Masc-Andro	Masc-F¢
1	31	17	10	6
2	10	7	5	1
3	13	0	7	10
4	18	33	43	33
5	3	7	6	8
6	15	13	13	13
7	2	0	4	1
8	8	20	8	13
9	0	3	3	15

group for these individuals and 9 to 11 as the Lower. The distributions across PAQ categories for each of these groups are also shown
in Table 11-11. In all three couple types, proportionally more Androgynous and fewer Undifferentiated girls were found in the Upper than
in the Lower groups, again suggesting the influence of parent behavior, with couple type held constant. A reanalysis of the Masculine-
Feminine group in which the constellation split matched that of the
Androgynous-Androgynous group revealed, as did the parallel analysis in males, that couple type continued to be related to the girls' PAQ
category, particularly in the Upper group (1–5). In the latter, 60%
of the females with Androgynous parents were Androgynous and 3%
were Undifferentiated, as opposed to 28% and 21%, respectively, for
those with Masculine-Feminine parents.

BEHAVIORAL CONSTELLATIONS AND SELF-ESTEEM

The behavioral constellations were built around relationships between
the parent behavior scales and the Self-esteem measure. We were interested in determining whether Self-esteem differences among behavioral constellations would continue to be observed if the PAQ category to which students were assigned was taken into account or
whether they would disappear. Accordingly, the mean Self-esteem
score was found for students in each of the four masculinity and
femininity categories within each of the behavioral constellations.
These means are reported in Table 11-12. Despite the small N's in a
number of cells (those with five cases or less are identified by an
asterisk), systematic trends can be noted in each PAQ category. Mean
Self-esteem tends to decrease from the first to the lowest ranked behavioral constellation for those in each PAQ category. These trends
are much more marked than in the parallel analyses for each of the
eight couple types (see Table 10-9). The data thus support two conclusions. First, perceived parent behaviors may affect Self-esteem independently of perceived parental attributes. Second, the influence of

Masc-Masc	Masc-Undiff	Undiff-Fem	Undiff-Undiff	Total N
6	2	0	0	48
2	2	0	2	21
10	2	6	2	38
17	11	12	3	131
12	20	0	2	41
12	11	25	15	93
17	13	6	7	28
6	15	12	21	63
19	24	38	49	97

Table 11-8. Distribution (in Percent) of PAQ Couple Types within Each Behavioral Constellation for High School Females

Couple type (Father-Mother)	Behavioral Constellation											Total %*
	1	2	3	4	5	6	7	8	9	10	11	
Andro-Andro	51	32	44	19	15	53	38	8	12	8	7	26
Andro-Fem	22	21	13	5	12	13	10	2	2	3	2	8
Masc-Andro	19	26	22	26	27	13	10	19	10	16	10	18
Masc-Fem	8	21	14	31	19	9	10	27	21	28	12	19
Masc-Masc	0	0	2	5	0	3	10	11	10	8	14	6
Masc-Undiff	0	0	3	4	8	9	13	22	22	15	25	11
Undiff-Fem	0	0	3	8	8	0	0	5	3	16	8	5
Undiff-Undiff	0	0	0	1	12	0	10	6	20	5	22	6

*These figures represent the percentage of each couple type within the total group of eight types.

parent behaviors on Self-esteem does not appear to be completely mediated through their influence on students' masculinity and femininity; even when PAQ category is held constant, striking differences in
Self-esteem across behavioral constellations continue to be observed.

Parent Behaviors and Achievement Motivation

Correlations were computed between the eleven parent behavior scales
and the achievement scales derived from WOFO-1 and WOFO-2.
Paralleling results obtained with parental attributes, correlations were
generally small. Again the relationships with the more reliable scales
of WOFO-2 tended to be larger and more consistent, and further
analyses were limited to the sample completing this instrument. Correlations with the WOFO-2 scales are shown in Table 11-13.

In males, significant correlations occurred most frequently with
the Competitiveness scale, positive relationships (ranging from .24 to
.30) being found with Father Positivity, Male Family Harmony, Female Family Harmony, and Male Achievement. For females, significant correlations were found most frequently with the Work scale,
positive relationships (ranging from .14 to .31) being found with
Father Positivity, Mother Democracy, Rule Enforcement, Male and
Female Family Harmony, Female Standards, and Male Achievement.
A number of positive correlations from the group of parent scales just
described were also found in females with the Mastery and Personal
Unconcern scales. Most consistently implicated in relationships with
the WOFO scales in females were Father Positivity and Male Achievement, these scales being significantly correlated with Work, Mastery,
and Personal Unconcern. In males, these two scales correlated only
with Competitiveness.

Although a number of correlations were significant, overall the
bivariate relationships between the achievement and parent scales
were weak. In order to explore the possibility that parental variables
interacted in a complex fashion to determine achievement scores, still
further analyses were undertaken. Using the median split technique
employed with the achievement scales in Chapter 10, the students
were assigned to one of eight groups on the basis of their scores,
above or below the median, on Competitiveness, Personal Unconcern,
and a composite of Work and Mastery. Three-way analyses of variance (high or low on each of the three scales) were then computed
separately for each sex on each of the eleven parent behavior scales.
The function of these analyses was to indicate whether a particular
parent behavior related directly to one or more of the components of
achievement motivation (main effects) or to a particular constellation of achievement orientation (interaction effects). One or more
significant effects were found for eight of the parent behavior scales.
(The three scales showing no significant effects were Mother Democracy and Positivity and Female Standards. The lack of significance of
the Mother scales suggests that fathers tend to play a more critical

role in the development of achievement motivation in both sexes.) Means on each of these eight parent scales in the eight achievement categories are shown in Table 11-14, along with the results of the analyses of variance.

Looking first at the data for males, significant $(p < .01)$ main effects were found only for the Competitiveness factor, as could have been expected from the correlational data. Those higher in Competitiveness were higher in Male Achievement and Female Family Harmony. An effect of borderline significance $(p < .10)$ was found with Male Family Harmony. For the Father Positivity and Father Democracy scales, significant $(p < .05)$ two-way interactions were found, both between Work-Mastery and Competitiveness. In the case of Father Positivity, males high in Work-Mastery and Competitiveness received the most paternal reinforcement while those high in Work-Mastery and low in Competitiveness reported the least, with the groups low in Work-Mastery intermediate. A similar pattern was also found on Father Democracy for males high in Work-Mastery but, for those with low work orientation, low competitiveness was associated with a highly democratic father and high competitiveness with less democratic treatment. Finally, a significant $(p < .05)$ three-way interaction was found on the Rule Enforcement scale. This interaction reflects the fact that rule enforcement varies sharply across the eight groups with males high in Work-Mastery, low in Competitiveness, and high in Personal Unconcern having the strongest rule enforcement, while low levels are found in the low Work-Mastery, high Competitiveness, and high Personal Unconcern group.

In females, one significant $(p < .01)$ main effect was found for Competitiveness: on the Family Protectiveness scale those from more protective families tended to be more competitive. A borderline main effect was also found for Work-Mastery; however, a highly significant $(p < .01)$ two-way interaction between Work-Mastery and Competi-

Table 11-9. *Distribution (in Percent) of Constellations of Parent Behaviors within Each PAQ Couple Type for Female High School Students*

Constellation	Andro-Andro	Andro-Fem	Masc-Andro	Masc-F
1	12	16	6	3
2	4	8	4	4
3	11	8	4	3
4	9	8	17	20
5	43	40	30	19
6	3	2	11	15
7	3	6	6	4
8	5	4	2	2
9	4	2	4	9
10	3	4	9	15
11	3	2	6	6

tiveness was present for the variable. The nature of this interaction was such that high Work-Mastery was related to low protectiveness while, for those low in Work-Mastery, high competitiveness was associated with the highest level of protectiveness and low competitiveness with an intermediate level. Main effects of borderline significance ($p < .10$) related to Work-Mastery were also found with Male Achievement and Father Positivity. In both cases a stronger expression of the parent behavior was associated with higher motivation, as was expected from the correlations reported earlier. One significant ($p < .05$) three-way interaction was also found for the Male Family Harmony scale ($p < .03$). Females high in Work-Mastery tended to experience a moderately high level of harmony while, for those low in

Table 11-10. *Percentages in the Four PAQ Categories within Each Behavioral Constellation for High School Students*

PAQ category

	Males					Females			
Constell	Undiff	Fem	Masc	Andro	Constell	Undiff	Fem	Masc	Andro
1	6	6	38	50	1	9	19	13	59
2	15	10	30	45	2	4	34	4	58
3	10	5	45	40	3	5	26	14	55
4	17	5	53	25	4	18	26	18	38
5	20	5	61	14	5	11	34	11	43
6	27	5	44	24	6	17	33	17	33
7	28	3	52	17	7	7	41	18	34
8	29	11	35	25	8	25	39	6	30
9	35	10	36	19	9	25	38	18	19
					10	28	35	11	25
					11	33	31	16	20

Masc-Masc	Masc-Undiff	Undiff-Fem	Undiff-Undiff	Total N
0	0	0	0	46
0	0	0	0	24
3	0	0	0	58
11	4	19	3	88
9	7	13	0	196
20	10	10	11	85
0	3	6	8	43
6	5	0	6	36
14	28	3	29	70
14	8	32	4	77
23	36	16	38	77

Work-Mastery and high in Competitiveness, high Personal Unconcern was associated with a high level of harmony and low unconcern with very low harmony.

The major import of these analyses is to suggest that parent behaviors may influence the components of achievement motivation in a complex, interactive manner. It seems likely that, as in the case of self-esteem and masculinity and femininity, constellations of parent behaviors play a significant role in determining constellations of achievement motivation. However, the present sample was too limited in size to permit any extensive, multivariate exploration of these relationships.

We did, however, conduct one additional set of analyses to see if we could relate composites of parent behaviors to particular patterns of motivation. Because these variables showed the most consistent relationships, we limited the analysis to Work-Mastery and Competitiveness as the subject variables. As in the analyses just reported, four groups were defined for each sex specifying those high and low in Work-Mastery and high and low in Competitiveness. Stepwise discriminant function analyses were then computed for each sex using Wilks' method in the SPSS statistical package (Nie et al. 1975). The eight parent behavior scales which related significantly to one or more of the achievement scales were used as dependent variables. The means of each group for the parent behaviors and results of the discriminant analyses are presented in Table 11-15.

For each sex one significant discriminant function was specified. However, the solution for males was better than that obtained for fe-

Table 11-11. *Percentage in Each PAQ Category for Upper and Lower Behavioral Constellations within Each of Three Couple Types for High School Students*

	N	Undiff	Males Fem	Masc	An
Andro-Andro couple					
Constell 1–3	33	9	6	30	
Constell 4–9	27	11	7	41	
Masc-Fem couple					
Constell 1–4	40	10	2	58	
Constell 5–9	40	28	17	38	
Undiff-Undiff couple					
Constell 1–8	27	33	4	41	
Constell 9	27	41	11	41	

Note: Family constellations were ranked according to the mean Self-esteem score of the students belonging to that constellation, Constellation 1 having the highest mean. Within each couple type, the split between the upper and lower ranked constellations was based on a median split or the closest approximation to it for males and on a split between the modal category and above vs. below the modal category for females.

males (Wilks' Lambda = .61 for males and .78 for females). The percentage of cases correctly classified by the solution was highly significant ($p < .005$) by chi square in each sex (44% correct for males and 40% for females).

Perhaps the best representation of the constellations of parent behaviors comes from examining the relative values of the means in each of the four groups. In males, the two groups which showed the most extreme difference in terms of centroids in the discriminant analysis were the low Work-Mastery, low and high Competitive categories. The low Work-Mastery, low Competitive group scored as moderately high on all the parental scales except Male Achievement. In contrast, low Work-Mastery, high Competitive males scored lower on Father Positivity, Father Democracy, and Rule Enforcement while rating higher on Sex-Role Enforcement and Male Achievement. In terms of emphases in the home, it appears that the noncompetitive males low in Work Orientation and Mastery receive a fair amount of warmth and acceptance but little tuition in achievement-related areas. In contrast, males who are highly competitive but low in Work Orientation and Mastery seem to have less positive and democratic fathers and parents who place considerable emphasis on interpersonal achievement and competitiveness (as is specified by the Male Achievement factor).

Contrasting the two groups high on Work-Mastery, it can be seen that the high Work-Mastery, high Competitive group has highly positive and democratic fathers, high family harmony, low rule and sex-role enforcement, and high emphasis on competitive achievement.

	N	Undiff	Females Fem	Masc	Andro
Constell 1–5	120	3	24	13	60
Constell 6–11	29	24	38	7	31
Constell 1–6	70	19	34	17	30
Constell 7–11	41	27	32	19	22
Constell 1–8	10	20	40	10	30
Constell 9–11	23	43	22	22	13

The high Work-Mastery, low Competitive group reflects a quite different constellation of parent behaviors. These males reported fathers low on democracy and positivity, a low level of family harmony, and less encouragement for competitive achievement. They also reported, however, high levels of family protectiveness and rule enforcement and moderately high sex-role enforcement.

The patterns of parent behaviors associated with achievement are strikingly different in females. The high Work-Mastery, low Competitive females reported the highest scores on Father Positivity, Father Democracy, Male and Female Family Harmony, Rule Enforcement, and Male Achievement. This group was also lowest in Family Protectiveness. Those high in both work orientation and competitiveness differed subtly from those low in competitiveness, reporting moderate levels of Father Democracy, Family Harmony, and Rule Enforcement and the least emphasis on Sex-Role Enforcement. The group low in Work-Mastery but high in Competitiveness was lowest in Father Positivity and Democracy and Rule Enforcement but highest in Family Protectiveness and Sex-Role Enforcement. Finally, the low achievement, noncompetitive females were lowest on Male Achievement and Family Harmony and intermediate on the remaining scales.

Because of the exploratory nature of these analyses, not too much faith should be placed in them until they are replicated in a larger research population. Interpretation should also await more detailed analyses. Nonetheless, it is fascinating to contrast the patterns of parent behaviors associated with high achievement orientations in the two sexes. A constellation of highly supportive father, family harmony, and emphasis on achievement is associated with high work

Table 11-12. *Mean Self-esteem Score for Each PAQ Category within Each Behavioral Constellation for High School Students*

| | Males | | | | |
| | | | | | Gra |
Constell	Undiff	Fem	Masc	Andro	me:
1	41.67*	41.00*	46.83	48.46	46.
2	33.00*	36.50*	44.33	50.22	44.
3	33.50*	24.50*	42.64	44.60	41.
4	34.59	30.43	42.54	42.06	40.
5	30.00	39.00*	41.68	43.83	39.
6	30.80	36.20*	40.33	42.78	38.
7	33.57	33.00*	40.40	37.40*	37.
8	33.47	30.86	36.81	43.00	36.
9	31.23	33.20	35.54	37.56	34.

*Based on cell N's of five or less.

and mastery motivation and high competitiveness in males but with high work and mastery and *low* competitiveness in females. Subtle differences in the types of achievement pressures, not picked up by the Male Achievement scale, may be imposed on the two sexes, girls being encouraged to "do their best" and boys to "be the best." Or the sexes may learn from other sources that competitiveness is expected and rewarded more in males than females.

In contrast, males high in Work-Mastery and low in Competitiveness and females high in Work-Mastery and *high* in Competitiveness report less democratic fathers and lower family harmony. These girls, however, report stronger achievement pressures than the boys, as reflected on the Male Achievement scale. In girls, competitiveness, in addition to work and mastery needs, may thrive (echoing Hoffman 1975) when achievement standards are high and the family atmosphere not highly supportive or completely harmonious. High achievement motivation and low competitiveness are, however, associated with high rule enforcement in both sexes.

It is also interesting to note that, with the exception of low Male Achievement in girls, noncompetitiveness coupled with low mastery and work orientation is not associated with extremes on any of the parent behaviors.

Overall, results suggest that the examination of patterns of behaviors may be the most fruitful approach to understanding the antecedents of achievement motivation. Such investigations will necessarily involve large samples, extensive multivariate analyses, and successful replications before strong inferences can be made.

		Females			
Constell	Undiff	Fem	Masc	Andro	Grand mean
1	41.0*	40.78	51.00	46.81	45.67
2	32.00*	42.50	49.00	46.86*	44.88
3	25.00*	37.67	44.42	45.64	42.25
4	36.81	39.04	43.62	45.72	41.98
5	33.63	37.72	42.50	44.59	40.78
6	31.20	33.57	41.06	45.74	38.34
7	29.67*	33.17	39.25	43.21	37.33
8	31.33	34.39	46.00*	40.72	36.22
9	30.64	33.42	41.23	38.46	35.16
10	29.05	31.78	42.78	39.42	34.21
11	27.22	29.92	37.84	41.18	32.83

Table 11-13. *Correlations between Parent Behavior Scales and WOFO-2 Achievement Scales for 111 Male and 220 Female High School Students*

	Males				Females			
	Work	Mast	Comp	Pers Unc	Work	Mast	Comp	Pers Unc
Fa Posit	.09	−.03	.26	−.06	.20	.20	.01	.16
Mo Posit	.17	.08	.16	.20	.11	.06	−.09	.11
Fa Democ	.05	.02	.10	−.02	.10	.11	−.12	.11
Mo Democ	.17	.01	.16	.02	.16	.06	−.06	.04
Rule Enforce	.08	.07	−.11	−.01	.14	.15	.07	.10
Fam Protect	.00	−.08	−.10	−.04	.01	−.12	.10	−.06
Sex-Role	−.03	−.07	.02	−.01	−.04	−.12	.01	−.02
Male Fam Harm	−.04	−.04	.24	.01	.18	.13	.00	.14
Fem Fam Harm	.14	.00	.30	.12	.21	.13	−.02	.14
Fem Stand	−.06	.09	−.04	−.21	.18	.16	.21	.06
Male Ach	.18	−.01	.30	.04	.31	.24	.13	.18

Note: For $df = 109$, $r_{.05} = .19$; for $df = 278$, $r_{.05} = .14$.

Table 11-14. *Means for Selected Behavior Scales Broken Down by Work-Mastery, Competitiveness, and Personal Unconcern for High School Students Completing WOFO-2 and Analysis of Variance Probabilities*

	Males							
	Fa Posit	Fa Democ	Fam Prot	Rule Enf	Male Fam Harm	Fem Fam Harm	Male Ach	Sex-Role
Lo W-M								
Lo Comp								
Lo Pers Unc	28.50	19.70	7.26	14.32	16.13	40.29	24.48	10.16
Hi Pers Unc	26.38	17.58	7.38	12.67	16.23	41.50	24.33	10.75
Hi Comp								
Lo Pers Unc	28.00	14.67	7.23	12.33	16.77	45.00	27.25	10.67
Hi Pers Unc	26.85	15.15	6.94	14.46	17.44	47.63	27.38	11.38
Hi W-M								
Lo Comp								
Lo Pers Unc	25.25	14.67	6.83	13.58	14.08	43.42	25.33	10.27
Hi Pers Unc	25.11	15.11	7.22	15.22	14.00	39.11	24.56	11.00
Hi Comp								
Lo Pers Unc	30.00	19.69	6.14	13.62	16.86	44.00	26.62	9.46
Hi Pers Unc	30.72	19.83	6.53	13.11	17.32	47.00	27.39	10.06
Probabilities from ANOVAs								
W-M Main								
Comp Main					<.094	<.004	<.008	
W-M x Comp	<.047	<.001						
W-M x Pers Unc								
W-M x Comp x Pers Unc				<.032				

	Females							
	Fa Posit	Fa Democ	Fam Prot	Rule Enf	Male Fam Harm	Fem Fam Harm	Male Ach	Sex-Role
Lo W-M								
Lo Comp								
Lo Pers Unc	27.12	18.41	6.92	14.14	15.91	41.08	23.76	7.56
Hi Pers Unc	26.95	19.43	6.68	13.36	15.41	42.07	24.00	6.39
Hi Comp								
Lo Pers Unc	22.18	15.09	8.91	14.00	12.45	40.82	24.00	7.27
Hi Pers Unc	29.00	18.92	9.08	13.25	18.58	48.75	26.83	7.83
Hi W-M								
Lo Comp								
Lo Pers Unc	27.29	19.50	5.96	14.55	16.26	43.65	24.29	6.25
Hi Pers Unc	29.95	20.33	6.76	15.33	18.02	47.22	26.30	7.29
Hi Comp								
Lo Pers Unc	30.88	19.63	7.20	12.14	17.80	43.90	26.25	6.00
Hi Pers Unc	29.19	18.67	6.29	14.54	16.95	43.54	26.08	6.46
Probabilities from ANOVAs								
W-M Main	<.080		<.064				<.063	
Comp Main			<.013					
W-M x Comp			<.007					
W-M x Pers Unc								<.070
W-M x Comp x Pers Unc				<.033				

Summary

1. In both sexes, but to a somewhat greater degree in males, positive and usually significant correlations were found between the M scale and the parent behavior scales loading on the second-order factors of Mother and Family Acceptance and Father Acceptance. The F scale was positively related to the same parent scales, although the correlations were usually smaller and less often significant. Few significant correlations were found with M-F.

2. The same cluster of parent scales that was correlated with M and F was also significantly related to Self-esteem. The relationships with the AWS were essentially orthogonal, except for the Sex-Role Enforcement scale; students of both sexes who were more traditional in their attitudes toward women's roles tended to report having fathers and mothers who were more traditional parents.

Table 11-15. *Parent Behavior Means and Results of Discriminant Analysis for High School Students Completing the WOFO-2 and Classified on the Basis of Work-Mastery and Competitiveness*

	Males			
	Lo Work-Mast Lo Comp	Lo Work-Mast Hi Comp	Hi Work-Mast Lo Comp	Hi Work-M Hi Comp
Fa Posit	28.9	27.4	24.3	30.4
Fa Democ	19.8	14.9	14.2	19.8
Fam Prot	6.8	6.6	7.0	6.2
Fem Fam Harm	42.0	46.6	40.8	46.0
Male Fam Harm	16.9	16.7	13.6	16.9
Rule Enforce	13.7	13.4	14.3	13.3
Sex-Role	10.4	11.0	10.6	9.8
Male Ach	24.2	27.3	24.9	27.1

Discrimin

Males			
Standardized discriminant function coefficients		Centroids of groups	
Fa Posit	− .05	Lo W-M Lo Comp	−.77
Fa Democ	−1.15	Lo W-M Hi Comp	.82
Fam Prot	− .22	Hi W-M Lo Comp	.48
Fem Fam Harm	.96	Hi W-M Hi Comp	−.24
Male Fam Harm	− .42		
Rule Enforce	− .05		
Sex-Role	.13		
Male Ach	.12		

Function 1 Canonical $r = .53$,
Wilks' Lambda $= .61$, $\chi^2 = 48.89$, $p = .002$

3. Females from Lower- and Lower-middle-class families reported that both their parents were significantly less positive and democratic and that their families were less harmonious, set lower achievement standards, and were more protective than did females from the two upper socioeconomic groups. In males, similar class differences were noted for the achievement standards and protectiveness scales. Upperclass parents of males were also reported to be most concerned with rule enforcement and Lower-class parents least.

4. Significant sex differences were found on a number of parent behavior scales, males reporting that their parents were more concerned about sex-role training, were less positive and democratic, had stricter standards, and were less protective.

5. The relationships between parent behaviors and students' identification with the mother or father (based on a question about similar-

| | | Females | |
Lo Work-Mast Lo Comp	Lo Work-Mast Hi Comp	Hi Work-Mast Lo Comp	Hi Work-Mast Hi Comp
27.1	25.7	29.4	29.7
18.7	17.1	18.9	20.0
6.4	9.0	6.5	6.4
42.0	45.0	44.0	46.1
15.5	15.6	16.7	17.4
13.8	13.6	14.1	15.2
7.0	7.6	6.4	7.0
23.9	25.6	26.1	26.1

ses

| | Females | | |
Standardized discriminant function coefficients		Centroids of groups	
Fa Posit	.20	Lo W-M Lo Comp	− .01
Fa Democ	.23	Lo W-M Hi Comp	−1.01
Fam Prot	− .98	Hi W-M Lo Comp	.28
Fem Fam Harm	− .54	Hi W-M Hi Comp	.18
Male Fam Harm	.41		
Rule Enforce	.42		
Sex-Role	− .08		
Male Ach	.28		

Function 1 Canonical $r = .36$, Wilks' Lambda $= .78$, $\chi^2 = 45.46$, $p = .005$.

ity to mother's or father's ideals) were examined. Males choosing the Father alternative had the highest means on the Father Positivity and Democracy scales and on Family Harmony; those choosing the Mother alternative had the lowest means. Similar results were found in females on the Father Positivity and Democracy scales, and the reverse pattern was found on the two parallel Mother scales. Significant relationships were also found for females with the Female Family Harmony, Female Standards, and Rule Enforcement scales.

6. Comparisons of the parent behavior scores for students assigned to the four PAQ categories revealed significant differences in males for all but the Sex-Role and Female Standards scales. On the remaining scales, Androgynous males fell at the overall mean on Protectiveness but were above average on the others, particularly on Female Family Harmony and Male Achievement. The Masculine males were lower than the Androgynous on all scales but Father Democracy. The lowest means were found in the Undifferentiated males. Feminine boys were below average on Father Positivity and Democracy but above average on Mother Democracy, Rule Enforcement, and Protectiveness. Despite this pattern, there was no evidence that Feminine boys identified more frequently with their mothers (as reflected in the item about similarity of ideals) than the other groups.

7. In females, nonsignificant differences among PAQ groups were found for the Protectiveness scale, and only borderline differences were found on Sex-Role Enforcement (the Feminine girls having the highest mean). On the remaining parent scales the Androgynous females tended to have the highest means, followed by the Feminine, Masculine, and Undifferentiated. The Masculine group, however, was strikingly high on the Female Standards scale.

8. Parent behaviors were also related to the couple type to which the parents had been assigned on the basis of their joint PAQ category. In both males and females, Androgynous-Androgynous and Androgynous-Feminine couples were the highest of the eight most frequent types on the cluster of scales reflecting father and mother acceptance. Lower but still above average means were obtained on these scales by the Masculine-Androgynous couples and means near the overall mean by the Masculine-Feminine couples. In the four nontraditional types, the means on this cluster of scales were below average, the lowest tending to be reported for the Undifferentiated couples.

A similar pattern of results was observed on the Male Achievement scale. On the Female Standards scale, however, Masculine-Masculine and Masculine-Undifferentiated couples were reported to be strictest with their daughters and the Masculine-Masculine couples strictest with their sons. On Rule Enforcement, the couple types with the lowest means were those in which the father was Undifferentiated. Although parents in these homes were reported to be relatively nonsupportive and authoritarian, they also appeared to be relatively ineffectual disciplinarians. Finally, on the Sex-Role Enforcement scale, couples in which the father was Masculine were reported to be most traditional by males, and couples in which one or both parents were Undifferentiated were similarly described by females. In females, couples in which the father was Androgynous were the most liberal.

9. In an attempt to determine the independent contributions to the students' PAQ of their perceptions of parents' PAQ and parents' behavior, a series of constellations of parent behaviors were sought which could be specified independently of parental classification on the PAQ scales. Data were analyzed by means of the Automatic Interaction Detection (AID) technique using Self-esteem scores as the criterion measure. Nine discrete patterns were identified for males and eleven for females. Constellations were ordered according to mean Self-esteem scores of students belonging to each one, the constellation producing the highest mean being ranked 1.

10. The percentage of each of the eight frequent couple types falling in each constellation produced the anticipated ordering. For example, Androgynous-Androgynous couples were overrepresented in both sexes in the higher ranked constellations, Masculine-Feminine in the intermediate ranks, and Undifferentiated-Undifferentiated in the lowest. However, there was considerable variability in the constellations to which parents belonging to each couple type were assigned. When the percentage of students falling into each of the four PAQ categories was determined for each constellation, the expected patterning again occurred, the higher ranking constellations having the largest percentage of Androgynous individuals and the lower ranking the highest percentage of Undifferentiated individuals.

11. Three representative couple types with sufficient N were selected for further study: Androgynous-Androgynous, Masculine-Feminine, and Undifferentiated-Undifferentiated. Within each type male and female students were split into an Upper and Lower Self-esteem group. Next, the distribution across PAQ categories was determined for each group. Within each type for each sex, the Upper group contained a greater percentage of Androgynous and a lower percentage of Undifferentiated individuals than the Lower group. These data thus suggest that constellations of parent behaviors are related to students' masculinity and femininity even when their parents' PAQ couple type is held constant. However, differences in the PAQ distributions across couple types remained even when behavioral constellations were taken into account. Thus parent behaviors and attributes may contribute independently as well as jointly to students' masculinity and femininity. A similar conclusion was reached from an analysis of the mean Self-esteem scores of students in each PAQ category in each behavioral constellation. Even with students' PAQ category held constant, mean Self-esteem tended to decline systematically from the highest to the lowest ranked constellation.

12. Correlations of the parent behavior scales with the four scales of

the WOFO-2 were modest in size, significant correlations occurring most frequently in males with the Competitiveness scale and, in females, with the Work scale, followed by Mastery and Personal Unconcern. The parent scales most consistently related to the achievement scales in females were Father Positivity and Male Achievement.

13. After respondents were classified on the basis of median splits on Work-Mastery, Competitiveness, and Personal Unconcern, three-way analyses of variance were computed for the parent behavior scales. Both main effects and interactions were found in each sex involving eight of the eleven parent scales, those above the medians on the achievement scales having higher means on the latter. Of the three scales not entering into significant relationships, two (Mother Positivity and Democracy) involved the mother's behavior exclusively, and the third (Female Standards) involved the mother more than the father. Thus the father appears to play a more critical role than the mother in the development of achievement motives in both sexes.

14. The presence of significant interactions suggested, first, that a particular type of parent behavior might differentially affect several components of achievement motivation and, second, that constellations of parent behavior might relate more consistently to constellations of achievement motivation than to individual components.

In order to explore the latter possibility, four subgroups were specified by median splits on Work-Mastery and Competitiveness, and eight parent behavior scales were employed in a stepwise discriminant analysis. One significant function was found in each sex. Markedly different patterns of behavior were associated with the several achievement groups in each sex. One consistent relationship was that a strong emphasis on rule enforcement in the family was associated with high mastery and work orientation and low competitiveness in both sexes, while an emphasis on achievement, as reflected on the Male Achievement scale, tended to be associated, particularly in males, with high competitiveness.

Although the results must be regarded tentatively because of the small samples involved, they strongly suggest that constellations of behaviors are more critical than any single type of parent behavior in determining achievement motivation.

12. The Influence of Parental Attributes and Behaviors: A Summing Up

Strong relationships were found between the students' report of their masculine and feminine characteristics and their perceptions of their parents' characteristics and child-rearing attitudes and behaviors. Before attempting to summarize these findings and interpret their significance, we shall take up troublesome methodological issues related to the use of children's perceptions of their parents vs. other sources of information about the parents such as self-report or behavioral observations by outsiders.

Perceptions vs. "Reality"

The justification most frequently offered for obtaining information about the parents from their children is that the relationships with children's behaviors and attributes are likely to be strongest when this type of parent measure is used. We concur with this position but, at the same time, disagree with the contention of strict phenomenologists and field theorists that fully satisfactory psychological theories can be developed solely by reconstructing the person's inner world and psychological environment from such behavioral indicators as verbal self-report and by using these perceptual measures to predict other behaviors. Such theories imply that the empirical laws of psychology need only be correlational, describing the associations between classes of responses. However, the relationship between behavior and its determining situational variables cannot safely be ignored (Spence 1963). A child, for example, who insists that her or his parents are warm, loving, and supportive in their treatment when the most casual observer can note that they are rejecting and psychologically if not physically abusive is a very different child from one whose description matches observers' assessments. One simply would not make the same set of inferences about the characteristics of each of these children or, over the long run, the same predictions about their behaviors. However, this type of gross discrepancy between perception and actuality is relatively rare. Across a large group of individuals, substantial correspondence would undoubtedly be found between the accounts of parent-child interactions (or any other type of social interaction) given by that fictive creature, the completely objective, all-seeing but unseen observer, and by the participants in those interactions, particularly if these accounts are limited to the immediately observable. However, our reactions to the behaviors of others are not based solely on what was said and done on each particular occasion; typically another's behavior is interpreted and given added meaning or significance. It is in the more subtle realm of interpretation that discrepancies ordinarily occur among individuals' perceptions of one another, and it is here that the case rests for children's perceptions about their parents having greater predictive utility than other sources of information about them.

Behaviorally oriented investigators, however, tend to be uneasy about the usefulness of self-report instruments, the best of which must be conceded to be imperfect, and to raise important and legitimate questions about the degree to which children's perceptions of their parents, as determined by such instruments, tell us anything about the parents themselves. The answer is not easy to obtain. The interpretation of an event by observers, participant or nonparticipant, is jointly influenced by their prior knowledge of the individual being observed and by their own unique experiences and biases. When faced with two nonidentical sets of perceptions of parents—one supplied by outside observers based on limited behavioral samples that may be distorted by the observers' very presence, the other supplied by children, who have had intimate and long-term interactions with their parents—how is one to judge which is more accurate? The former have the advantage of being more dispassionate and hence more likely to be "objective," and the latter have the advantage of having enormously greater information. Still further confusion is introduced when the parents' perceptions of their own behaviors and characteristics are sought. Prior investigations (e.g., Coopersmith 1967; Schaefer & Bayley 1967) as well as our own suggest that, when measurement techniques with satisfactory reliability and other psychometric properties are used, moderate correlations among these three types of perceptions typically emerge. Such results suggest not only that each type of data provides unique information, valuable in its own right, but also that each reflects, however imperfectly, something about "real" parental characteristics and behaviors.

A concrete question about the relative accuracy of two sources of data is raised by the results of our analyses showing that, when students' perceptions of their fathers' and mothers' characteristics were used to assign parents to PAQ categories, replicable relationships emerged between the distribution of college and high school students across the four masculinity-femininity categories and parental couple type. These findings suggest that important relationships exist between students' instrumental and expressive characteristics and the characteristics they perceive in their parents. The correlations between the college students' ratings of their parents on the PAQ and their fathers' and mothers' self-ratings were not only significant but also larger than the correlations between the students' self-ratings and their ratings of their parents, thus suggesting some verdicality between the parents' instrumental and expressive behaviors in the family setting and their children's inferences from these behaviors about parental attributes. However, when parents' self-reports were substituted for student perceptions, the patterns of relationships between student PAQ category and parent couple type were considerably diluted in males and survived only minimally in females.

While the latter findings are disquieting, they do not necessarily demonstrate that the students' perceptions were without foundation. It is reasonable to assume, as we argued above, that a fairly substantial relationship exists between parental self-concepts of their instrumental and expressive characteristics and the manifestations of these characteristics within the home as an objective observer would describe them and between these behaviors and their children's perceptions of them. However, there are multiple slippages between parents' perceptions of themselves and students' perceptions of their parents. Both fathers and mothers may behave somewhat differently at home than in other settings; their actions toward a particular child may be shaped by their attitudes toward that child and by that child's behavior toward them; children's interpretation of their parents' behavior and hence their inferences about their parents' attributes are filtered through their own needs and temperamental characteristics. These slippages, coupled with the imperfections of our measuring instrument and the crudeness of our four-way categorical system, may put too heavy a load on the data derived from parents' self-concepts to reproduce with any fidelity the relationships found between students' perceptions of their parents and their perceptions of themselves.

Relationships between Masculinity and Femininity and Perceptions of the Parents

Both males and females, we have shown, differ widely in the degree to which they possess both expressive, feminine characteristics and instrumental, masculine ones, the variability within each sex being at least as impressive as the difference between them. Our analyses further indicated that the relationships between masculinity and femininity and other characteristics, such as self-esteem, are often similar in both sexes. Data such as these suggested to us that the nature of the relationships between students' perceptions of parent behaviors and attributes and their own masculinity and femininity would also have many points of similarity in males and females. Still further, they led us in our exploration of the influence of child-rearing practices to focus on patterns of parent behaviors with general significance for psychological masculinity and femininity rather than on isolation of very particular differences in the rearing of boys and girls that might contribute to temperamental differences between the typical male and female. While some sex differences were expected and indeed did occur, our expectation of a substantial correspondence between the findings for males and females was amply confirmed.

In the discussion of our major results that follows, we shall first consider the general findings, mentioning discrepancies between the sexes only when necessary, and then specifically take up differences between the sexes.

RELATIONSHIPS WITH COUPLE TYPE

Family dynamics are complex, involving mutually supportive or antagonistic interactions among family members. It was therefore not surprising that clearer patterns emerged when analyses involved not mothers alone or fathers alone but parents as couples.

Students tended to perceive their same-sex parent as possessing stereotypical characteristics of their sex to a greater degree than themselves, that is, males rated their fathers somewhat higher on the M and M-F scales than themselves and females rated their mothers somewhat higher on F. The distributions of mothers and fathers across the four PAQ categories were nonetheless quite comparable to those produced by students' self-ratings. Classification of the parents into the sixteen possible couple types, based on the joint M and F scores of each parent, indicated that, in both high school and college samples, the usual state of affairs was one in which each parent was above the median on the sexually appropriate attributes, over 50% falling into the four categories we have described as traditional (Masculine father, Feminine mother) or near-traditional (Androgynous-Androgynous, Androgynous-Feminine, or Masculine-Androgynous). There was some indication, however, that Androgynous women were more likely to be married to Androgynous than to Masculine men than the base rate figures for each sex would suggest. Similarly, among the nontraditional couple types, Undifferentiated men have a higher probability of being married to Undifferentiated women.

The conclusion to be drawn from several lines of evidence is that, overall, the homes in which both parents are perceived as Androgynous are most likely to be "healthy," in the sense of producing an atmosphere in which children develop socially desirable characteristics that allow them to function effectively and to achieve a sense of self-worth. Following closely is the Androgynous-Feminine couple, then Masculine-Androgynous and Masculine-Feminine. Among the four nontraditional types that occurred frequently, the two combinations in which the father was Masculine (Masculine-Masculine and Masculine-Undifferentiated) were associated with relatively less favorable outcomes than the traditional or near-traditional combinations but tended to be better than the Undifferentiated-Feminine combination. Worst of all was the Undifferentiated-Undifferentiated couple.

A major source of data leading to this ordering of favorability is found in the association between couple type and the patterns of parental behaviors that high school students attributed to their parents. Parental warmth and supportiveness, which are typically found to be correlated with democratic treatment, have unambiguously been established as making long-term contributions to an individual's psychological well-being. Among the eight frequent couple types, both fathers and mothers in the Androgynous-Androgynous and Androgynous-Feminine combinations were rated highest on the cluster of scales related to warmth, democracy, and family harmony, and Undifferentiated parents were rated lowest, with the intermediate groups tending to follow the order described above. Similarly, Androgynous parents were rated highest in encouraging achievement in their children (Male Achievement scale), and Undifferentiated parents rated lowest, with the traditional Masculine-Feminine couples at an intermediate level. In short, the associations between parent behaviors and couple type were quite uniform for all the scales implicated in the second-order factors of Mother-Family Acceptance and Father Acceptance.

The scales contributing to the second-order permissiveness-control factor (with the exception of the Male Achievement scale, which loaded on this as well as the Acceptance factors) were related in a more complicated way to couple type. The overall relationships can most easily be described by referring to the patterns Baumrind (1968) has identified as *authoritative* and *authoritarian*. The authoritative pattern describes quite accurately the constellation of behaviors attributed to the Androgynous and Androgynous-Feminine couples. These parents, in addition to having high expectations for their children, set clear rules for them to follow and were moderately firm in enforcing these rules. At the same time, they respected their children's wishes and needs and were more likely to praise and encourage their positive behaviors than to punish and criticize their deficiencies. The homes in which the father was Masculine and the mother Masculine or Undifferentiated, in contrast, quite closely approximated the authoritarian pattern. In these families the father, the mother, or both were perceived as being undemocratic in their treatment, quite strict and critical, and (in girls) firm in rule enforcement. The Masculine-Androgynous and Masculine-Feminine couples exhibited behaviors somewhere between these authoritative and authoritarian patterns.

The two types of couples in which the father was Undifferentiated (Undifferentiated-Feminine and Undifferentiated-Undifferentiated), in addition to being emotionally nonsupportive, were low in democracy, just as were the two nontraditional couples in which the father was Masculine. Unlike the latter, however, they were reported as setting relatively low standards for the child and as lacking in firmness or consistency of rule enforcement. The impression one gains here is of a home in which the family members are emotionally distant from one another and the parents, while of an authoritarian bent, are ineffective as disciplinarians. One interesting sex difference was found in these homes: girls rated their parents high on the Sex-Role Enforcement scale while boys rated them relatively low. Perhaps girls, being perceived as tractable, were more likely to have been pressured into conventional behaviors, while boys (many of whom did report masculine attributes and might therefore have been resistant to parental efforts to control their behavior) were more likely to be simply left alone in this and other areas.

An ordering of couple types is also apparent in the students' self-esteem scores, those reporting their parents as Androgynous tending to report the highest self-esteem and social competence, those with Undifferentiated parents the least, and so on. These self-esteem data can be predicted from the different distributions of the students' PAQ categories in the various couple types. Inspection of these distributions revealed that, for males, the proportion classified as Feminine was consistently low in all couple types (with but one exception to be described below). However, reciprocal variations across couple types were noted in the other three categories. For the sons of Androgynous parents, Androgyny was the most likely outcome, with the proportion falling into the Masculine and Undifferentiated categories being correspondingly depressed. As one moves from this father-mother combination to Androgynous-Feminine, Masculine-Androgynous, Masculine-Feminine, and finally to Masculine-Masculine, the proportion of Androgynous males decreases, more and more being classified as Masculine and as Undifferentiated. These data clearly suggest a strong association between the sons' and the fathers' characteristics, with the mothers' contributions being secondary. In two of the remaining couple types—Masculine-Undifferentiated and Undifferentiated-Undifferentiated—the percentage not only of Androgynous but also of Masculine males decreased, with a marked elevation being noted in the Undifferentiated category.

In both college and high school samples, a striking deviation from the overall pattern occurred in males whose parents were classified as Undifferentiated-Feminine. A substantial proportion of males from these homes were classified as Feminine, the elevation in this category being accompanied by a lower proportion of Undifferentiated males than in the two combinations in which the mother was Undifferentiated (Masculine-Undifferentiated, Undifferentiated-Undifferentiated). In this instance where the father fails to manifest strongly either masculine or feminine characteristics, the potential salvaging role of the mother with socially desirable expressive attributes becomes apparent.

The configuration of a decreasing proportion of Androgynous individuals and an increasing proportion of Undifferentiated individuals as one goes from couples in which both father and mother are Androgynous to couples in which both are Undifferentiated is paralleled in the data from females. However, sex differences of considerable import also occurred. In males, the father contributed more than the mother in the couple types in which the father was high in masculinity (i.e., was Masculine or Androgynous). In females, the influence of the parents was more nearly equal. Further, females tended to be more responsive to the masculine characteristics of their parents than males to their feminine characteristics, whether or not the parent was Androgynous. This is shown most clearly in the relatively high proportion of Masculine females found in homes in which the parents were Masculine-Feminine or Masculine-Masculine.

In summary, different configurations of parent behaviors were associated with the eight couple types, which in turn were related to the frequency with which their sons and daughters exhibited masculine and feminine characteristics and to their level of self-esteem.

PARENT BEHAVIORS VS. PARENTAL ATTRIBUTES

In an attempt to determine the independent contributions of parent behaviors and parental attributes to children's characteristics, a series of discrete behavioral constellations was identified for each sex, using Self-esteem as the criterion measure. Because the focus of our interest was elsewhere, we have not presented verbal descriptions of each of the resulting constellations. We will note only in passing that they revealed complex, interactive patterns that often reflected discrepancies in the scores of the father and mother on parallel scales. As anticipated from our initial analyses, favorability of the constellations (as indicated by the mean self-esteem of the children) was associated with overall desirability of the couple type, Androgynous couples tending to be concentrated in the more favorable constellations, Undifferentiated couples in the least, and so forth. However, it is equally important to note that a variety of couple types was to be found within each behavioral constellation.

The results of analyses based on these behavioral constellations suggested that both parental attributes (couple type) and parent behaviors continued to be related to the students' masculinity and femininity and self-esteem when the other was held constant. Thus parent behaviors and attributes may be inferred to contribute independently as well as jointly to their children's characteristics. Although our results pinpoint some of the parental factors associated with masculinity and femininity, the nature of their influence can only be surmised. The kinds of parent behaviors we assessed, as noted in an earlier discussion, may influence children's characteristics in a number of ways. The experimental literature suggests that they may serve to augment or to detract from the parent's attractiveness as a model, thereby affecting the probability that the child will imitate and thus acquire the parent's instrumental or expressive characteristics. Parent behaviors may themselves be imitated and have some influence on personality development. Children whose parents are warm, supportive, and respectful of their legitimate needs, for example, may develop the predisposition to treat those with whom they interact in the same way, that is, they acquire expressive characteristics. Parent behaviors may also have less specific effects, setting up supportive conditions that allow the child to realize his or her potentialities or creating an atmosphere in which the child's development is inhibited or distorted.

In designing our parent behavior measure, we made no systematic attempt to assess parental efforts to inculcate directly particular instrumental and expressive characteristics or their opposites. Not only is such tuition frequent, but the kind of person the parent values and tries to teach the child to be is probably related both to the general patterns of child-rearing practices the parents have adopted and to their own attributes.

The role of the parents as models in bringing about parent-child resemblances is particularly difficult to discern from correlational data of the type we have collected. Some of the resemblances we have uncovered may reasonably be attributed (at least in part) to modeling, but others may have other roots. Both the formal empirical evidence (such as responses to the questions about the parent whom the student most resembled or felt closest to) and commonsense considerations suggest, for example, that the Androgynous son or daughter of Androgynous parents finds them worthy of emulation and attempts to become like them. The Masculine male who reports himself as closer or more similar to his Masculine father than to his Feminine mother may also be inferred to have acquired his father's instrumental qualities in part because he has adopted the father as a model. However, while his relative deficiency in expressive characteristics suggests that he has largely rejected his mother as an exemplar, it is quite unclear whether his low expressiveness is due to the lack of an influential model or to a more active imitation of his father's interpersonal indifference. In the case of the Undifferentiated children of Undifferentiated parents, one strongly suspects that they have rejected both parents as models and resemble them primarily because the conditions that would allow them to develop instrumental or expressive attributes are absent.

Equally important to identify are the factors that lead individuals whose parents are perceived as exhibiting both desirable behaviors and personal characteristics to *fail* to acquire those attributes or, conversely, that lead those whose parents do not exhibit these qualities to develop a high degree of instrumentality or expressiveness. Other social influences within and outside the family that we did not attempt to measure, as well as the temperamental, physical, and cognitive characteristics of the individuals themselves, may be assumed to play a part. Even within the context of the present Parental Attitudes Questionnaire, additional information about the role of parents might have been obtained by determining the configurations of parental behaviors, within each couple type, for students falling into each of the four PAQ categories. This type of refined analysis would require data from massive numbers of individuals, considerably more than we had available.

SEX DIFFERENCES

We have already commented on the asymmetrical relations found in males and females between patterns of parent-child resemblances in masculinity and femininity. Males were more responsive to the socially desirable characteristics of their fathers than to the characteristics of their mothers and were likely to exhibit expressive, feminine qualities only if one or both parents were Androgynous. Females were more likely than males to exhibit the socially desirable characteristics of either parent without regard to their stereotypic appropriateness. These findings confirm the observations of other investigators (e.g., Block 1973; Biller 1971; Lynn 1969) that the influence of the father in child development has been systematically underestimated. However, they contradict some of the implications of Johnson's (1963) reciprocal role theory about the contribution of the father to the development of his daughter's expressiveness. In many couple types the consequence of having a father high in masculine, instrumental attributes is to *increase* the probability that she will also possess these qualities.

Johnson's primary intent, however, was to explain the acquisition of *sex-role behaviors*, and our evidence does nothing to disconfirm that portion of her theorizing. It does point up, once more, the necessity of distinguishing both empirically and conceptually between expressiveness and instrumentality as properties of the individual's *personality* and "expressive" vs. "instrumental" *roles*.

The sexes also differed in their reports of parent behaviors. High school boys perceived their parents as being more concerned with sex-role enforcement than high school girls, thus confirming a consistent finding in studies in which similar information was elicited from the parents themselves. The boys also reported that their parents were stricter and more critical (Female Standards scale), less positive and democratic, and less protective. Similar results have been found in other investigations in which older children and young adolescents were questioned about their parents, boys in comparison to girls indicating that their parents were less affectionate and nurturant and more often physically punished them or deprived them of privileges (e.g., Droppleman & Schaefer 1963; Siegelman 1965; Hoffman & Saltzstein 1967). Young boys have been observed to be more active and disruptive in their behavior than girls and to be less likely to be responsive to adult directives both at home and at school, thereby more frequently eliciting critical, negative reactions from adult caretakers (Minton, Kagan, & Levine 1971; Serbin, O'Leary, Kent, & Tonick 1973; Good, Sikes, & Brophy 1973). These findings suggest both that the discrepancies in the reports of the sexes reflect genuine differences in the treatment they receive and that these sex differences are in part the consequence of the greater resistance to control exhibited by boys rather than purely the unilateral tendency of parents to use differential socialization practices with their female and male children. The differences between the sexes in their perceptions of parent behaviors, however, should not be overemphasized. Far more striking were the variations within each sex and the implications of constellations of parent behaviors for their children's attributes and self-esteem.

Although the pressures on boys to achieve are commonly believed to be far greater than the pressures on girls, significant differences were not found between the sexes on the Male Achievement scale. This failure is echoed in other studies. Examination of the data reported by Kelly and Worell (1976) in their investigation of college students reveals that men and women were similar in their responses to scales tapping their perceptions of maternal and paternal encouragement of cognitive independence, competence, and curiosity. Similarly, Maccoby and Jacklin's (1974) survey of the literature led them to conclude that there are no consistent differences in the demands placed on boys and girls for intellectual performance, although there is some suggestion that boys are expected to be more competitive than girls (Block 1973). Parents do have higher educational aspirations for sons than for daughters, as reflected in their greater expectation that boys will go on to college (e.g., Hilton & Berglund 1971), and also, it seems safe to assume, higher vocational aspirations for their sons. These differential aspirations are reflected in the data from our high school sample, boys reporting higher educational goals and a stronger career orientation than girls. However, if there are differences between the parents of boys and girls in their attempts to instill the kinds of achievement needs that make intellectual and vocational success more probable, the instruments devised to measure parental behaviors have not been sufficient to detect them.

The Antecedents of Achievement Motivation

Our explorations of the parental attributes and behaviors associated with the several components of achievement motivation can at best be regarded as tentative. Among parental characteristics, fathers' and mothers' achievement motives could be expected to be most strongly related to their children's but, since the amount of information we could gather from each student was limited and the focus of our investigation was on the development of masculinity and femininity, data on these parental characteristics were not obtained. Similarly, our Parental Attitudes Questionnaire was not specifically designed to determine in detail techniques that parents might use to inculcate the need to achieve in their children. Our efforts were further hampered by the relatively small sample given the second and more psychometrically satisfactory version of our achievement instrument (WOFO-2). While the data we have obtained give tantalizing glimpses at the origins of achievement motivation, they permit us only to speculate on the combination of forces acting to nurture these motives and to lay out a template for more extensive study.

The major trends in our data can be briefly summarized. A number of significant or near-significant correlations were found between students' achievement scores and parental masculinity and femininity, most of them involving the father rather than the mother. Relationships between parent couple type were also found, particularly in the case of Work Orientation and Mastery. Students of both sexes from traditional or near-traditional homes were high in these two components of achievement motivation proportionately more often than those from nontraditional homes. A similar pattern of relationships was found in females with Competitiveness, but the results found in males (the majority of whom were above the median established for the pooled sample of both sexes) were more ambiguous.

It was not surprising to find that, among the parent behavior scales, Male Achievement was most consistently implicated in both sexes in significant correlations with students' achievement scores. In the full parent behavior–student achievement matrix, the highest correlation (.30) in boys was between Competitiveness and Male Achievement while, in girls, the highest correlation (.31) was between the latter and Work Orientation. This difference between the sexes was also noted in other parent behavior scales, significant correlations tending to occur most often with Competitiveness in boys and with Work in girls. The nature of achievement pressures differs in the sexes, these data seem to imply, girls being expected to be devoted to hard work for its own sake and boys being expected to have being better than others as a major goal.

Attention is also called to the finding that paternal variables were more likely to be related to achievement scores in both sexes than maternal behaviors. Once again our evidence suggests that the father is more influential than the mother in instilling needs to achieve in his children. The strongest indication of maternal influence was on Work Orientation in females, relationships that may reflect mothers' recognition of what is required to run a household and the expectation that their daughters should not only be prepared to assume similar responsibilities when they marry but should also help with domestic chores while they are growing up.

Aside from the kinds of behaviors assessed by the Male Achievement scale (and quite secondarily by the Female Standards scale), it is quite difficult to discern what direct causal influence, if any, parent behaviors have on their children's achievement needs or to disentangle the role of parent behaviors from their instrumentality and expressiveness. The couple types and the parent behaviors that were most likely to be associated with high scores on the achievement scales, it will be noted, are themselves correlated.

It is not unlikely that the development of achievement motivation is mediated to a considerable extent by the acquisition of masculine and feminine attributes. The logic for this assertion is that these instrumental and expressive characteristics provide basic orientations that can facilitate or hinder the development and manifestation of the various components of achievement motivation. Instrumentality may serve as a precursor for mastery, work, and competitiveness, facilitating the expression of these motives as they develop. Expressiveness may mediate achievement motivation through instilling the willingness both to work and to accept the responsibility of caring for others and through making the individual more sensitive to the interpersonal components of achievement behavior. Expressiveness may also facilitate the social comparisons needed to evaluate performance and set realistic levels of aspiration. Androgynous individuals may thus not only acquire higher levels of motivation than Feminine or Undifferentiated individuals but also be better able than Masculine individuals to cope with the social aspects of their expression. According to this line of reasoning, parental masculinity and femininity should play a mediating role both in indirect training for achievement, as through modeling, and through the associated family climate. Our data from the Male Achievement scale further suggest that these parental characteristics may also be associated, particularly in the father, with direct tuition of achievement-related behaviors.

Although causal linkages unquestionably exist between parental attributes and behaviors and the development of achievement motivation, it is unlikely that large relationships, whether direct or mediated through other variables such as M and F, can be found. This should be the case because the influence of other individual characteristics and extraparental factors is, of necessity, particularly strong in the case of achievement motivation. The child's abilities and talents, for example, must play a pervasive and continuing role, shaping not only parental treatment but especially the responses and reinforcements of peers and teachers.

Veroff (1969), as we have noted, has stressed the importance of social comparison processes involving peers as a prime determinant of integrated achievement motivation. The expectancies both peers and teachers hold for the child's performance, as Rosenthal and Jacobson (1968) and others have suggested, can influence treatment and resultant motivation, thus becoming self-fulfilling prophecies. The role of the family, in concert with the characteristics of the child, is probably central during preschool years but diminishes when schoolmates and other adults come to occupy more of the growing child's work and social universe.

Still further complications are introduced into the study of the development of achievement motivation by our demonstration that its various components do not necessarily combine linearly to determine achievement behaviors but interact in a complex fashion. These data illustrate the necessity of determining the very particular configurations of parental attributes and behaviors that contribute to combinations of the components of achievement motivation rather than studying total achievement motivation, treated as a unitary concept, or individual components in isolation. For example, in our analysis of the data from students given the second version of our achievement instrument (WOFO-2), significant differences were reported in the parent behavior of males with high work, mastery, and competitive needs and those high in work and mastery but low in competitiveness. Having high needs in all three dimensions was associated with strongly positive families, supportive fathers, and emphasis on achievement while, in contrast, being low in competitiveness while high in the other two was associated with a much less positive family climate. Given the data suggesting that, at least in some types of activities, strong interpersonal competitiveness may have a negative influence on attainments, this seemingly paradoxical finding clearly merits further explication. This may be a case where folk wisdom and reality are in conflict, with most parents assuming that high competitiveness is essential for sustained achievement (at least in males) and attempting to provide tuition and reinforcement for competitive strivings.

Attempts to discover the interplay of causal forces serving as precursors of achievement motivations must, of necessity, involve multiple approaches and multivariate studies of considerable magnitude. In looking at antecedents of achievement orientation in young children, a longitudinal approach is needed which assesses a broad range of parental attributes, parental attitudes, and behaviors (both through expressed values and observed actions toward the child) and considers the family as a unit defined by the joint contribution of each parent and responses to the child's behavior in achievement situations. Potentially relevant characteristics of the child, such as ability measures, are also important to include. It should also be profitable not only to study the family structure but also to follow the child through interactions in school with peers and teachers. Although massive in scope, such an approach would seem to offer the greatest chance of uncovering the relative contribution and causal patterns among the many constituents implicated by more limited studies.

A second essential research strategy involves large-scale, cross-sectional studies of individuals at various stages of the life cycle that include groups with unique aspirations and objectively measurable levels of attainment. The possible disadvantages of reliance on self-report measures of achievement motivation would be somewhat offset by relating such variables to real achievement behaviors.

The value of the complex research sketched above is unquestionable. Given the type of interactions suggested by the studies conducted to date, limited studies encompassing a narrow range of concepts such as the behaviors of a single parent, a global measure of achievement, or a contrived, uninvolving operationalization of achievement behavior can provide only a restricted and potentially misleading picture of achievement and its development.

Although we have been more successful in isolating some of the antecedents of masculinity and femininity than of achievement motivation, similar multivariate approaches to the former are also required. We regard the evidence we have reported here not as definitive but as richly suggestive, pointing to directions in which future research might usefully go.

Appendices

A. Measuring Instruments

Table I. *Family Information Sheet*

Tel. No. _____ Birthday _____

_____ Sex _____ School _____

1. For each of the 3 age periods listed at the right, indicate (by checking) the adults with whom you lived (all or most of the time) who were responsible for your upbringing:

	Birth–5 yrs.	*6–10 yrs.*	*11 yrs.* +
a) Mother & father (natural or adoptive)	_____	_____	_____
b) Mother only	_____	_____	_____
c) Father only	_____	_____	_____
d) Mother & stepfather	_____	_____	_____
e) Father & stepmother	_____	_____	_____
f) Other (specify) _____	_____	_____	_____

2. Over the past 5 years, what was your parents' (or other adult guardians' with whom you live) employment?

	Mother	*Father*
No paid employment	_____	_____
Part-time employment	_____	_____
Full-time employment	_____	_____

3. How much education have your parents (or other adult guardians with whom you live) completed?

	Mother	*Father*
Grade school	_____	_____
Some high school	_____	_____
High school graduate	_____	_____
Training beyond high school	_____	_____
Some college	_____	_____
College graduate	_____	_____
Postgraduate work	_____	_____

4. What is your family's religious affiliation?

____ Catholic ____ Greek Orthodox ____ Protestant ____ Jewish
____ None ____ Other (specify) _____

5. To what ethnic or racial group do you belong? _____

6. List below the brothers and sisters (include step- and foster brothers and sisters) with whom you grew up. List them from *oldest* to *youngest*, specifying their sex (M or F) and current age. Put yourself in the list where you belong, writing "SELF" and your age.

Sex (M or F)	Age		Sex (M or F)	Age
1. _____	___		4. _____	___
2. _____	___		5. _____	___
3. _____	___		6. _____	___

Table II. *Personal Attributes Questionnaire*

The items below inquire about what kind of a person you think you are. Each items consists of *a pair* of characteristics, with the letters A–E in between. For example:

Not at all Artistic   A . . . . B . . . . . C . . . . D . . . . E   Very Artistic

Each pair describes contradictory characteristics—that is, you cannot be both at the same time, such as very artistic and not at all artistic.

The letters form a scale between the two extremes. You are to chose a letter which describes where *you* fall on the scale. For example, if you think you have no artistic ability, you would choose A. If you think you are pretty good, you might choose D. If you are only medium, you might choose C, and so forth.

Scale*

M-F	1. Not at all aggressive	A . . . . B . . . . . C . . . . D . . . . E	*Very aggressive***
M	2. Not at all independent	A . . . . B . . . . . C . . . . D . . . . E	*Very independent*
F	3. Not at all emotional	A . . . . B . . . . . C . . . . D . . . . E	*Very emotional*
M-F	4. Very submissive	A . . . . B . . . . . C . . . . D . . . . E	*Very dominant*

* The scale to which each item is assigned is indicated below by M (Masculinity), F (Femininity), and M-F (Masculinity-Femininity).
** Italics indicate the extreme masculine response for the M and M-F scales and the extreme feminine response for the F scale. Each extreme masculine response on the M and M-F scales and extreme feminine response on the F scale are scored 4, the next most extreme scored 3, etc.

Table II, cont'd.

			Right
M-F	5. *Not at all excitable in a major crisis*	A . . . . B . . . . C . . . . D . . . . E	Very excitable in a major crisis
M	6. Very passive	A . . . . B . . . . C . . . . D . . . . E	*Very active*
F	7. Not at all able to devote self completely to others	A . . . . B . . . . C . . . . D . . . . E	*Able to devote self completely to others*
F	8. Very rough	A . . . . B . . . . C . . . . D . . . . E	*Very gentle*
F	9. Not at all helpful to others	A . . . . B . . . . C . . . . D . . . . E	*Very helpful to others*
M	10. Not at all competitive	A . . . . B . . . . C . . . . D . . . . E	*Very competitive*
M-F	11. Very home oriented	A . . . . B . . . . C . . . . D . . . . E	*Very worldly*
F	12. Not at all kind	A . . . . B . . . . C . . . . D . . . . E	*Very kind*
M-F	13. *Indifferent to others' approval*	A . . . . B . . . . C . . . . D . . . . E	Highly needful of others' approval
M-F	14. *Feelings not easily hurt*	A . . . . B . . . . C . . . . D . . . . E	Feelings easily hurt
F	15. Not at all aware of feelings of others	A . . . . B . . . . C . . . . D . . . . E	*Very aware of feelings of others*

16. . . . . to make decisions   Has difficulty making

			Scale		
M	19. Not at all self-confident	A....B....C....D....E	*Very self-confident*
M	20. Feels very inferior	A....B....C....D....E	*Feels very superior*
F	21. Not at all understanding of others	A....B....C....D....E	*Very understanding of others*
F	22. Very cold in relations with others	A....B....C....D....E	*Very warm in relations with others*
M-F	23. *Very little need for security*	A....B....C....D....E	Very strong need for security
M	24. Goes to pieces under pressure	A....B....C....D....E	*Stands up well under pressure*

Table III. *Texas Social Behavior Inventory*

The Social Behavior Inventory asks you to describe your reactions and feelings when you are around other people. Each item has a scale, marked with the letters A, B, C, D, and E, with (A) indicating "not at all characteristic of me" and (E) "very characteristic of me," and the other letters, points in between.

For each item, choose the letter which best describes how characteristic the item is of *you*.

1. I am not likely to speak to people until they speak to me.

A	B	C	D	E
Not at all characteristic of me	Not very	Slightly	Fairly	Very much characteristic of me

2. I would describe myself as self-confident.

A	B	C	D	E
Not at all characteristic of me	Not very	Slightly	Fairly	Very much characteristic of me

3. I feel confident of my appearance.

A	B	C	D	E
Not at all characteristic of me	Not very	Slightly	Fairly	Very much characteristic of me

4. I am a good mixer.

A	B	C	D	E
Not at all characteristic of me	Not very	Slightly	Fairly	Very much characteristic of me

5. When in a group of people, I have trouble thinking of the right things to say.

A	B	C	D	E
Not at all characteristic of me	Not very	Slightly	Fairly	Very much characteristic of me

6. When in a group of people, I usually do what the others want rather than make suggestions.

A	B	C	D	E

Not at all characteristic of me	Not very	Slightly	Fairly	Very much characteristic of me

7. When I am in disagreement with other people, my opinion usually prevails.

A	B	C	D	E

Not at all characteristic of me	Not very	Slightly	Fairly	Very much characteristic of me

8. I would describe myself as one who attempts to master situations.

A	B	C	D	E

Not at all characteristic of me	Not very	Slightly	Fairly	Very much characteristic of me

9. Other people look up to me.

A	B	C	D	E

Not at all characteristic of me	Not very	Slightly	Fairly	Very much characteristic of me

10. I enjoy social gatherings just to be with people.

A	B	C	D	E

Not at all characteristic of me	Not very	Slightly	Fairly	Very much characteristic of me

11. I make a point of looking other people in the eye.

A	B	C	D	E

Not at all characteristic of me	Not very	Slightly	Fairly	Very much characteristic of me

12. I cannot seem to get others to notice me.

A	B	C	D	E
Not at all characteristic of me	Not very	Slightly	Fairly	Very much characteristic of me

13. I would rather not have very much responsibility for other people.

A	B	C	D	E
Not at all characteristic of me	Not very	Slightly	Fairly	Very much characteristic of me

14. I feel comfortable being approached by someone in a position of authority.

A	B	C	D	E
Not at all characteristic of me	Not very	Slightly	Fairly	Very much characteristic of me

15. I would describe myself as indecisive.

A	B	C	D	E
Not at all characteristic of me	Not very	Slightly	Fairly	Very much characteristic of me

16. I have no doubts about my social competence.

A	B	C	D	E
Not at all characteristic of me	Not very	Slightly	Fairly	Very much characteristic of me

Table IV. *Attitudes toward Women*

The statements listed below describe attitudes toward the roles of women in society which different people have. There are no right or wrong answers, only opinions. You are asked to express your feeling about each statement by indicating whether you (A) agree strongly, (B) agree mildly, (C) disagree mildly, or (D) disagree strongly.

1. Swearing and obscenity are more repulsive in the speech of a woman than a man.

A	B	C	D
Agree strongly	Agree mildly	Disagree mildly	Disagree strongly

2. Under modern economic conditions with women being active outside the home, men should share in household tasks such as washing dishes and doing the laundry.

A	B	C	D
Agree strongly	Agree mildly	Disagree mildly	Disagree strongly

3. It is insulting to women to have the "obey" clause remain in the marriage service.

A	B	C	D
Agree strongly	Agree mildly	Disagree mildly	Disagree strongly

4. A woman should be as free as a man to propose marriage.

A	B	C	D
Agree strongly	Agree mildly	Disagree mildly	Disagree strongly

5. Women should worry less about their rights and more about becoming good wives and mothers.

A	B	C	D
Agree strongly	Agree mildly	Disagree mildly	Disagree strongly

6. Women should assume their rightful place in business and all the professions along with men.

A	B	C	D

A	B	C	D
Agree strongly	Agree mildly	Disagree mildly	Disagree strongly

7. A woman should not expect to go to exactly the same places or to have quite the same freedom of action as a man.

A	B	C	D

A	B	C	D
Agree strongly	Agree mildly	Disagree mildly	Disagree strongly

8. It is ridiculous for a woman to run a locomotive and for a man to darn socks.

A	B	C	D

A	B	C	D
Agree strongly	Agree mildly	Disagree mildly	Disagree strongly

9. The intellectual leadership of a community should be largely in the hands of men.

A	B	C	D

A	B	C	D
Agree strongly	Agree mildly	Disagree mildly	Disagree strongly

10. Women should be given equal opportunity with men for apprenticeship in the various trades.

A	B	C	D

A	B	C	D
Agree strongly	Agree mildly	Disagree mildly	Disagree strongly

11. Women earning as much as their dates should bear equally the expense when they go out together.

A	B	C	D

A	B	C	D
Agree strongly	Agree mildly	Disagree mildly	Disagree strongly

12. Sons in a family should be given more encouragement to go to college than daughters.

A	B	C	D

Agree strongly	Agree mildly	Disagree mildly	Disagree strongly

13. In general, the father should have greater authority than the mother in the bringing up of children.

A	B	C	D

Agree strongly	Agree mildly	Disagree mildly	Disagree strongly

14. Economic and social freedom is worth far more to women than acceptance of the ideal of femininity which has been set up by men.

A	B	C	D

Agree strongly	Agree mildly	Disagree mildly	Disagree strongly

15. There are many jobs in which men should be given preference over women in being hired or promoted.

A	B	C	D

Agree strongly	Agree mildly	Disagree mildly	Disagree strongly

Table V. *Initial Version of the Work and Family Orientation Questionnaire (WOFO-1)*

The following statements describe reactions to conditions of work and challenging situations. For each item, indicate how much you *agree* or *disagree* with the statement, as it refers to yourself, by choosing the appropriate letter on the scale A, B, C, D, or E.

1. I more often attempt difficult tasks that I am not sure I can do than easier tasks I believe I can do.

A	B	C	D	E
Strongly agree	Slightly agree	Neither agree nor disagree	Slightly disagree	Strongly disagree

2. It is very important for me to do my work as well as I can even if it isn't popular with my co-workers.

A	B	C	D	E
Strongly agree	Slightly agree	Neither agree nor disagree	Slightly disagree	Strongly disagree

3. I would rather do something at which I feel confident and relaxed than something which is challenging and difficult.

A	B	C	D	E
Strongly agree	Slightly agree	Neither agree nor disagree	Slightly disagree	Strongly disagree

4. I would rather learn fun games that most people know than a difficult thought game.

A	B	C	D	E
Strongly agree	Slightly agree	Neither agree nor disagree	Slightly disagree	Strongly disagree

5. If I am not good at something I would rather keep struggling to master it than move on to something I may be good at.

A	B	C	D	E
Strongly agree	Slightly agree	Neither agree nor disagree	Slightly disagree	Strongly disagree

6. I really enjoy working in situations involving skill and competition.

A	B	C	D	E
Strongly agree	Slightly agree	Neither agree nor disagree	Slightly disagree	Strongly disagree

7. When a group I belong to plans an activity, I would rather organize it myself than have someone else organize it and just help out.

A	B	C	D	E
Strongly agree	Slightly agree	Neither agree nor disagree	Slightly disagree	Strongly disagree

8. Once I undertake a task, I dislike goofing up and not doing the best job I can.

A	B	C	D	E
Strongly agree	Slightly agree	Neither agree nor disagree	Slightly disagree	Strongly disagree

9. I think more of the future than of the present and past.

A	B	C	D	E
Strongly agree	Slightly agree	Neither agree nor disagree	Slightly disagree	Strongly disagree

10. If money were no problem, I'd rather pursue my own interests and hobbies after I finish my education, rather than working, even for myself.

A	B	C	D	E
Strongly agree	Slightly agree	Neither agree nor disagree	Slightly disagree	Strongly disagree

11. It is important for me to get a job after I finish school in which there is opportunity for promotion and advancement.

A	B	C	D	E
Strongly agree	Slightly agree	Neither agree nor disagree	Slightly disagree	Strongly disagree

12. The main satisfaction I expect I would get from a full-time job is being around people and not the work itself.

A	B	C	D	E
Strongly agree	Slightly agree	Neither agree nor disagree	Slightly disagree	Strongly disagree

13. It is important to my future satisfaction in life to have a job or career which pays well.

A	B	C	D	E
Strongly agree	Slightly agree	Neither agree nor disagree	Slightly disagree	Strongly disagree

14. It is important to me to have a job or career that will bring me prestige and recognition from others.

A	B	C	D	E
Strongly agree	Slightly agree	Neither agree nor disagree	Slightly disagree	Strongly disagree

15. I wouldn't mind spending more than 40 hours a week working at a job that interested me, even if I didn't get paid more for the overtime.

A	B	C	D	E
Strongly agree	Slightly agree	Neither agree nor disagree	Slightly disagree	Strongly disagree

16. People who work hard all their lives, even at jobs they enjoy, make more sacrifices than it's worth.

A	B	C	D	E
Strongly agree	Slightly agree	Neither agree nor disagree	Slightly disagree	Strongly disagree

17. After I complete my schooling I would like a job or career which has responsibility and demands a lot of me.

A	B	C	D	E
Strongly agree	Slightly agree	Neither agree nor disagree	Slightly disagree	Strongly disagree

18. Assuming that I get married, I would like my husband or my wife to have a job or career which pays well.

A	B	C	D	E
Strongly agree	Slightly agree	Neither agree nor disagree	Slightly disagree	Strongly disagree

19. Assuming that I get married, I would like my husband or my wife to have a job or career which brings recognition and prestige from others.

A	B	C	D	E
Strongly agree	Slightly agree	Neither agree nor disagree	Slightly disagree	Strongly disagree

20. What is the *least* amount of education that will satisfy you?

   a. graduate from high school
   b. some special vocational training beyond high school (electronics, auto mechanics, nursing, secretarial school, etc.)
   c. some college
   d. graduate from college
   e. advanced professional degree (Ph.D., MD, law degree, etc.)

21. How important do you think marriage will be to your satisfaction in life, in comparison to a job?

   a. the most important thing; I will work primarily for financial reasons
   b. marriage relatively *more* important than my work
   c. marriage and my work equally important
   d. marriage relatively *less* important than my work
   e. marriage is unimportant; I would be reasonably content if I did not marry

22. How many children would you ideally like to have?

   a. 0
   b. 1
   c. 2
   d. 3
   e. 4 or more

Table VI. *Achievement Items from the Initial Version of the Work and Family Orientation Questionnaire (WOFO-1): Scale Assignment and Factor Loadings from Male High School Student Data*

Item	Scale	Factor loadings					
		Mast	Job	Spouse	Eff	Comp	Work
1	Mast	.45	−.02	−.01	.00	.18	−.08
2	Work	.02	.17	.03	.15	.23	−.36
3	Mast	−.56	.05	−.17	.08	.04	.22
4	Mast	−.38	.12	.02	−.06	.21	.11
5	Mast	.32	−.01	.03	−.00	.24	.05
6	Comp	.24	.16	−.01	.04	.38	.01
7	Mast	.41	.02	−.12	.06	−.01	.05
8	Work	−.04	.11	−.06	.23	.20	.41
9	(None)	.10	.16	−.05	.11	−.02	.16
10	Comp	−.01	−.03	−.01	.00	.29	.00
11	Job	−.01	.56	.00	−.01	−.02	.02
12	Work	−.05	.08	.00	.03	.09	.28
13	Job	−.09	.78	.04	−.18	.01	.06
14	Job	.04	.48	−.23	.01	−.02	.12
15	Eff	.00	−.07	.02	.62	.06	.05
16	Eff	.02	.07	−.06	−.39	.05	.07
17	Mast	.40	.24	.01	.27	−.15	.02
18	Spouse	−.07	.00	−.53	−.09	−.05	−.07
19	Spouse	.09	−.02	−.75	.01	−.05	.02

Note: Mast = Mastery; Job = Job Concerns; Spouse = Spouse Career Aspirations; Eff = Effort; Comp = Competitiveness; Work = Work Orientation.

Table VII. *Achievement Items from the Initial Version of the Work and Family Orientation Questionnaire (WOFO-1): Scale Assignment and Factor Loadings from Female High School Student Data*

Item	Scale	Factor 1	Factor 2	Factor 3	Factor 4	Factor 5
1	Mast	.06	.42	.06	−.09	−.15
2	Work	−.03	.31	.21	.08	−.06
3	Mast	−.03	−.38	−.04	.17	.37
4	Mast	.01	−.14	−.01	.08	.44
5	Mast	−.09	.46	−.01	.02	.06
6	Comp	.05	.47	−.04	−.01	−.13
7	Mast	.10	.26	.12	−.02	.02
8	Work	.01	.18	.22	.18	.03
9	(None)	−.00	.25	−.04	.12	.11
10	Comp	.01	.05	.02	−.10	.33
11	Job	.08	.13	.04	55	−.09
12	Work	.20	.01	−.06	−.01	.20
13	Job	.25	−.10	−.12	.61	−.04
14	Job	.63	−.01	.04	.18	.05
15	Eff	.06	.01	.61	−.12	.12
16	Eff	.09	.09	−.52	−.04	.07
17	Mast	.18	.28	.28	−.05	−.15
18	Spouse	.30	−.07	−.12	.37	−.02
19	Spouse	.78	−.01	−.01	.05	−.04

Note: The factor analysis for the total group of females did not yield a coherent structure. Accordingly, the factors are not named. Scale assignments are based on the data from males (see Table VI).

Table VIII. *Intercorrelations and Cronbach Alphas for the Six Scales of WOFO-1*

Males are above the diagonal and females below

	Alpha (Female)	Work	Mast	Comp	Eff	Job	Spouse	Alpha (Male)
Work	.14		.26	.06	.20	.06	−.01	.50
Mast	.56	.32		.15	.22	.00	.00	.35
Comp*		.16	.31		.05	.11	.05	
Eff*		.22	.26	.05		−.10	−.10	
Job	.65	.00	.00	.08	−.11		.36	.59
Spouse*		−.06	−.01	.04	−.14	.61		

* Because there are only two items on these scales, alphas cannot be computed.

Table IX. *Second Version of the Work and Family Orientation Questionnaire (WOFO-2)*

1. I would rather work in a situation where group effort is stressed and more important rather than one in which my individual effort is stressed.

A	B	C	D	E
Strongly agree	Slightly agree	Neither agree nor disagree	Slightly disagree	Strongly disagree

2. I more often attempt difficult tasks that I am not sure I can do than easier tasks I believe I can do.

A	B	C	D	E
Strongly agree	Slightly agree	Neither agree nor disagree	Slightly disagree	Strongly disagree

3. It is very important for me to do my work as well as I can even if it isn't popular with my co-workers.

A	B	C	D	E
Strongly agree	Slightly agree	Neither agree nor disagree	Slightly disagree	Strongly disagree

4. I would rather do something at which I feel confident and relaxed than something which is challenging and difficult.

A	B	C	D	E
Strongly agree	Slightly agree	Neither agree nor disagree	Slightly disagree	Strongly disagree

5. I would rather learn fun games that most people know than a difficult thought game.

A	B	C	D	E
Strongly agree	Slightly agree	Neither agree nor disagree	Slightly disagree	Strongly disagree

6. If I am not good at something I would rather keep struggling to master it than move on to something I may be good at.

A	B	C	D	E
Strongly agree	Slightly agree	Neither agree nor disagree	Slightly disagree	Strongly disagree

7. I really enjoy working in situations involving skill and competition.

A	B	C	D	E
Strongly agree	Slightly agree	Neither agree nor disagree	Slightly disagree	Strongly disagree

8. When a group I belong to plans an activity, I would rather organize it myself than have someone else organize it and just help out.

A	B	C	D	E
Strongly agree	Slightly agree	Neither agree nor disagree	Slightly disagree	Strongly disagree

9. Once I undertake a task, I dislike goofing up and not doing the best job I can.

A	B	C	D	E
Strongly agree	Slightly agree	Neither agree nor disagree	Slightly disagree	Strongly disagree

10. I think more of the future than of the present and past.

A	B	C	D	E
Strongly agree	Slightly agree	Neither agree nor disagree	Slightly disagree	Strongly disagree

11. I hate losing more than I like winning.

A	B	C	D	E
Strongly agree	Slightly agree	Neither agree nor disagree	Slightly disagree	Strongly disagree

12. I worry because my success may cause others to dislike me.

A	B	C	D	E
Strongly agree	Slightly agree	Neither agree nor disagree	Slightly disagree	Strongly disagree

13. It is important to me to perform better than others on a task.

A	B	C	D	E
Strongly agree	Slightly agree	Neither agree nor disagree	Slightly disagree	Strongly disagree

14. I feel that winning is very important in both work and games.

A	B	C	D	E
Strongly agree	Slightly agree	Neither agree nor disagree	Slightly disagree	Strongly disagree

Table X. *Achievement Items for the Second Version of the Work and Family Orientation Questionnaire (WOFO-2): Scale Assignment and Factor Loadings*

Item	Scale	Factor loadings			
		Mast	Comp	Pers Unconcern	Work
1	Pers Unconcern	−.07	−.18	.55	−.18
2	Work	−.08	−.05	.01	−.66
3	Work	.16	.02	.26	−.30
4	Mast; Work	.48	−.02	.05	−.44
5	Mast	.55	−.03	.07	.14
6	Mast	.40	.05	−.03	−.19
7	Comp	.09	−.48	.02	−.16
8	Comp	.34	−.35	−.26	−.03
9	Pers Unconcern	.26	−.10	.37	.10
10	(None)	−.05	−.16	.05	.03
11	(None)	.00	.05	−.15	−.03
12	Pers Unconcern	.06	.13	.49	.06
13	Comp	.05	−.52	.00	.02
14	Comp	−.17	−.71	.06	.06

Note: The factor analysis was performed on the data from male scientists.

Table XI. *Intercorrelations and Cronbach Alphas for the Four Scales of the WOFO-2 (Male Scientists)*

	Alpha	Work	Mast	Comp	Pers Unconcern
Work	.39	1.00	.45	.37	.25
Mast	.60		1.00	.39	.33
Comp	.54			1.00	.10
Pers Unconcern	.55				1.00

Table XII. *Parental Attitudes Questionnaire*

The questions ask for information about your parents' attitudes and actions. "Parent" includes stepparent, foster parent or any other adult guardian who had been responsible for you all or most of your life.

If a question asks about "parents" and you were brought up by only one, answer for him or her.

Answer every item by picking the letter on the scale below which best describes how characteristic or uncharacteristic it is as it applies to *your* experience in your family.

I.

A	B	C	D	E
Very characteristic				Very uncharacteristic

1. Members of my family are very close and get along amazingly well.
2. When I was little, my parents considered it their business to know what I was up to all the time.
3. At home I had a quite definite daily schedule I was expected to follow.
4. If I go on after I finish my education and have a very successful career, my parents will be very pleased.
5. Relative to friends my age, there were fewer family rules and regulations I was expected to follow.
6. If I have any children, I expect to bring them up very similarly to how I was brought up.
7. Our family has always done lots of things together.
8. My parents encouraged me to stick up for my rights and to fight back if anybody tried to push me around.

II. All the questions in this section refer to your *mother* or other female guardian. If you grew up without a mother or female guardian, leave this section blank and go to Section III, question 34.

A	B	C	D	E
Very characteristic				Very uncharacteristic

9. My mother believed there was no reason why she should have her own way all the time any more than I should have mine.
10. My mother encouraged me to talk to her about my troubles.
11. There were rules in my family but lots of times my mother didn't really care if I lived up to them.
12. I was discouraged from ever questioning my mother's way of thinking or doing things.
13. My mother didn't mind if I played with toys that were supposed to be for the opposite sex.
14. When I did something I shouldn't my mother tried to get me to understand why I was wrong rather than simply punishing me.
15. My mother encouraged me to do my best on everything I did.

16. My mother didn't want me to bother her with unimportant little problems.
17. I received a good deal of physical affection from my mother.
18. I would describe my mother as a strict parent.
19. When I look back, I think my mother criticized me or punished me a lot more than I deserved.
20. I was expected to do what my mother told me to with little discussion or explanation.
21. My mother always has set up high standards for me to meet.
22. I was encouraged to tell my mother if I believed a family rule was unfair.
23. I feel that my mother has almost always approved of me and the things I do.
24. My mother is very sympathetic to "women's lib."
25. My mother frequently praised me for doing well.
26. My mother tried to impress upon me that getting along with people was one of the most important things I could learn.
27. My mother and I argued a lot about what I should be doing or how I should behave.
28. My mother always took an interest in my activities.
29. My mother frequently criticized what I was doing.
30. My mother was always careful and cautious about what she'd let me do for fear I'd get hurt.
31. My mother was so inconsistent in what she expected of me I just gave up trying to understand her.
32. My mother believed I had a right to my own point of view and allowed me to express it.
33. When I did something I wasn't supposed to and my mother found out about it, she very often let me get away with it.

III. All the questions in this section refer to your *father* or other male guardian. If you grew up all or most of the time without your father or a male guardian in your home, leave this section blank.

A	B	C	D	E
Very characteristic				Very uncharacteristic

34. My father believed there was no reason why he should have his own way all the time any more than I should have mine.
35. My father encouraged me to talk to him about my troubles.
36. There were rules in my family but lots of times my father didn't really care if I lived up to them.
37. I was discouraged from ever questioning my father's way of thinking or doing things.
38. My father didn't mind if I played with toys that were supposed to be for the opposite sex.
39. When I did something I shouldn't my father tried to get me to understand why I was wrong rather than simply punishing me.
40. My father encouraged me to do my best on everything I did.
41. My father didn't want me to bother him with unimportant little problems.
42. I received a good deal of physical affection from my father.
43. I would describe my father as a strict parent.

44. When I look back, I think my father criticized me or punished me a lot more than I deserved.
45. I was expected to do what my father told me to with little discussion or explanation.
46. My father always has set up high standards for me to meet.
47. I was encouraged to tell my father if I believed a family rule was unfair.
48. I feel that my father has almost always approved of me and the things I do.
49. My father is very sympathetic to "women's lib."
50. My father frequently praised me for doing well.
51. My father tried to impress upon me that getting along with people was one of the most important things I could learn.
52. My father and I argued a lot about what I should be doing or how I should behave.
53. My father always took an interest in my activities.
54. My father frequently criticized what I was doing.
55. My father was always careful and cautious about what he'd let me do for fear I'd get hurt.
56. My father was so inconsistent in what he expected of me I just gave up trying to understand him.
57. My father believed I had a right to my own point of view and allowed me to express it.
58. When I did something I wasn't supposed to and my father found out about it, he very often let me get away with it.

IV. If you did not grow up with both your mother and father (or step- or foster parents) all or most of the time, leave this section blank.

59. When you had a problem, whom did you confide in?
    a. My father almost always
    b. My father more often than my mother
    c. My father and mother equally
    d. My mother more often than my father
    e. My mother almost always

60. My mother and father have always agreed quite closely on how children should be brought up.
    a. Very characteristic
    b. Often characteristic
    c. Only sometimes characteristic
    d. Often uncharacteristic
    e. Very uncharacteristic

61. While I was growing up, I felt:
    a. Much closer to my father than my mother
    b. Somewhat closer to my father than my mother
    c. Equally close to my mother and my father (or not close to either)
    d. Somewhat closer to my mother than my father
    e. Much closer to my mother than my father

62. My ideals are:
    a. Much more similar to my father's than my mother's
    b. Somewhat more similar to my father's than my mother's
    c. Equally similar to both my parents (or not similar to either)
    d. Somewhat more similar to my mother's than my father's
    e. Much more similar to my mother's than my father's

63. My personality is:
    a. Much more similar to my father's than my mother's
    b. Somewhat more similar to my father's than my mother's
    c. Equally similar to both my parents (or not similar to either)
    d. Somewhat more similar to my mother's than my father's
    e. Much more similar to my mother's than my father's

Table XIII. *Composition and Factor Loadings for the Parent Behavior Items of the Parental Attitudes Questionnaire Scales, High School Students*

Factor loadings

| | Father Positivity | | | Mother Positivity | |
Item	Males	Females	Item	Males	Females
35	.50	.60	16	.45	.30
39	.41	.49	19	.57	.49
40	.45	.58	20	.30	.30
41	−.41	−.42	23	−.34	−.54
42	.31	.49	27	.49	.52
47	.51	.53	29	.54	.51
48	.31	.50	31	.52	.50
50	.51	.55	32	−.32	−.34
53	.54	.60			
56	−.31	−.41			

| | Father Democracy | | | Mother Democracy | |
Item	Males	Females	Item	Males	Females
39	−.32	−.40	9	.40	.44
43	.46	.61	10	.34	.36
44	.53	.57	14	.37	.37
45	.44	.53	22	.50	.51
52	.58	.44	23	.34	.29
54	.56	.40	26	.30	.33
56	.36	.36	32	.46	.45
57	−.45	−.42	47	.33	.32

Table XIII, cont'd.

Rule Enforcement			Family Protectiveness		
Item	Males	Females	Item	Males	Females
5	.42	.40	2	.34	.38
11	.49	.51	30	.50	.67
18	−.40	−.33	55	.59	.52
33	.41	.57			
36	.42	.51	Sex-Role Enforcement		
58	.41	.48	Item	Males	Females
			13	.43	.48
			24	.40	.52
			38	.64	.45
			49	.41	.50

Sex-specific factors

Male only		Female only	
Male Family Harmony		Female Family Harmony	
Item	Males	Item	Females
1	.43	1	.31
6	.35	4	.34
7	.49	6	.35
8	.32	8	.33
17	.37	10	.41
35	.32	14	.36
42	.42	15	.58
		16	−.30
		17	.39
		22	.32
		23	.35
		25	.35
		26	.43
		28	.39
		31	−.29
		32	.38

Male only		Female only	
Male Achievement Standards		Female Standards	
Item	Males	Item	Females
4	.49	3	.40
15	.50	18	.49
25	.29	19	.38
26	.35	21	.56
28	.38	46	.37
40	.44		
45	.32		
46	.31		
48	.29		

Table XIV. *Cronbach Alphas and Intercorrelations of the Eleven Scales from the Parental Attitudes Questionnaire for High School Students*

Males are above the diagonal and females below.

	Alpha (Fem)	Fa Posit	Mo Posit	Fa Democ	Mo Democ	Rule Enforce	Male Fam Harm	Fem Fam Harm	Male Ach	Fem Stand	Fam Protect	Sex-Role	Alpha (Males)
Fa Posit	.87		.34	.64	.55	.05	.69	.57	.58	.00	-.10	-.11	.83
Mo Posit	.82	.35		.35	.61	-.03	.35	.70	.33	-.44	-.13	.02	.71
Fa Democ	.81	.70	.40		.36	-.09	.38	.32	.20	-.21	-.13	-.14	.78
Mo Democ	.85	.51	.74	.39		-.05	.70	.83	.58	-.09	.40	-.10	.84
Rule Enforce	.65	.02	-.10	-.18	-.09		.10	.11	.18	.40	.16	.07	.58
Male Fam Harm	.82	.73	.56	.47	.77	.06		.66	.47	.03	.48	-.06	.59
Fem Fam Harm	.89	.49	.80	.38	.89	.00	.78		.76	-.10	.08	.01	.54
Male Ach	.67	.60	.47	.31	.63	.10	.62	.75		.19	.14	.02	.82
Fem Stand	.58	-.02	-.49	-.27	-.22	.38	-.08	-.21	.15		.28	-.02	.82
Fam Protect	.67	.13	-.13	-.07	.27	.18	.37	.07	.37	.22		.02	.68
Sex-Role	.53	-.26	-.22	-.23	-.22	.09	-.25	-.23	-.21	.06	.13		.55

Table XV. Loadings from Second-order Factor Analyses of Scale Scores on the Parental Attitudes Questionnaire, High School Sample

Scale	Males			Females		
	Mother-Family Acceptance	Father Acceptance	Family Rules & Stand	Mother-Family Acceptance	Father Acceptance	Family Rules & Stand
Father Positivity	.46	.79	.30	.28	.85	.18
Mother Positivity	.71	.11	−.22	.81	.21	−.33
Father Democracy	.29	.69	−.23	.18	.80	−.21
Mother Democracy	.84	.20	−.01	.83	.32	−.02
Rule Enforcement	.01	−.06	.36	.00	−.09	.49
Family Protectiveness	−.01	−.04	.42	.01	.03	.38
Sex-Role Enforcement	.00	−.17	.07	−.16	−.25	.08
Male Fam Harmony	.49	.45	.32			
Female Fam Harmony				.95	.27	.06
Male Ach Standards	.60	.19	.43			
Female Standards				.26	−.08	.68

Table XVI. *Parental Attributes Questionnaire*

A. Mother's Attributes

The following items refer to your perceptions of your *mother*. If you were brought up most of your life by a stepmother, foster mother, or other female guardian, please answer for her instead. If there was no woman regularly in your household who was responsible for your upbringing, go to Section B.

1. Not at all independent — Very independent
   A....B....C....D....E
2. Not at all emotional — Very emotional
   A....B....C....D....E
3. Very passive — Very active
   A....B....C....D....E
4. Not at all able to devote self completely to others — Able to devote self completely to others
   A....B....C....D....E
5. Very rough — Very gentle
   A....B....C....D....E
6. Not at all helpful — Very helpful to others
   A....B....C....D....E
7. Not at all competitive — Very competitive
   A....B....C....D....E
8. Not at all kind — Very kind
   A....B....C....D....E
9. Not at all aware of feelings of others — Very aware of feelings of others
   A....B....C....D....E
10. Can make decisions easily — Has difficulty making decisions
    A....B....C....D....E
11. Gives up very easily — Never gives up easily
    A....B....C....D....E
12. Not at all self-confident — Very self-confident
    A....B....C....D....E
13. Feels very inferior — Feels very superior
    A....B....C....D....E
14. Not at all understanding of others — Very understanding of others
    A....B....C....D....E
15. Very cold in relations with others — Very warm in relations with others
    A....B....C....D....E
16. Goes to pieces under pressure — Stands up well under pressure
    A....B....C....D....E

B. Father's Attributes

The following items refer to your perceptions of your *father*. If you were brought up most of your life by a stepfather, foster father, or other male guardian, please answer for him instead.

If you had no father or other male guardian, please omit this section.

17.	Not at all independent	Very independent
	A....B....C....D....E	
18.	Not at all emotional	Very emotional
	A....B....C....D....E	
19.	Very passive	Very active
	A....B....C....D....E	
20.	Not at all able to devote self completely to others	Able to devote self completely to others
	A....B....C....D....E	
21.	Very rough	Very gentle
	A....B....C....D....E	
22.	Not at all helpful to others	Very helpful to others
	A....B....C....D....E	
23.	Not at all competitive	Very competitive
	A....B....C....D....E	
24.	Not at all kind	Very kind
	A....B....C....D....E	
25.	Not at all aware of feelings of others	Very aware of feelings of others
	A....B....C....D....E	
26.	Can make decisions easily	Has difficulty making decisions
	A....B....C....D....E	
27.	Gives up very easily	Never gives up easily
	A....B....C....D....E	
28.	Not at all self-confident	Very self-confident
	A....B....C....D....E	
29.	Feels very inferior	Feels very superior
	A....B....C....D....E	
30.	Not at all understanding of others	Very understanding of others
	A....B....C....D....E	
31.	Very cold in relations with others	Very warm in relations with others
	A....B....C....D....E	
32.	Goes to pieces under pressure	Stands up well under pressure
	A....B....C....D....E	

B. Demographic Characteristics of High School Samples

Table I. Percentage of Mothers and Fathers in Each Educational Category within the Four Socioeconomic Classes

Table II. Percentage of Intact Homes at Three Age Periods within Each Socioeconomic Class

Table III. Distribution of Family Sizes (Number of Children) in Each Socioeconomic Group and in Each Religious Group

Table IV. Percentages of Mothers and Fathers in Each Employment Group within Each Socioeconomic Group

Table I. *Percentage of Mothers and Fathers in Each Educational Category within the Four Socioeconomic Classes*

Education	Fathers				Mothers			
	Upper	Upper mid	Lower mid	Lower	Upper	Upper mid	Lower mid	Lower
Grade school	0	1	4	7	1	0	1	6
Some high school	0	2	12	15	0	4	7	15
H. S. graduate	2	13	32	47	18	39	47	60
Voc. training beyond H. S.	1	6	16	14	14	13	14	6
Some college	2	11	12	9	13	13	10	8
College graduate	20	50	22	6	32	26	18	4
Postgraduate	75	17	2	1	22	5	3	1

Table II. *Percentage of Intact Homes at Three Age Periods within Each Socioeconomic Class*

Age period	Upper	Upper mid	Social class Lower mid	Lower	Total
Birth–5 years	96	99	98	98	98
6–10 years	92	96	94	94	94
10+ years	91	92	92	89	92

Table III. *Distribution of Family Sizes (Number of Children) in Each Socioeconomic Group and in Each Religious Group*

	1	2	3	4	5–6	7–8	9–10	>10
Class								
Upper	2	18	34	22	17	4	3	0
Upper middle	3	18	31	22	21	4	1	0
Lower middle	4	19	29	22	18	6	2	0
Lower	5	18	18	23	23	7	3	3
Religion								
Catholic	4	16	24	21	25	6	3	1
Protestant	4	22	32	24	14	3	1	0
Jewish	7	27	46	13	5	2	0	0
None	2	30	36	18	9	3	2	0
Other	0	22	15	7	35	14	7	0

Note: The cell entries represent the percentage in each socioeconomic or religious group of the given family size. The increasing family size with decreasing level of class is largely due to the increasing proportion of Catholic families in going from the Upper to Lower groups. Although Lower-class Catholics tended to have larger families than the other groups, Catholicism was associated with greater family size in every socioeconomic class.

Table IV. *Percentages of Mothers and Fathers in Each Employment Group within Each Socioeconomic Group*

Class	Fathers			Mothers		
	None	Part-time	Full-time	None	Part-time	Full-time
Upper	0	0	100	48	35	17
Upper middle	0	1	99	42	36	22
Lower middle	0	1	99	37	33	30
Lower	0	1	99	42	34	24

C. Subsidiary Analyses, Chapter 7: Relationships with Achievement Scales

Table I. Correlations of WOFO-1 Achievement Scales with PAQ Scales, Self-esteem, and AWS for High School Students Aspiring to College and Professional Degrees

PAQ scale	Work	Mast	Comp	Effort	Job	Spouse
Masc (M)						
Males	.23	.39	.22	.03	.07	.07
Females	.25	.42	.34	.07	.04	−.01
Fem (F)						
Males	.01	.18	.00	.14	.02	.01
Females	.15	.02	−.13	.17	−.12	−.01
Masc-Fem (M-F)						
Males	.09	.20	−.01	.01	−.03	.04
Females	.12	.23	.22	−.02	.06	−.10
Self-esteem						
Males	.11	.43	.15	.10	.11	.07
Females	.15	.38	.26	.14	.05	.06
AWS						
Males	.08	.08	−.05	.15	−.23	.12
Females	.14	.14	−.03	.19	−.11	−.13

Note: For $df = 350$, $r_{.05} = .10$.

D. Subsidiary Analyses, Chapter 10: Relationships with Parental Attributes

Table I. Percentage of Students in Each Masculinity and Femininity Group in Each of the Sixteen Couple Types for High School Students

Table II. Percentage of Males and Females in Each Masculinity and Femininity Category, Broken Down by Couple Type and Perception of Themselves as More Similar in Ideals to Mother, Father, or Equal to Both

Table III. Intercorrelations for College Students among PAQ Scales (Parent Self-ratings, Student Ratings of Parents, and Student Self-ratings) and AWS (Parents' and Students' Self-report)

Table IV. Percentages in Masculinity and Femininity Categories for College Students' Ratings of Parents (Males and Females Combined), Parents' Self-ratings, and Male and Female Students' Self-ratings

Table V. Means and Standard Deviations on the PAQ Scales for College Students' Self-report, Parent Self-report, and Student Ratings of Parents

Table VI. Percentage of College Students in Each Masculinity and Femininity Category for the Sixteen Couple Types

Table VII. Percentage of College Students in Each of the PAQ Categories within Each of the Sixteen Couple Types Classified by Parent Self-report

Table I. *Percentage of Students in Each Masculinity and Femininity Group in Each of the Sixteen Couple Types for High School Students*

Couple type (Father-Mother)	Males					Females				
	N	Undiff	Fem	Masc	Andro	N	Undiff	Fem	Masc	Andro
Andro-Andro	63	10	6	33	51	151	7	27	11	55
Andro-Masc	11	18	9	36	36	34	15	21	12	53
Andro-Fem	29	17	7	35	41	48	6	42	12	40
Andro-Undiff	7	14	0	43	43	27	18	30	7	44
Masc-Andro	92	17	8	46	29	110	12	32	15	41
Masc-Masc	48	19	2	58	21	35	20	40	23	17
Masc-Fem	81	18	10	48	24	112	22	33	18	27
Masc-Undiff	43	33	2	44	21	64	22	39	14	25
Fem-Andro	4	25	0	0	75	10	10	60	0	30
Fem-Masc	2	50	0	50	0	4	25	0	25	50
Fem-Fem	1	100	0	0	0	10	20	70	0	10
Fem-Undiff	1	100	0	0	0	4	0	50	25	25
Undiff-Andro	12	8	0	75	17	35	14	31	9	46
Undiff-Masc	15	33	13	27	27	17	29	12	12	47
Undiff-Fem	16	31	19	31	19	29	38	28	10	24
Undiff-Undiff	56	38	7	39	16	34	38	26	18	18

Table II. *Percentage of Males and Females in Each Masculinity and Femininity Category, Broken Down by Couple Type and Perception of Themselves as More Similar in Ideals to Mother, Father, or Equal to Both*

Couple type (Father-Mother)	Sim	Males					Females				
		N	Undiff	Fem	Masc	Andro	N	Undiff	Fem	Masc	Andro
Andro-Andro	Fa	24	12	4	21	63	31	10	39	3	48
	Eq	33	3	9	42	46	84	6	21	16	57
	Mo	2	50	0	0	50	27	11	33	7	48
Andro-Fem	Fa	15	7	13	40	40	17	6	59	6	29
	Eq	13	31	0	31	38	24	8	29	8	54
	Mo	0					7	0	43	43	14
Masc-Andro	Fa	26	12	4	50	35	17	18	35	12	35
	Eq	46	20	9	43	28	50	12	24	14	50
	Mo	16	25	12	38	25	39	8	43	18	31
Masc-Fem	Fa	22	23	3	60	14	24	25	17	25	33
	Eq	29	14	17	38	31	57	26	32	21	21
	Mo	12	17	17	25	42	27	11	48	7	33
Masc-Masc	Fa	14	14	7	72	7	7	29	29	29	14
	Eq	23	22	0	52	26	18	17	44	22	17
	Mo	6	17	0	67	17	8	12	38	25	25
Masc-Undiff	Fa	22	27	0	50	23	21	19	43	14	24
	Eq	15	33	7	53	7	30	23	30	20	27
	Mo	3	67	0	0	33	9	22	44	0	33
Undiff-Fem	Fa	1	0	100	0	0	4	25	25	25	25
	Eq	7	43	29	14	14	10	30	30	10	30
	Mo	7	29	0	43	28	12	50	25	8	17
Undiff-Undiff	Fa	16	44	6	44	6	8	38	25	25	12
	Eq	29	31	7	41	20	21	38	29	19	14
	Mo	9	56	0	33	11	4	50	0	0	50

Table III. Intercorrelations for College Students among PAQ Scales (Parent Self-ratings, Student Ratings of Parents, and Student Self-ratings) and AWS (Parents' and Students' Self-report)

	Males						Females					
	Fathers			Mothers			Fathers			Mothers		
	M	F	M-F	M	F	M-F	M	F	M-F	M	F	M-F
Student ratings of parents												
M	1.00	.09	.50	1.00	.12	.55	1.00	.17	.54	1.00	.08	.66
F		1.00	-.29		1.00	-.25		1.00	-.23		1.00	-.26
M-F			1.00			1.00			1.00			1.00
Parent AWS	-.09	.09	-.01	.19	-.04	.21	-.08	.05	-.10	.20	-.08	.28
Parent self-ratings												
M	1.00	.30	.45	1.00	.20	.48	1.00	.16	.43	1.00	.09	.63
F		1.00	-.23		1.00	-.27		1.00	-.23		1.00	-.25
M-F			1.00			1.00			1.00			1.00
Parent AWS	.04	.15	.03	.15	-.08	.27	-.06	.04	-.03	.24	-.02	.26

	Males			Females		
	M	F	M-F	M	F	M-F
Student self-ratings						
M	1.00	.19	.40	1.00	.13	.55
F		1.00	-.23		1.00	-.25
M-F			1.00			1.00
Student AWS	-.11	-.02	.05	.02	-.26	.23

Table IV. *Percentages in Masculinity and Femininity Categories for College Students' Ratings of Parents (Males and Females Combined), Parents' Self-ratings, and Male and Female Students' Self-ratings*

| | Male students or parents | | | |
	Undiff	Fem	Masc	Andro
Students' ratings of parents	16	6	44	35
Parents' self-ratings	19	6	44	32
Students' self-ratings	19	12	36	33

| | Female students or parents | | | |
	Undiff	Fem	Masc	Andro
Students' ratings of parents	13	39	10	38
Parents' self-ratings	22	33	14	31
Students' self-ratings	20	36	14	31

Table V. *Means and Standard Deviations on the PAQ Scales for College Students' Self-report, Parent Self-report, and Student Ratings of Parents*

| | Parent self-report | | Students' parent ratings | | Student self-report | |
PAQ scale	$\bar{X}$	SD	$\bar{X}$	SD	$\bar{X}$	SD
M						
Males*	23.21	4.24	24.13	5.25	22.46	4.24
Females**	19.58	4.84	19.46	5.80	19.88	4.48
F						
Males	21.06	4.29	20.83	5.98	21.96	4.14
Females	23.99	4.26	25.74	4.86	24.13	3.66
M-F						
Males	16.97	3.79	18.57	4.50	16.61	4.01
Females	12.88	3.95	11.53	4.48	12.63	4.13

* Male students or fathers.
** Female students or mothers.

Table VI. Percentage of College Students in Each Masculinity and Femininity Category for the Sixteen Couple Types

Couple type (Father-Mother)	PAQ category									
	Males					Females				
	N	Undiff	Fem	Masc	Andro	N	Undiff	Fem	Masc	Andro
Andro-Andro	87	9	7	25	59	132	11	33	10	46
Andro-Masc	12	17	8	67	8	30	23	30	13	33
Andro-Fem	54	13	15	37	35	84	17	44	4	36
Andro-Undiff	12	17	17	50	17	18	11	50	22	17
Masc-Andro	85	14	9	44	33	103	10	34	14	42
Masc-Masc	24	33	4	42	21	22	32	23	23	23
Masc-Fem	119	29	8	39	24	145	20	34	23	23
Masc-Undiff	44	32	2	36	30	45	31	33	13	22
Fem-Andro	12	25	8	0	67	8	0	75	0	25
Fem-Masc	5	40	20	20	20	9	11	56	11	22
Fem-Fem	10	10	20	50	20	10	40	30	10	20
Fem-Undiff	4	25	25	50	0	11	18	55	27	0
Undiff-Andro	31	13	10	45	32	30	13	43	20	23
Undiff-Masc	14	36	21	29	14	10	20	30	20	30
Undiff-Fem	42	19	24	38	19	33	39	30	12	18
Undiff-Undiff	26	61	8	12	19	31	42	32	10	16

Note: Parent classification is based on students' ratings of parents.

Table VII. *Percentage of College Students in Each of the PAQ Categories within Each of the Sixteen Couple Types Classified by Parent Self-report*

Couple type (Father-Mother)	Males					Females				
	N	Undiff	Fem	Masc	Andro	N	Undiff	Fem	Masc	Andro
Andro-Andro	39	3	18	44	36	31	19	45	13	23
Andro-Masc	7	29	14	29	29	18	11	22	17	50
Andro-Fem	23	9	9	44	39	29	21	35	14	31
Andro-Undiff	20	35	0	50	15	16	25	25	13	38
Masc-Andro	33	30	12	33	24	38	21	26	13	40
Masc-Masc	10	30	10	30	30	21	38	24	14	24
Masc-Fem	40	20	5	30	45	58	19	41	9	31
Masc-Undiff	21	24	5	43	29	39	13	41	10	36
Fem-Andro	4	25	50	0	25	7	14	43	0	43
Fem-Masc	5	20	0	80	0	3	33	66	0	0
Fem-Fem	6	0	50	33	17	5	20	80	0	0
Fem-Undiff	1	0	0	0	100	4	25	25	25	25
Undiff-Andro	13	23	15	23	39	15	27	20	27	27
Undiff-Masc	6	0	33	33	33	8	38	38	13	13
Undiff-Fem	18	22	6	44	28	21	10	38	14	38
Undiff-Undiff	12	33	0	42	25	15	33	20	20	27

E. Subsidiary Analyses, Chapter 11: Relationships with Parental Behaviors

Table I. Means on Each Parent Factor for Each Masculinity and Femininity Group for High School Students and Results of Sex x PAQ Analyses of Variance

Table II. Mean Self-esteem Score and Mean z Scores on the Parental Behavior Scales for the Nine Male Constellations and Eleven Female Constellations in High School Students

Table I. *Means on Each Parent Factor for Each Masculinity and Femininity Group for High School Students a⌁ Results of Sex x PAQ Analyses of Variance*

Parent Behavior scale

PAQ	Father Posit Male	Female	Mother Posit Male	Female	Father Democ Male	Female	Mother Democ Male	Female	Rule Enfor⌁ Male	Fem
Andro	28.27	29.60	19.62	21.47	17.43	19.10	20.99	22.51	14.69	15.
Masc	24.50	26.67	18.88	18.97	17.70	17.12	20.41	20.34	13.89	15.
Fem	24.46	27.33	17.98	20.26	15.12	19.06	21.33	21.07	15.13	14.
Undiff	24.62	24.61	16.75	18.85	15.80	17.87	18.81	19.90	14.21	13.
Total	26.42	27.59	18.52	20.26	17.01	18.60	20.26	21.26	14.26	14.
ANOVA	*p*		*p*		*p*		*p*		*p*	
Sex	<.09		<.001		<.001		<.002			
PAQ	<.007		<.001		<.026		<.001			<.026
Sex x PAQ					<.007					

Table II. *Mean Self-esteem Score and Mean z Scores on the Parental Behavior Scales for the Nine Male Constella⌁ and Eleven Female Constellations in High School Students*

Males

Constell	N	Self-esteem	Fa Posit	Mo Posit	Fa Democ	Mo Democ	Rule Enforce	Fam Prot	Sex-Role	Male Fam	Fem Fam	Male Ach	Fe⌁ Star
1	48	47.0	1.48	.96	1.07	.98	.17	−.29	−.30	.56	1.38	1.15	−.⌁
2	21	44.3	.72	.29	.22	−.10	.57	−.40	.43	.14	.80	1.52	.⌁
3	38	41.5	.01	.72	−.10	.77	−.35	−.30	.21	.17	1.03	.69	−.⌁
4	131	40.4	.34	.63	.24	−.10	.06	−.34	.03	−.03	.54	.53	−.⌁
5	41	39.6	.20	−.12	.30	−.51	−.20	−.38	.95	−.18	−.26	−.59	−.3
6	93	38.2	.12	−.80	−.35	−.51	.18	−.02	−.04	−.32	−.14	.51	.6⌁
7	28	37.9	−1.24	−.38	−.52	−1.20	−.38	−1.48	.25	−1.18	1.21	−1.31	−.5⌁
8	63	36.7	.12	−.15	.32	−.41	−.27	−.33	−.89	−.29	−.50	−.89	−.2⌁
9	97	34.2	−1.14	−.49	−.62	−.94	.04	−.12	.16	−.95	−.82	−.98	−.0⌁

Parent Behavior scale

ct emale	Sex-Role		Male Fam Harm		Fem Fam Harm		Male Ach		Fem Stand	
	Male	Female	Male	Female	Male	Female	Male	Female	Male	Female
8.07	10.66	7.02	17.72	18.81	44.35	47.10	26.55	26.79	10.01	8.77
7.50	10.69	7.11	17.38	16.61	41.61	41.10	25.15	25.54	9.45	9.83
8.08	10.69	7.65	16.95	17.42	40.18	43.49	24.79	25.33	9.71	8.48
8.11	10.41	7.24	17.05	16.62	38.31	39.79	23.72	23.85	9.86	8.56
6.00	10.62	7.28	17.35	17.65	41.46	43.79	25.18	25.63	9.71	8.79
	p		*p*		*p*		*p*		*p*	
44	<.001				<.004				<.012	
42			<.001		<.001		<.001			
			<.029						<.015	

Females

N	Self-esteem	Fa Posit	Mo Posit	Fa Democ	Mo Democ	Rule Enforce	Fam Prot	Sex-Role	Male Fam	Fem Fam	Male Ach	Fem Stand
46	45.7	1.49	.94	1.07	.93	-.12	-.48	-.55	1.08	1.19	1.02	-.16
24	44.9	.67	.77	-.31	.59	-.06	.04	.00	.48	.87	.69	-.08
58	42.3	.84	-.55	.52	-.67	.70	.06	.07	-.03	-.37	.26	.35
88	42.0	-.34	.29	-.34	.35	-.02	-.14	.01	-.11	.59	.50	.19
196	40.8	.65	.68	.79	.56	.00	-.13	-.28	.38	.81	.67	-.25
85	38.3	-.77	-.56	-1.13	-.92	.30	-.62	-.14	-.81	-.58	-.24	.39
43	37.3	-.50	.31	-.08	.28	-.47	-.44	.22	-.49	.10	-.87	-.76
36	36.2	.75	-.46	.71	-.72	-1.20	-.21	-.16	-.25	-.61	-.15	-.10
70	35.3	-.22	-.35	.36	-.78	-.34	-.70	-.04	-.59	-.45	-.37	.00
77	34.2	-.53	-.37	-.54	-.75	.34	.71	.19	-.51	-.31	-.12	.30
77	32.9	-1.30	-.96	-.80	-1.44	.04	-.56	.53	-1.35	-1.49	-1.84	-.09

References

Aaronson, B.S., & Grumpelt, H.R. Homosexuality and some MMPI measures of masculinity-femininity. *Journal of Clinical Psychology*, 1961, *17*, 245–247.

Ach, N. *Uber den Willensakt und das Temperament*. Leipzig: Quelle & Meyers, 1910.

Achenbach, T.M. Comparison of Stanford-Binet performances of retarded and non-retarded persons matched for MA and sex. *American Journal of Mental Deficiency*, 1970, 74, 488–494.

Aldis, O. *Play fighting*. New York: Academic Press, 1975.

Alper, T.G. Achievement motivation in college women: A now you see it now you don't phenomenon. *American Psychologist*, 1974, *29*, 194–203.

Alper, T.G., & Greenberger, E. Relationship of picture structure to achievement motivation in college women. *Journal of Personality and Social Psychology*, 1967, 7, 362–371.

Alpert, R., & Haber, R.N. Anxiety in academic achievement situations. *Journal of Abnormal and Social Psychology*, 1960, *61*, 207–215.

Angrist, S.A. The study of sex-roles. *Journal of Social Issues*, 1969, *15*, 215–232.

Archer, J. Biological explanation of psychological sex differences. In B. Lloyd & J. Archer (Eds.), *Exploring sex differences*. London: Academic Press, 1976.

Atkinson, J.W. Motivational determinants of risk-taking behavior. *Psychological Review*, 1957, 64, 359–372.

Atkinson, J.W. (Ed.). *Motives in fantasy, action and society*. Princeton: Van Nostrand, 1958.

Atkinson, J.W. *An introduction to motivation*. Princeton: Van Nostrand, 1964.

Atkinson, J.W. The mainsprings of achievement-oriented activity. In J.W. Atkinson & J.O. Raynor (Eds.), *Motivation and achievement*. Washington, D.C.: V.H. Winston & Sons, 1974.

Atkinson, J.W., & Feather, N.T. (Eds.). *A theory of achievement motivation*. New York: Wiley, 1966.

Atkinson, J.W., & McClelland, D.C. The projective expression of needs: II. The effect of different intensities of the hunger drive on thematic apperception. *Journal of Experimental Psychology*, 1948, *38*, 643–658.

Atkinson, J.W., & Raynor, J.O. (Eds.). *Motivation and achievement*. Washington, D.C.: V.H. Winston & Sons, 1974.

Bakan, D. *The duality of human existence*. Chicago: Rand McNally, 1966.

Bandura, A. *Principles of behavior modification.* New York: Holt, Rinehart, & Winston, 1969.

Bandura, A., & Huston, A.C. Identification as a process of incidental learning. *Journal of Abnormal and Social Psychology,* 1961, *63,* 311–318.

Bandura, A., Ross, D., & Ross, S. Transmission of aggression through imitation of aggressive models. *Journal of Abnormal and Social Psychology,* 1961, *63,* 575–582.

Bandura, A., Ross, D., & Ross, S. A comparative test of the status envy, social power, and secondary reinforcement theories of identification learning. *Journal of Abnormal and Social Psychology,* 1963, *67,* 527–534.

Barry, H., Bacon, M.K., & Child, I.L. A cross-cultural survey of some sex differences in socialization. *Journal of Abnormal and Social Psychology,* 1957, *55,* 527–534.

Bar-Tal, D., & Frieze, I. *Achievement motivation and gender as determinants of attributions for success and failure.* Unpublished manuscript, University of Pittsburgh, 1973.

Baumrind, D. Child care practices anteceding three patterns of preschool behavior. *Genetic Psychology Monographs,* 1967, *75,* 43–88.

Baumrind, D. Authoritarian vs. authoritative parental control. *Adolescence,* 1968, *3,* 255–272.

Baumrind, D. Current patterns of parental authority. *Developmental Psychology Monograph,* 1971, *4* (No. 1, pt. 2).

Baumrind, D., & Black, A.E. Socialization practices associated with dimensions of competence in preschool boys and girls. *Child Development,* 1967, *38,* 291–328.

Beane, W. *Life history and personality variables in scientific attainment.* Unpublished doctoral dissertation, University of Texas, Austin, 1976.

Bem, D., & Allen, A. On predicting some of the people some of the time: The search for cross-situational consistencies in behavior. *Psychological Review,* 1974, *81,* 506–520.

Bem, S.L. The measurement of psychological androgyny. *Journal of Consulting and Clinical Psychology,* 1974, *42,* 155–162.

Bem, S.L. Sex-role adaptability: One consequence of psychological androgyny. *Journal of Personality and Social Psychology,* 1975, *31,* 634–643.

Bem, S.L. On the utility of alternate procedures for assessing psychological androgyny. *Journal of Consulting and Clinical Psychology,* 1977, *45,* 196–205.

Bem, S.L., & Lenney, E. Sex-typing and the avoidance of cross-sex behavior. *Journal of Personality and Social Psychology,* 1976, *33,* 48–54.

Bem, S.L., Martyna, W., & Watson, C. Sex typing and androgyny: Further explorations of the expressive domain. *Journal of Personality and Social Psychology,* 1976, *34,* 1016–1023.

Berscheid, E., & Walster, E. Physical attractiveness. In L. Berkowitz

(Ed.), *Advances in experimental social psychology* (Vol. 7). New York: Academic Press, 1974.

Berzins, J.I., Welling, M.A., & Wetter, R.E. *The PRF ANDRO scale user's manual.* Unpublished manual, University of Kentucky, 1975.

Biller, H.B. *Father, child, and sex role: Paternal determinants of personality development.* Lexington: Heath Lexington Books, 1971.

Birnbaum, J.A. Life patterns and self-esteem in gifted family oriented and career committed women. In M.T.S. Mednick, S.S. Tangri, & L.W. Hoffman (Eds.), *Women and achievement: Social and motivational analyses.* Washington, D.C.: Hemisphere, 1975.

Block, J.H. Conceptions of sex roles: Some cross-cultural and longitudinal perspectives. *American Psychologist*, 1973, *28*, 512–526.

Bott, E. *Family and social network.* London: Tavistock Publications, 1957.

Bronfenbrenner, U. Freudian theories of identification and their derivatives. *Child Development*, 1960, *31*, 15–40.

Bronfenbrenner, U. The origins of alienation. *Scientific American*, 1974, *231*, 53–61.

Bronson, W.C. Dimensions of ego and infantile identification. *Journal of Personality*, 1959, *27*, 532–545.

Brown, D.G. Sex-role preference in young children. *Psychology Monographs*, 1956, *70* (14 Whole No. 421).

Brown, D.G. The development of sex-role inversion and homosexuality. *Journal of Pediatrics*, 1957, *50*, 613–619.

Brown, D.G. Inversion and homosexuality. *American Journal of Orthopsychiatry*, 1958, *28*, 424–429.

Brown, M. Motivational correlates of academic performance. *Psychological Reports*, 1974, *34*, 746.

Byrne, D. Attitudes and attraction. In L. Berkowitz (Ed.), *Advances in experimental social psychology* (Vol. 4). New York: Academic Press, 1969.

Callard, E. *Achievement motive in the four-year old and its relationship to the achievement expectancies of the mother.* Unpublished doctoral dissertation, University of Michigan, 1964.

Carlson, R. Sex differences in ego functioning. *Journal of Consulting and Clinical Psychology*, 1971, *37*, 267–277.

Carney, R.E., & McKeachie, W.J. Religion, sex, social class, probability of success, and student personality. *Journal of Science and Student Religion*, 1963, *3*, 32–42.

Cartwright, D.S. Trait and other sources of variance in the S-R inventory of anxiousness. *Journal of Personality and Social Psychology*, 1975, *32*, 408–415.

Child, I.L. Personality. *Annual Review of Psychology*, Palo Alto: Annual Reviews, 1954, *5*, 149–170.

Clark, R.A. The projective measurement of experimentally induced levels of sexual motivation. *Journal of Experimental Psychology*, 1952, *4*, 391–399.

278   *References*

Cole, J.R., & Cole, S. The Ortega hypothesis. *Science*, 1972, *178*, 368–375.

Cole, J.R., & Cole, S. Letter published in *Science*, 1974, *183*, 32–33.

Constantinople, A. Masculinity-femininity: An exception to the famous dictum? *Psychological Bulletin*, 1973, *80*, 389–407.

Coopersmith, S. *The antecedents of self-esteem*. San Francisco: Freeman, 1967.

Cowan, G., & Goldberg, F.J. Need achievement as a function of the race and sex of figures of selected TAT cards. *Journal of Personality and Social Psychology*, 1967, *5*, 245–249.

Crandall, V.C. Achievement behavior in young children. In W.W. Hartup & N.L. Smothergill (Eds.), *The young child: Reviews of research*. Washington, D.C.: National Association for the Education of Young Children, 1967.

Crowne, D.P., & Marlowe, D. A new scale of social desirability independent of psychopathology. *Journal of Consulting Psychology*, 1961, *24*, 349–354.

D'Andrade, R.G. Sex differences and cultural institutions. In E. Maccoby (Ed.), *The development of sex differences*. Stanford: Stanford University Press, 1966.

Deaux, K., & Emswiller, T. Explanations of successful performance on sex-linked tasks; what's skill for the male is luck for the female. *Journal of Personality and Social Psychology*, 1974, *29*, 80–85.

Derlega, V.J., & Chaikin, A.L. Norms affecting self-disclosure in men and women. *Journal of Consulting and Clinical Psychology*, 1976, *44*, 376–380.

Douvan, E., & Adelson, J. The psychodynamics of social mobility in adolescent boys. *Journal of Abnormal and Social Psychology*, 1958, *56*, 31–44.

Droppleman, L.F., & Schaefer, E.S. Boys' and girls' reports of maternal and paternal behavior. *Journal of Abnormal and Social Psychology*, 1963, *67*, 648–654.

Dymond, R.F. A scale for measurement of empathic ability. *Journal of Consulting Psychology*, 1949, *14*, 127–133.

Ellis, L.J., & Bentler, P.M. Traditional sex-determined role standards and sex stereotypes. *Journal of Personality and Social Psychology*, 1973, *25*, 28–34.

Erikson, E. Inner and outer space: Reflection on womanhood. *Daedalus*, 1964, *93*, 1–25.

Feather, N.T. Attribution of responsibility and valence of success and failure in relation to initial confidence and perceived locus of control. *Journal of Personality and Social Psychology*, 1969, *13*, 129–144.

Fishbein, M., & Ajzen, I. Attitudes towards objects as predictors of single and multiple behavioral criteria. *Psychological Review*, 1974, *81*, 26–43.

Foushee, H.C., Davis, M.H., & Archer, R.L. *Empathy, masculinity and femininity: Toward a redefinition*. Submitted for publication.

Foushee, H.C., Helmreich, R., & Spence, J.T. *Implicit theories of masculinity and femininity: Dualistic or bipolar?* Submitted for publication.

French, E., & Lesser, G.S. Some characteristics of the achievement motive in women. *Journal of Abnormal and Social Psychology*, 1964, *68*, 119–128.

Frieze, I. *Sex differences in perceiving the causes of success and failure.* Unpublished manuscript, University of Pittsburgh, 1973.

Garfield, E. Citation analysis. *Science*, 1975, *178*, 471–479.

Goldberg, S. *The inevitability of patriarchy.* New York: Morrow, 1973.

Good, T., Sikes, J.N., & Brophy, J. Effect of teacher sex and student sex on classroom interaction. *Journal of Educational Psychology*, 1973, *65*, 74–87.

Gordon, G. *Role theory and illness.* New Haven: University and College Press, 1966.

Goudsmit, S.A. Letter published in *Science*, 1974, *183*, 28.

Gough, H.G. Identifying psychological femininity. *Educational and Psychological Measurement*, 1952, *12*, 427–439.

Gough, H.G. *Manual for the California Personality Inventory.* Palo Alto: Consulting Psychologists' Press, 1957.

Gough, H.G. College attendance as predicted from the California Psychological Inventory. *Journal of Counseling Psychology*, 1968, *15*, 260–278.

Gough, H.G., & Heilbrun, A.B. *Joint manual for the Adjective Check List and the Needs Scales for the ACL.* Palo Alto: Consulting Psychologists' Press, 1965.

Gray, J.A. Sex differences in emotional behavior in mammals including man: Endocrine bases. *Acta Psychologica*, 1971, *35*, 29–46.

Gray, J.A., & Buffery, A.W.H. Sex differences in emotional and cognitive behavior in mammals including man: Adaptive and neural bases. *Acta Psychologica*, 1971, *35*, 89–111.

Green, R. *Sexual identity conflict in children and adults.* New York: Basic Books, 1974.

Gurin, G., Veroff, J., & Feld, S. *Americans view their mental health.* New York: Basic Books, 1960.

Gutman, D.L. Women and the conception of ego strength. *Merrill-Palmer Quarterly*, 1965, *11*, 229–240.

Haavio-Mannila, E. Convergences between East and West: Tradition and modernity in sex roles in Sweden, Finland, and the Soviet Union. In M.T.S. Mednick, S.S. Tangri, & L.W. Hoffman (Eds.), *Women and achievement: Social and motivational analyses.* Washington, D.C.: Hemisphere, 1975.

Hacker, L.M. New kinds of students and new ways of testing achievement. In *Proceedings of the 1956 International Conference on Testing Problems.* Princeton: Educational Testing Service, 1956, 95–102.

Hall, F.T., & Schroeder, M.P. Time spent on household tasks. *Journal of Home Economics*, 1970, *62*, 23–29.

Hathaway, S.R., & McKinley, J.C. *Minnesota Multiphasic Personality Inventory: Manual.* New York: Psychological Corporation, 1967.

Heckhausen, H. *Hoffnung und Furcht in der Leistungsmotivation.* Meisenheim 1 Glon: Horn, 1963.

Heckhausen, H. *The anatomy of achievement motivation.* New York: Academic, 1967.

Heilbrun, A.B., Jr. Sex-role, instrumental-expressive behavior and psychopathology in females. *Journal of Abnormal Psychology,* 1968, 73, 131–136.

Heilbrun, A.B., Jr. Parent identification and filial sex-role behavior: The importance of biological context. In J.K. Cole & R. Dienstbier (Eds.), *Nebraska Symposium on Motivation* (Vol. 21). Lincoln: University of Nebraska Press, 1973.

Heilbrun, A.B., Jr. Measurement of masculine and feminine sex role identities as independent dimensions. *Journal of Consulting and Clinical Psychology,* 1976, 44, 183–190.

Heilbrun, A.B., Jr., Kleemeier, C., & Piccola, G. Developmental situational correlates of achievement behavior in college females. *Journal of Personality,* 1974, 42, 420–436.

Heilbrun, K. *The derivation of negative sex stereotypes from the Adjective Check List.* Unpublished paper, 1976.

Heist, P., & Yonge, G. *Manual for the Omnibus Personality Inventory.* New York: Psychological Corporation, 1968.

Helmreich, R., Self-esteem and social behavior. In B. Wolman (Ed.), *International Encyclopedia of Neurology, Psychiatry, Psychoanalysis and Psychology.* New York: Van Nostrand Reinhold, 1977.

Helmreich, R., Aronson, E., & LeFan, J. To err is humanizing—sometimes: Effects of self-esteem, competence, and a pratfall on interpersonal attraction. *Journal of Personality and Social Psychology,* 1970, 16, 259–264.

Helmreich, R., Beane, W., Lucker, G.W., & Matthews, K.A. Achievement motivation among social psychologists, in preparation.

Helmreich, R., Beane, W., Lucker, G.W., & Spence, J.T. Achievement motivation and scientific attainment. *Personality and Social Psychology Bulletin,* in press.

Helmreich, R., & Spence, J.T. The Work and Family Orientation Scale (WOFO): An objective instrument to assess components of achievement motivation and attitudes toward family and career. JSAS *Catalog of Selected Documents in Psychology,* in press.

Helmreich, R., & Stapp, J. Short forms of the Texas Social Behavior Inventory, an objective measure of self-esteem. *Bulletin of the Psychonomic Society,* 1974, 4, 473–475.

Helmreich, R., Stapp, J., & Ervin, C. The Texas Social Behavior Inventory (TSBI): An objective measure of self-esteem or social competence. JSAS *Catalog of Selected Documents in Psychology,* 1974, 4, 79.

Herrenkohl, R.C. Factor analytic and criterion study of achievement motivation. *Journal of Educational Psychology*, 1972, *63*, 314–326.

Hetherington, E.M. A developmental study of the effects of sex of the dominant parent on sex-role preference, identification and imitation in children. *Journal of Personality and Social Psychology*, 1965, 2, 188–194.

Hetherington, E.M., & Frankie, G. Effects of parental dominance, warmth, and conflict on imitation in children. *Journal of Personality and Social Psychology*, 1967, 6, 119–125.

Hilton, T.L., & Berglund, G.W. Sex differences in mathematics achievement—a longitudinal study. *Educational Testing Service Research Bulletin*, 1971.

Hoffman, L.W. Fear of success in males and females: 1965 and 1972. *Journal of Consulting and Clinical Psychology*, 1974, 42, 353–358.

Hoffman, L.W. Early childhood experiences and women's achievement motives. In M.T.S. Mednick, S.S. Tangri, & L.W. Hoffman (Eds.), *Women and achievement: Social and motivational analyses*. Washington, D.C.: Hemisphere, 1975.

Hoffman, M.L., & Saltzstein, H.D. Parent discipline and the child's moral development. *Journal of Personality and Social Psychology*, 1967, 5, 45–57.

Holter, H. *Sex roles and social structure*. Islo-Bergen-Tromso: Universitets Forlaget, 1970.

Hooker, E. An empirical study of some relationships between sexual patterns and gender identity in male homosexuals. In J. Money (Ed.), *Sex research: New developments*, 1965. New York: Holt, Rinehart & Winston, 1965.

Horner, M. *Sex differences in achievement motivation and performance in competitive and non-competitive situations*. Unpublished doctoral dissertation, the University of Michigan, 1968.

Horrocks, J.E., & Jackson, D.W. *Self and role: A theory of self-process and role behavior*. Boston: Houghton Mifflin, 1972.

Hutt, C. *Males and females*. Harmondsworth: Penguin Books, 1972.

Inkeles, A., & Levinson, D.J. National character: The study of modal personality and sociocultural systems. In G. Lindzey (Ed.), *Handbook of social psychology* (First edition, Vol. 2). Reading, Mass.: Addison-Wesley, 1954.

Jackson, D.N. *Personality Research Form manual*. Goshen, New York: Research Psychologists' Press, 1967.

Jackson, D.N., Ahmed, S.A., & Heapy, N.A. Is achievement motivation a unitary construct? *Journal of Research in Personality*, 1976, *10*, 1–21.

Janeway, E. *Man's world, women's place: A study in social mythology*. New York: William Morrow, 1971.

Jenkin, N., & Vroegh, K. Contemporary concepts of masculinity and femininity. *Psychological Reports*, 1969, 25, 279–297.

Johnson, M.M. Sex role learning in the nuclear family. *Child Development*, 1963, *34*, 319–333.

Jones, E.E., & Nisbett, E. The actor and the observer: Divergent perceptions of the causes of behavior. In E.E. Jones et al. (Eds.), *Attribution: Perceiving the causes of behavior.* Morristown, New Jersey: General Learning Press, 1972.

Kaberry, P. *Women of the grassfields.* London: Her Majesty's Stationery Office, 1952.

Kagan, J. Acquisition and significance of sex typing and sex role identity. In M.L. Hoffman & L.W. Hoffman (Eds.), *Review of child development research* (Vol. 2). New York: Russell Sage, 1964.

Kehoe, P. *Psychological factors in the experience of pre-menstrual and menstrual symptomatology,* unpublished doctoral dissertation, the University of Texas, Austin, 1977.

Kelly, J.A., Caudill, S., Hathorn, S., & O'Brien, C.G. Socially undesirable sex-correlated characteristics: Implications for androgyny and adjustment. *Journal of Consulting and Clinical Psychology,* in press.

Kelly, J.A., & Worell, L. Parent behaviors related to masculine, feminine, and androgynous sex role orientations. *Journal of Consulting and Clinical Psychology,* 1976, 44, 843–851.

Kohlberg, L.A. Cognitive-developmental analysis of children's sex-role concepts and attitudes. In E.E. Maccoby (Ed.), *The development of sex differences.* Stanford: Stanford University Press, 1966.

Kohn, M.L. Social class and the exercise of parental authority. *American Sociological Review,* 1959, 24, 352–366.

Kristal, J., Sanders, D., Spence, J.T., & Helmreich, R. Inferences about femininity of competent women and their implications for likability. *Sex Roles,* 1975, 1, 33–40.

Lee, P.C. Psychology and sex differences. In P.C. Lee & R.S. Stewart (Eds.), *Sex differences: Cultural and developmental.* New York: Urizen Books, 1976.

Leslie, G.R., & Leslie, E.M. *Marriage in a changing world.* New York: Wiley, 1977.

Lesser, G.S., Krawitz, R.N., & Packard, R. Experimental arousal of achievement motivation in adolescent girls. *Journal of Abnormal and Social Psychology,* 1963, 66, 59–66.

Lewin, K. Wille und Badürfnis. *Psychologische Forschung,* 1926, 1, 294–385.

Lewin, K., Dembo, T., Festinger, L., & Sears, P.S. Level of aspiration. In J.McV. Hunt (Ed.), *Personality and the behavior disorders* (Vol. 1). New York: Ronald Press, 1944.

Littig, L.W., & Yericaris, C.A. Achievement motivation and intergenerational occupational mobility. *Journal of Personality and Social Psychology,* 1965, 1, 386–389.

Loevinger, J. The meaning and measurement of ego development. *American Psychologist,* 1966, 21, 195–206.

Loevinger, J., & Wessler, R. *Measuring ego development* (Vol. 1). San Francisco: Jossey-Bass, 1970.

Looft, W.R. Socialization and personality throughout the life span: An examination of contemporary psychological approaches. In P.B. Baltes & K.W. Schaie (Eds.), *Life-span developmental psychology.* New York: Academic Press, 1973.

Lynn, D.B. *Parental and sex-role identification: A theoretical formulation.* Berkeley: McCutchan, 1969.

Maccoby, E.E. Sex differentiation during childhood. JSAS *Catalog of Selected Documents in Psychology,* 1976, 6, 97.

Maccoby, E.E., & Jacklin, C.N. *The psychology of sex differences.* Stanford: Stanford University Press, 1974.

Maccoby, E.E., & Wilson, W.C. Identification and observational learning from films. *Journal of Abnormal and Social Psychology,* 1957, 55, 76–87.

Maccoby, M. *Gamesmen, the new corporate leaders.* New York: Simon & Schuster, 1977.

Mandler, G., & Sarason, S.B. A study of anxiety and learning. *Journal of Abnormal and Social Psychology,* 1952, 47, 166–173.

Manosevitz, M. Education and MMPI MF scores in homosexual and heterosexual males. *Journal of Consulting and Clinical Psychology,* 1971, 36, 395–399.

Martin, B. Parent-child relations. In F.D. Horowitz (Ed.), *Review of child development research* (Vol. 4). Chicago: University of Chicago Press, 1975.

McClelland, D.C. *Personality.* New York: William Sloane, 1951.

McClelland, D.C., Atkinson, J.W., Clark, R.A., & Lowell, E.L. *The achievement motive.* New York: Appleton-Century-Crofts, 1953.

McMahan, I.D. *Sex differences in causal attributions following success and failure.* Paper presented at the meeting of the Eastern Psychological Association, April 1971.

Mead, M. *Sex and temperament.* New York: William Morrow & Mendor, 1935.

Mednick, M.T.S. Social change and sex role inertia: The case of the kibbutz. In M.T.S. Mednick, S.S. Tangri, & L.W. Hoffman (Eds.), *Women and achievement: Social and motivational analyses.* Washington, D.C.: Hemisphere, 1975.

Mednick, M.T.S., Tangri, S.S., & Hoffman, L.W. (Eds.). *Women and achievement: Social and motivational analyses.* Washington, D.C.: Hemisphere, 1975.

Mehrabian, A. Male and female scales of tendency to achieve. *Educational and Psychological Measurement,* 1968, 28, 493–502.

Mehrabian, A. Measures of achieving tendency. *Educational and Psychological Measurement,* 1969, 29, 445–451.

Mehrabian, A., & Epstein, N.A. A measure of emotional empathy. *Journal of Personality,* 1972, 40, 525–543.

Miller, D.R., & Swanson, G.E. *The changing American parent.* New York: Wiley, 1958.

Minton, C., Kagan, J., & Levine, J.A. Maternal obedience and control in the two-year-old. *Child Development,* 1971, 42, 1873–1894.

Mischel, W. Sex-typing and socialization. In P.H. Mussen (Ed.), *Carmichael's manual of child psychology* (Vol. 2). New York: Wiley, 1970.

Mischel, W. *Introduction to personality* (Second edition). New York: Holt, Rinehart & Winston, 1976.

Mischel, W. On the future of personality measurement. *American Psychologist*, 1977, 32, 246–254.

Mischel, W., & Grusec, J. Determinants of the rehearsal and transmission of neutral and aversive behaviors. *Journal of Personality and Social Psychology*, 1966, 2, 197–205.

Mitchell, J.V. An analysis of the factorial dimensions of the achievement motivation construct. *Journal of Educational Psychology*, 1961, 52, 179–187.

Monahan, L., Kuhn, M., & Shaver, P. Intrapsychic versus cultural explanations of the "fear of success" motive. *Journal of Personality and Social Psychology*, 1974, 29, 60–64.

Monday, L.A., Hout, D.P., & Lutz, S.W. *College student profiles: American College Testing Program.* Iowa City: ACT Publications, 1967.

Money, J., & Ehrhardt, A.E. *Man and woman, boy and girl.* Baltimore: Johns Hopkins University Press, 1972.

Montague, A. *The nature of human aggression.* New York: Oxford University Press, 1976.

Moore, L.L. The relationship of academic group membership to the motive to avoid success in women. (Doctoral dissertation, University of Michigan, 1972.) *Dissertation Abstracts International*, 1972, 32, 43–55.

Morgan, S.W., & Mausner, B. Behavioral and fantasied indicators of avoidance of success in men and women. *Journal of Personality*, 1973, 41, 457–469.

Moulton, R.W. *Motivational implications of individual differences in competence.* Paper presented at the meeting of the American Psychological Association, 1967.

Moulton, R.W., Liberty, P.G., Jr., Burnstein, E., & Altucher, N. Patterning of parental affection and disciplinary dominance as a determinant of guilt and sex typing. *Journal of Personality and Social Psychology*, 1966, 4, 356–363.

Mowrer, O.H. *Learning theory and personality dynamics.* New York: Ronald, 1950.

Murdock, G.P. *Social structure.* New York: Macmillan, 1949.

Murray, H.A. *Explorations in personality.* New York: Oxford University Press, 1938.

Mussen, P., & Distler, L. Masculinity, identification, and father-son relationships. *Journal of Abnormal and Social Psychology*, 1959, 59, 350–356.

Mussen, P., & Parker, A.L. Mother nurturance and girls' incidental imitative learning. *Journal of Personality and Social Psychology*, 1965, 2, 94–97.

Mussen, P., & Rutherford, E. Parent-child relations and parental personality in relation to young children's sex-role preferences. *Child Development*, 1963, *34*, 589–607.

Nie, N., Hull, H., Jenkins, J., Steinbrenner, K., & Bent, P. *SPSS: Statistical Package for the Social Sciences.* New York: McGraw-Hill, 1975.

Parsons, T. Age and sex in the social structure of the United States. *American Sociological Review*, 1942, *7*, 604–616.

Parsons, T. Family structure and the socialization of the child. In T. Parsons & R.F. Bales (Eds.), *Family, socialization, and interaction process.* Glencoe: Free Press, 1955.

Parsons, T. Social structure and the development of personality: Freud's contribution to the integration of psychology and sociology. *Psychiatry*, 1958, *21*, 321–340.

Parsons, T., & Bales, R.F. *Family socialization and interaction process.* Glencoe: Free Press, 1955.

Payne, D.E., & Mussen, P.H. Parent-child relations and father identification among adolescent boys. *Journal of Abnormal and Social Psychology*, 1956, *52*, 358–362.

Peplau, L.A. *The impact of fear of success, sex-role attitudes and opposite sex relationships on women's intellectual performance.* Unpublished doctoral dissertation, Harvard University, 1973.

Radin, N. Father-child interaction and the intellectual functioning of four-year-old boys. *Developmental Psychology*, 1972, *6*, 353–361.

Radloff, R., & Helmreich, R. The Life History Questionnaire. JSAS *Catalog of Selected Documents in Psychology*, 1972, *2*, 13–14. (Ms. No. 71)

Raven, B.H., & Rubin, J.Z. *Social psychology: People in groups.* New York: Wiley & Sons, 1976.

Raven, J., Molloy, E., & Corcoran, R. Toward a questionnaire measure of achievement motivation. *Human Relations*, 1972, *25*, 469–492.

Raynor, J.O. *The relationship between distant future goals and achievement motivation.* Unpublished doctoral dissertation, University of Michigan, 1968.

Raynor, J.O. Future orientation and motivation of immediate activity. *Psychological Review*, 1969, *76*, 606–610.

Raynor, J.O. Relationships between achievement-related motives, future orientation, and academic performance. *Journal of Personality and Social Psychology*, 1970, *15*, 28–33.

Raynor, J.O. Future orientation in the study of achievement motivation. In J.W. Atkinson & J.O. Raynor (Eds.), *Motivation and achievement.* New York: V.H. Winston & Sons, 1974.

Raynor, J.O., & Rubin, I.S. Effects of achievement motivation and future orientation on level of performance. *Journal of Personality and Social Psychology*, 1971, *17*, 36–41.

Revelle, W., & Michaels, E.J. The theory of achievement motivation revisited: The implications of inertial tendencies. *Psychological Review*, 1976, *83*, 394–404.

Rosekrans, M.A. Imitation in children as a function of perceived similarity to a social model and vicarious reinforcement. *Journal of Personality and Social Psychology*, 1967, 7, 307–315.

Rosen, B.C. The achievement syndrome. *American Sociological Review*, 1956, *21*, 203–211.

Rosen, B.C. Family structure and achievement motivation. *American Sociological Review*, 1962, *26*, 574–585.

Rosen, B.C. Race, ethnicity, and the achievement syndrome. In S.S. Guterman (Ed.), *Black psyche: The modal personality patterns of Black Americans*. Berkeley: Glendessary, 1972.

Rosen, B.C. Social change, migration and family interaction in Brazil. *American Sociological Review*, 1973, *38*, 198–212.

Rosen, B.C., & D'Andrade, R. The psychosocial origins of achievement motivation. *Sociometry*, 1959, *22*, 185–218.

Rosenberg, M. *Society and the adolescent self-image*. Princeton: Princeton University Press, 1965.

Rosenkrantz, P.S., Vogel, S.R., Bee, H., Broverman, I. K., & Broverman, D.M. Sex role stereotypes and self concepts in college students. *Journal of Consulting and Clinical Psychology*, 1968, *32*, 287–295.

Rosenthal, R., & Jacobson, L. *Pygmalion in the classroom*. New York: Holt, Rinehart, & Winston, 1968.

Rossi, A.S. Transition to parenthood. *Journal of Marriage and the Family*, 1968, *30*, 26–39.

Sarason, S.B., Davidson, K.S., Lighthall, F.F., Waite, R.R., & Ruebush, B.V. *Anxiety in elementary school children*. New York: John Wiley & Sons, 1960.

Sarnoff, I. Identification with the aggressor: Some personality correlates of anti-semitism among Jews. *Journal of Personality*, 1951, *20*, 199–218.

Scanzoni, J.H. *Sex roles, life styles, and child bearing*. New York: The Free Press, 1975.

Schaefer, E.S. A circumplex model for maternal behavior. *Journal of Abnormal and Social Psychology*, 1959, *59*, 226–235.

Schaefer, E.S., & Bayley, N. Validity and consistency of mother-infant observations, adolescent maternal interviews, and adult retrospective reports of maternal behavior. *Proceeding of 75th Annual Convention, American Psychological Association*, 1967, 147–148.

Scott, J.W., & Tilly, L.A. Women's work and the family in nineteenth-century Europe. In C.E. Rosenberg (Ed.), *The family in history*. Philadelphia: the University of Pennsylvania Press, 1975.

Sears, R.R. Identification as a form of behavior development. In P.B. Harris (Ed.), *The concept of development*. Minneapolis: University of Minneapolis Press, 1957.

Sears, R.R., Maccoby, E.E., & Levin, H. *Patterns of child rearing.* Evanston, Ill.: Row & Peterson, 1957.

Serbin, L.A., O'Leary, K.D., Kent, R.N., & Tonick, I.J. A comparison of teacher response to the pre-academic and problem behavior of boys and girls. *Child Development*, 1973, *44*, 796–804.

Shrable, V.K., & Moulton, R.W. Achievement fantasy as a function of variations in self-rated competence. *Perceptual and Motor Skills*, 1968, *27*, 515–528.

Siegelman, M. Evaluation of Bronfenbrenner's questionnaire for children concerning parental behavior. *Child Development*, 1965, *36*, 163–174.

Slaby, R.G., & Frey, K.S. Development of gender constancy and selective attention to same-sex models. *Child Development*, 1975, *47*, 849–856.

Smith, C.P. *Achievement-related motives in children.* New York: Russell Sage Foundation, 1969.

Sonquist, J., Baker, E., & Morgan, J. *Searching for structure.* Ann Arbor, Michigan: Institute for Social Research, University of Michigan, 1973.

Spence, J.T. Learning theory and personality. In J.M. Wepman & R.W. Heine (Eds.), *Concepts of personality.* Chicago: Aldine Publishing Company, 1963.

Spence, J.T. The Thematic Apperception Test and attitudes toward achievement in women: A new look at the motive to avoid success and a new method of measurement. *Journal of Consulting and Clinical Psychology*, 1974, *42*, 427–437.

Spence, J.T., & Helmreich, R. Who likes competent women? Competence, sex-role congruence of interests, and subjects' attitudes toward women as determinants of interpersonal attraction. *Journal of Applied Social Psychology*, 1972, *2*, 197–213. (a)

Spence, J.T., & Helmreich, R. The Attitudes toward Women Scale: An objective instrument to measure attitudes toward the rights and roles of women in contemporary society. JSAS *Catalog of Selected Documents in Psychology*, 1972, *2*, 66. (b)

Spence, J.T., Helmreich, R., & Stapp, J. A short version of the Attitudes toward Women Scale (AWS). *Bulletin of the Psychonomic Society*, 1973, *2*, 219–220.

Spence, J.T., Helmreich, R., & Stapp, J. The Personal Attributes Questionnaire: A measure of sex-role stereotypes and masculinity-femininity. JSAS *Catalog of Selected Documents in Psychology*, 1974, *4*, 43

Spence, J.T., Helmreich, R., & Stapp, J. Ratings of self and peers on sex-role attributes and their relation to self-esteem and conceptions of masculinity and feminity. *Journal of Personality and Social Psychology*, 1975, *32*, 29–39.

Stapp, J. *Antecedents of self-esteem and psychological masculinity and femininity.* Unpublished doctoral dissertation, University of Texas, Austin, 1975.

Stephens, W.N. *The family in cross-cultural perspective.* New York:
    Holt, Rinehart, & Winston, 1963.
Stotland, E., Zander, A., & Natsoulas, T. The generalization of inter-
    personal similarity. *Journal of Abnormal and Social Psychol-
    ogy,* 1961, 62, 250–256.
Stricker, G. Implications of research for psychotherapeutic treatment
    of women. *American Psychologist,* 1977, 32, 14–22.
Tangri, S.S. *Role-innovation in occupational choice among college
    women.* Doctoral dissertation, University of Michigan, 1969.
Tangri, S.S. Determinants of occupational role innovation among
    college women. *Journal of Social Issues,* 1972, 28, 177–199.
Taylor, J.A. A personality scale of manifest anxiety. *Journal of
    Abnormal and Social Psychology,* 1953, 48, 285–290.
Thompson, N.L., Schwartz, D.M., McCandless, B.R., & Edwards, D.A.
    Parent-child relationships and sexual identity in male and
    female homosexuals and heterosexuals. *Journal of Consulting
    and Clinical Psychology,* 1973, 41, 120–127.
Tiger, L., & Fox, R. *The imperial animal.* New York: Holt, Rinehart,
    & Winston, 1971.
Tiller, P.O. *Isolation: Identification and parent figure preference in
    doll play.* Oslo, Norway: Institute for Social Research, 1964.
Tressemer, D. Fear of success: Popular but unproven. *Psychology
    Today,* 1974, 7, 82–85.
Veroff, J. Development and validation of a projective measure of
    power motivation. *Journal of Abnormal and Social Psychology,*
    1957, 54, 1–8.
Veroff, J. Social comparison and the development of achievement
    motivation. In C.P. Smith (Ed.), *Achievement-related motives
    in children.* New York: Russell Sage, 1969.
Veroff, J., Atkinson, J.W., Feld, S.C., & Gurin, G. The use of thematic
    apperception to assess motivation in a nation-wide interview
    study. *Psychological Monographs,* 1960, 74 (12, Whole No.
    499).
Veroff, J., & Feld, S.C. *Marriage and work in America.* New York:
    Van Nostrand-Reinhold, 1970.
Veroff, J., Feld, S.C., & Gurin, G. Achievement motivation and re-
    ligious background. *American Sociological Review,* 1962, 27,
    205–217.
Veroff, J., McClelland, L., & Ruhland, D. Varieties of achievement
    motivation. In M.T.S. Mednick, S.S. Tangri, & L.W. Hoffman
    (Eds.), *Women and achievement: Social and motivational
    analyses.* Washington, D.C.: Hemisphere, 1975.
Veroff, J., Wilcox, S., & Atkinson, J.W. The achievement motive in
    high school and college age women. *Journal of Abnormal and
    Social Psychology,* 1953, 48, 108–119.
Wakefield, J.A., Jr., Sasek, J., Friedman, A.F., & Bowden, J.D.
    Androgyny and other measures of masculinity-femininity.
    Journal of Consulting and Clinical Psychology, 1976, 44,
    766–770.

Walker, E.L., & Atkinson, J.W. The expression of fear-related motivation in thematic apperception as a function of proximity to an atomic explosion. In J.W. Atkinson (Ed.), *Motives in fantasy, action and society*. Princeton: Van Nostrand, 1958.

Ward, S. *Range of sex-role identity and self-esteem in a homosexual sample*. Unpublished honors thesis, University of Texas, Austin, 1974.

Watson, J.D. *The double helix*. New York: Atheneum, 1968.

Weiner, B. New conceptions in the study of achievement motivation. In B.A. Maher (Ed.), *Progress in experimental personality research* (Vol. 5). New York: Academic Press, 1970.

Weiner, B. *Theories of motivation*. New York: Markham, 1972.

Weinstein, M. Achievement motivation and risk preference. *Journal of Personality and Social Psychology*, 1969, *13*, 153–173.

Wellens, G.J. The motive to avoid success in high school seniors: Achievement shifts and psychological correlates. *Dissertation Abstracts International*, 1973, *33*, 5529.

Wertheim, E.G., Widom, C.S., & Wortzel, L.H. Multivariate professional career choice. *Journal of Applied Psychology*, in press.

Wessman, A.E., & Ricks, D.F. *Mood and personality*. New York: Holt, Rinehart, & Winston, 1966.

Wetter, R.E. Levels of self-esteem associated with four sex role categories. In R. Bednar (Chair), *Sex roles: Masculine, feminine, androgynous, or none of the above?* Symposium presented at the meeting of the American Psychological Association, Chicago, 1975.

White, R.W. Motivation reconsidered: The concept of competence. *Psychological Review*, 1959, *66*, 297–333.

Whiting, J.W.M. Sorcery, sin, and the superego. A cross-cultural study of some mechanisms of social control. In M.R. Jones (Ed.), *Nebraska Symposium on Motivation*. Lincoln: University of Nebraska Press, 1959.

Wilson, E.O. *Sociobiology*. Cambridge: Belknap Press, 1975.

Winterbottom, M.R. The relation of need for achievement to learning experiences in independence and mastery. In J. W. Atkinson (Ed.), *Motives in fantasy, action and society*. Princeton: D. Van Nostrand, Co., 1958.

Witkin, H.A. Social conformity and psychological differentiation. *International Journal of Psychology*, 1974, *9*, 11–29.

Woolf, V. *A room of one's own*. New York: Harcourt, Brace, & World, 1929.

Worell, L., & Worell, J. *The Parent Behavior Form*. Unpublished manual, 1974.

Zanna, M.P., & Pack, S.J. On the self-fulfilling nature of apparent sex differences in behavior. *Journal of Experimental Social Psychology*, 1975, *11*, 583–591.

Zuckerman, M., & Wheeler, L. To dispel fantasies about the fantasy-based measure of fear of success. *Psychological Bulletin*, 1975, *82*, 932–946.

Author Index

Subject Index